ROUTLEDGE LIBRARY EDITIONS:
GERMAN HISTORY

Volume 34

THE POLITICAL RE-EDUCATION
OF GERMANY AND HER ALLIES

THE POLITICAL RE-EDUCATION
OF GERMANY AND HER ALLIES
After World War II

Edited by
NICHOLAS PRONAY AND KEITH WILSON

Routledge
Taylor & Francis Group

NEW YORK AND LONDON

First published in 1985 by Croom Helm Ltd

This edition first published in 2020
by Routledge
52 Vanderbilt Avenue, New York, NY 10017

and by Routledge
2 Park Square, Milton Park, Abingdon, Oxon OX14 4RN

Routledge is an imprint of the Taylor & Francis Group, an informa business

British Library Cataloguing in Publication Data
A catalogue record for this book is available from the British Library

ISBN: 978-0-367-02813-8 (Set)
ISBN: 978-0-429-27806-8 (Set) (ebk)
ISBN: 978-0-367-24788-1 (Volume 34) (hbk)
ISBN: 978-0-367-24793-5 (Volume 34) (pbk)
ISBN: 978-0-429-28443-4 (Volume 34) (ebk)

Publisher's Note
The publisher has gone to great lengths to ensure the quality of this reprint but points out that some imperfections in the original copies may be apparent.

Disclaimer
The publisher has made every effort to trace copyright holders and would welcome correspondence from those they have been unable to trace.

The POLITICAL RE-EDUCATION OF GERMANY & HER ALLIES

After World War II

Edited by Nicholas Pronay and Keith Wilson

CROOM HELM
London & Sydney

©1985 Nicholas Pronay and Keith Wilson
Croom Helm Ltd, Provident House, Burrell Row,
Beckenham, Kent BR3 1AT
Croom Helm Australia Pty Ltd, First Floor,
139 King Street, Sydney, NSW 2001, Australia

British Library Cataloguing in Publication Data

The Political re-education of Germany and her
    allies after World War II.
    1. Germany (West)—Politics and government
    I. Pronay, Nicholas   II. Wilson, Keith M. *1951-*
    320'.07'043   JN3971
    ISBN 0-7099-2091-1

Printed and bound in Great Britain
by Billing & Sons Limited, Worcester.

CONTENTS

Preface

PREFACE

This volume is the most recent outcome of the work of the Inter University History Film Consortium, founded in 1967 for the purpose of encouraging the study of the part played by modern persuasion techniques, including film and other mass media as well as publicity and propaganda agencies, in the political and social history of the twentieth century. Presently, the Consortium consists of the History departments of the Universities of Birmingham, Leeds, Nottingham, Reading, Wales, the London School of Economics and Political Science, Queen Mary College, London, the College of St Mark and St John, Plymouth and Westminster College, Oxford. The articles printed here have been prepared at the invitation of the Consortium. With the exception of those dealing with the first world war antecedents of the policy of re-education and that of Japan, they have been read at an international conference held in London in April 1983 and revised in the light of the discussion held with the participation of many of those involved in its planning and execution after 1945. I should like express our gratitude to Lord Annan, Sir Hugh Greene, Sir Duncan Wilson (whose last public appearance this Conference had sadly proved) Professor George Allen and Professor A.J. Ryder amongst others for their personal contributions, and to thank Dr Marcus Phillips and Professor Karl Stadler for their talks on the German film industry in the Adenauer period and on Austrian re-education.

In planning this volume, the Consortium hoped to provide, first, a 'reader' on major aspects of the policy of re-education for undergraduates and others turning to the study of the post-war period, and second, to bring to the attention of the English speaking reader some of the fruits and perspectives of the extensive German work on this central, and intriguing, part of German and European history since 1945 .

The Consortium wishes to acknowledge the financial assistance provided by the British Academy and the German Academic Exchange Service; the help and advice in planning the volume given by Dr Lothar Kettenacker, Professor Michael Balfour and Professor J.A.S. Grenville, and to thank Dr Josef Foschepoth and Rolf Steiniger for making available the bibliography of German work on re-education prepared for their volume Die Britische Deutschland und Besatzungspolitik to be published under the aegis of the German Historical Institute.

It gives me personal pleasure to be able to express as Chairman on behalf of the Consortium the warmest thanks to Mrs Ann Dale and Mrs Margaret Walkington for preparing the volume for the press by 'wordprocessor technology' - and for their good humour and efficiency at moments of crisis arising out of it - and to Mrs. Ann Hall for the Index.

Nicholas Pronay

INTRODUCTION

'TO STAMP OUT THE WHOLE TRADITION....'

NICHOLAS PRONAY

Political re-education was the alternative put forward by Britain during the common wartime search for a policy which would prevent the resurgence of Germany for a third time as a hostile military power. Both the Americans and the Russians initially thought in terms of destroying the material capacity of Germany for going to war again in the foreseeable future. The Americans proposed, principally, the destruction of the economic and industrial capacity of Germany for making war by a ruthless and thorough demolition of what was left of it after the war. By flooding her mines, dismantling her heavy industry and similar measures, Germany was to be reduced, in the phrase of the so-called Morgenthau Plan, to 'a pastoral economy'. Political dismemberment would complete the job. The Soviet Union thought in much the same terms of 'de-industrialisation' but wished to complete it by the once-and for-all 'removal' of Germany's political and social elite, a policy modelled on the same principles which the Soviets had already applied in the case of the Kulaks and the Polish officer class. [1]

The British alternative in fact was to go for the mind instead of the body. It sought to eradicate, by all the means available to the Military Government of an occupied country, the ideas and the ideals on which the authoritarian and militaristic political systems of Germany had been based - and to substitute for them the ethical, philosophical and political ideas of Britain and her transatlantic descendants. The Germans were to be re-educated to embrace the 'rule of law'; 'rechstat' instead of 'real-politik'; philosophical pragmatism instead of idealism in the Hegelian sense; constitutionalism instead of étatism. They were to be cured of militarism by learning to think of the soldier as the paid servant of the community rather than as the elite of the nation, and to unlearn that it was the state which legitimated the individual rather than the other way around. The realisation of this policy was to involve the control and manipulation not only of the media of opinion formation but also the agencies of attitude formation. It was to be effected by re-structuring the media of opinion formation, such as the press, radio and cinema to ensure a pluralist approach to 'kultur'. By remaking and as far as possible re-staffing the

1

educational system and reorienting the curricular and scholarly vehicles for attitude formation - including the rewriting of the nation's history that perhaps most powerful formulator of basic attitudes - a long term change of outlook and attitudes would be secured. In all ways, the Germans were to be taught to look to Great Britain and to the English speaking world as their exemplar.

The British policy of re-education gradually gained American acceptance, was extended to Japan and was formally incorporated into the Potsdam Agreement. Although there were some in the USA, principally the officials of the State Department, who had themselves favoured 're-education' in place of the Morgenthau ideas – though as part of a package with political dismemberment – it remained essentially a British approach consistently central only to British thinking and practice after victory. Apart from the inevitable differences of opinion as to the political philosophy to be inculcated as distinct from being eradicated, it also occupied a rather different place in the priorities of the three allies within that cluster of short-term and long-term plans and objectives described at Potsdam as the 'Four D's': De-militarisation, De-nazification, Democratisation, and De-industrialisation (now only in the sense of using the German industry as a quarry for reparation payments, and of not helping the Germans to rebuild their economic prosperity). Given a free hand, the British would have been quite happy to do without any of these essentially physical measures, or at least to apply them only in a short, sharp, shock period immediately after the collapse of Germany. Even as far as de-nazification was concerned, after the removal of the active and to some degree prominent Nazis, the British would have preferred to see in-depth denazification emerge as the result of the change of the German mind instead of a continuing witch-hunt by the Military Government.

The same applied to democratisation. As far as the British were concerned, the form of government - whether a popular democracy or an indirect constitutional democracy, or even a mildly socialist system - should emerge from a Germany imbued with the principles of the rule of law, rather than come by action of the Military Government. Least of all should it result from any root-and-branch, social-cum-political, reform imposed by the occupying power, whether it entailed land-reform (such as was carried out in Japan) or the nationalisation of key industries. The British were even against forcibly uniting the divided parties of the left or centre as bulwarks against the rise of a new party of the right. As far as de-industrialisation, heavy reparations payments and, even more, the policy of keeping down the living standards of the Germans was concerned, these were provisions the British had to accept as part of the compromise. They were operated by them in their own Zone as little as practicable within Allied unity. Even in education itself the British, unlike the Americans or the Russians, would use administrative measures to change the social basis or authoritarian structure of the educational system as little as possible. Altogether, though the Americans did prepare extensive plans in the closing months of the war, and initially at any rate, went about

2

Introduction

re-education as well as 'denazification, demilitarisation and democratisation' with a characteristically missionary zeal, and although the Soviets brutally forced through a fundamental, ideological as well as social and political, re-orientation resulting in Soviet-style states and societies in all the areas they occupied, only the British placed the central emphasis, indeed sought to rely almost wholly, on 're-education' as against physical measures. The emphasis of the studies in this volume reflects the centrality of Britain in the history of re-education.

*

The history of the political re-education of Germany and her Allies belongs to the most recent historical period, the last decade for which the records have been opened. As an Allied policy it formally concluded at the restoration of sovereign governments and the signing of peace treaties with them. The history of re-education therefore runs up to the beginning of the 1950s both in the archival and in the practical sense of being an Allied policy for the period of occupation. On the other hand, the aims of the policy were long-term, the success or failure of which was to be measured by what happened, or perhaps more exactly, what did not happen during the decades following the restoration of sovereign governments to the defeated peoples. As a historical subject re-education is thus particularly affected by the constraints which generally operate in respect of the most recent periods of history: the story can be told historically since there is access to the records, or at least a substantial part of them, but it is not yet possible to put it into its broader historical perspective in the sense of answering the basic question: did it succeed? The essays in this volume therefore concentrate on describing, largely for the first time in English, the actual process of the planning of the 're-education' of the enemy after victory and some of the major aspects of the actual carrying out of that policy in the years immediately after 1945, based on the historical record material opened under the Thirty Year Rule. They do not seek to pass broader historical judgements on the place of re-education in the history of Germany, in particular, since 1945. For answers to that large question about the long-term effects and the historical significance of the policy of 're-education' we will have to wait until the records of the post-1950 decades become available. To some extent we also need as yet more research amongst some parts of the voluminous record material of the period and the policy itself, such as the Control Commission papers held in Germany, some of which are just about to become available. We also lack as yet perhaps the broader historical perspectives for the later 1940s in general which are just beginning to emerge from research work currently being published. Finally, it is only in fact in the English speaking part of the world, and in areas occupied by them after the war, that the records for even this period are actually so available, and therefore the essays deal only with those areas for which 'history' does indeed begin at around 1950. This excludes both the French and Russian Zones. For the French Zone the records have only partially and very recently been opened – and for the Soviet Zone, and indeed for the Soviet Union as a state, in a sense, history has not yet begun at all.

This volume, therefore, published close on the fortieth anniversary of the adoption of re-education as a central part of post-victory policy during the second world war, cannot as yet provide answers to those larger questions which it raises especially concerning its effects. On the other hand, it is already possible to define at least some of the questions on which further research will have to concentrate in exploring the record material as it becomes available during the next decades. The central question is the relationship between re-education and the remarkable fact that so far neither Germany nor Japan show signs of reverting to former habits of thought or ambitions. There is no doubt that they are today still as close to the Anglo-Saxon idea of a polity as the planners of the re-education policy could possibly have hoped : but what was the relative rôle of the re-education policy and of the work of the re-educators as against the other factors affecting the evolution of Germany since 1945? What was the rôle of the partitioning of Germany; the separation of Prussia and the brutal destruction of the Junker-class, economically, socially and, all too often, physically, in the Soviet Zone/East Germany? And, what might have been the rôle of the continuing (de facto) presence of Allied forces in both halves of Germany – and well beyond in fact the 20-30 years which had been thought a necessary period of Allied presence for completing the job of re-education? Thirty years from now, when the records of that complex, successful and apparently so thoroughly altered society of West Germany (and of Japan with different parallel factors operating there) will have been studied, such questions will surely be the stuff of examination papers.

Until at least some of the record material becomes available for the later 1950s there is simply not sufficient factual information available even to attempt a speculative discussion of these fascinating questions central for a historical perspective on the policy of re-education. As far as the other part of a broader perspective is concerned, the historical context of the making of the policy during the second world war, much work has also yet to be done. But there is perhaps enough already known to raise, at least in the form of a preliminary discussion, two of the central questions about the policy designed 'to stamp out the whole tradition' on which Germany, a great, European and by many standards highly successful modern nation has been built: (i) Was the policy necessary as far as Germany was concerned? (ii) How did this remarkable idea, the more breathtaking in its implications for both those who conceived it and those on whom it was to be practised the more one thinks about it, actually arise: where did the historical, political, even psychological, roots of the assumptions lie on which such an idea could be perceived as both a legitimate and a practical proposition?

Introduction

(i) Even given the premise of the policy - that there had in fact been historically deep-seated ideas in German (and Japanese) society which so long as they remained the dominant ones would continue to prevent them from settling down to a peaceful membership of the community of their neighbours - was an imposed policy of 're-education' actually necessary? Would not the magnitude of defeat, which followed upon such monumental effort to win, by itself have led to a fundamental re-thinking quite spontaneously anyway? No people could have tried harder than the German nation to obtain by war what it believed was its right to have and what it believed was within its capacity to attain if it put everything it had into the struggle. Yet they were defeated by enemies whom they had believed to be morally and politically inferior to them because they lacked their inborn capacity for war. Was it then still necessary for an external agency to initiate and carry through the re-thinking implied in that defeat, after 1945?

There can be no doubt that in the second world war the German people had been willing to give every ounce of heroism and self-sacrifice of which they were capable in order to gain that domination, that high position in the world which they perceived their rightful place to be. Fired by the belief that they could attain such domination despite their limited resources by devoting more totally what they did have to the national purpose than it lay in their opponents to do they gave all they could be expected to give - and more. The German people were willing to accept casualties on any scale, bear the destruction of their magnificent architectural and industrial heritage, together with those living standards and home comforts of which they as people had been also so proud to have created. To be sure, other nations, the Russians and the British in particular, had been as willing to accept such sacrifices, albeit in defence.

The German people however were willing to sacrifice even more. They were willing to sacrifice ethical and cultural principles which, at different levels of society, they had held dear and were conscious and proud of having attained to. They believed with Hitler that the reason why they had lost the first world war was because they had been too soft; too bound by codes of chivalry in their conduct on the front, too bound by legality at home to strike down their own weaker-willed or misguided brethren; too unwilling to listen to those who advocated total ruthlessness, and too unwilling to enlist the services of the brutal and criminal elements whose talents suited them to the vicious business of war. In the second war, they willingly threw all that too into the furnace of war. In peacetime, just in preparation for war, their ruling class - once so insistent on the highest standards of education, and of being a 'gentleman' for public office - handed power to a coterie of men straight from what they regarded as the gutter, in the belief that they would have the ruthlessness, cunning and unscrupulousness with which the nation could be totally organised for war. They allowed the perversion of what before they had proudly regarded as the finest educational system in the world maintaining the most uncompromising academic standards into a machine for turning out callous and brutalised warriors. They were willing to convert what they had once proudly regarded as a singularly learned and punctilious judicial system into a brutish and simplicistic machine for maintaining blind obedience not to laws but orders; in effect put the nation under drumhead courtmartials in peacetime. When the longed for and prepared for war came, they fought not only with all the heroism, obedience, and dedication of which they were capable, but also with utter ruthlessness, shrinking from nothing, and knowingly burning all their bridges as far as the rest of the world was concerned. They gave their best, did their worst, did everything which in the light of their 'weltanschaung' should have brought them victory. Yet they lost, they were totally and indubitably defeated, their country utterly destroyed.

With empathy, it could thus be argued that the 're-education' of the German nation was the second world war itself. That it was bound to have destroyed the credibility of the militarist political tradition on which the nation had been built.

It could further be argued that the manner in which they were defeated went even deeper in terms of 're-education'. Whatever the western allies might have thought and irrespective of with what degree of historical truth, the Germans in 1945 knew that it was on the Eastern Front that they had been defeated. [2] It was there in 1941-42 that for all practical purposes the whole of the first-line strength of the largest, best equipped and best trained army which Germany ever had and could ever hope to muster was launched, in a spirit of total ruthlessness and with elemental treachery, against an unprepared Russia. Despite all that, it was first fought to a standstill and then remorselessly, efficiently and irresistibly beaten back and back – by the despised Slav. The historical roots of the German 'herrenvolk-untermensch' mentality lay in the perception of an historical struggle between the 'German and the Slav'. It was in that perception too that the sense of a mission to dominate took its roots. The fundamental, philosophical and psychological, re-education of Germany can therefore be said to have started at Moscow when they were routed by a superbly organised, perfectly timed, counter-attack by Russian divisions which they did not believe could still exist - and which had manifestly better equipment, training and leadership.

Hitler might have been able to preserve his own hold on his beliefs by ordering that he was never again to be given intelligence figures showing that the Russians were outbuilding Germany in tanks in a ratio of ten to one. But German soldiers knew that Russian tanks were not only infinitely more numerous than their own but also that as fighting machines they were a generation ahead of their own at each stage of the war; that Russian artillery outnumbered their own and its guns were of such advanced technological features that captured Soviet anti-tank guns became a treasured prize being, at times, the only guns capable of stopping Soviet armour at anything like a normal range. [3] Their officers knew that in addition to technological superiority and at least equal fighting qualities, once the Red Army recovered from the shock and losses caused by their treacherous attack, they were also up against the ability of the Soviet High Command to spring total tactical surprises at them time after time. It is probable that they were spared from knowing the particularly painful, and educational, fact that in suffering defeat after defeat from Stalingrad onward they were being beaten by an army which was actually in numerical inferiority right up until the spring of 1944, but they certainly knew that it had a massive and ever increasing superiority in tanks, guns and aircraft.

By 1945 the Germans knew - in their hearts, as Hitler would say - that they had been outfought, out-built, out-designed and out-generalled by the Slav. [4] It could therefore be argued that when the position was reached that to be 'sent to the East', transferred to a command on the Eastern front, came to be seen as a punishment for a German officer, then the warrior ethos, the German mission to rule over the primitive masses of the East, the historic base of all that, could never again revive after 1945. And, it could be argued, with it went the Prussian (junker) military aristocracy's raison d'être, and so did in a fundamental sense 'Prussia' itself as an element in the German make up. As Lothar Kettenacker so nicely puts it - looking at the destruction of the Prussian aristocracy by Hitler, and thus of 'Prussian militarism', and the manifestation of that destruction by its inability to stop the fighting when they recognised that the war was lost and thus save Germany and the Army - 'by 1945 Berlin was a ruin in every sense of the word...'. [5]

Could the German people therefore, after their experiences in the war, on the Eastern Front in particular, ever again believe that as a race they possessed such special military qualities that they could overcome the facts of geography and of numbers? Could the German people ever again believe that the 'natural form of German society was a marching column'? Could they again come to believe that for Germans 'battle is to men what giving birth is to women' as even a highly educated, multilingual, non-Prussian, catholic aristocrat, von Papen, could once put it? Could therefore the Army ever again be seen as the 'schule des Nation'? This is a question of historical perspective, not an implied criticism of the wartime planners. The brutal and bloody experience of the trenches in the first world war had manifestly not had that effect on the German people; and the skilful and determined resistance of the German armies in 1944-45, their continued display of an appetite for action and brutality of spirit, on the battlefront as in captivity, coupled with a remarkably strong home front almost to the point of occupation, certainly made it look, that militarism was as strong as ever. Nevertheless, one of the questions which future researchers and historians will doubtless ask is whether re-education was necessary at all, at least in the negative sense of stamping out 'Prussian militarism'; the objective on which all the Allies agreed and which was taken still in 1945 as the central task of re-education. [7]

*

(ii) The other question raised by the policy of re-education which will no doubt also be asked increasingly as further work proceeds on this extraordinary story is not about the Germans or the Japanese, but about the British and the Americans. What elements in their past, their culture and political system made them believe that it was both legitimate and practicable to attempt what might fairly be described, even though the word itself did not come into use until 1950, as brainwashing whole nations?

There were several historical roots from which the policy of re-education grew during the second world war, the longest of which went far back into the 19th century in both Britain and the USA. In Britain they came together in the discovery by the British ruling elite that by educating the elites of their subject peoples into British ways, from cricket to the rule of law, they were able to maintain their rule by indirect control rather than by the more costly and troublesome overtly military-administrative direct methods of control. The success of this cultural and educational method in India and elsewhere fostered a particular predilection towards the belief that no matter how distant or alien or deep-rooted the political tradition or culture of another society might be, it was always possible to bring about a change of attitudes in depth through a combination of occupation and 'education'. A similar predilection grew in the USA from their own historical experience of the moulding of the 'American Nation'.

In a sense, there was an even deeper historical root in English society and culture itself. It was the assumption that the right kind of education could transform a boy born of the lower orders into a gentleman, manifested and fostered in the Public School Movement of the later 19th century and in the form taken by the development of Oxford and Cambridge in the same period. The acceptance into English society, and into the political ruling circle itself, the offspring of (at least fairly wealthy) men from the lower classes, provided the son had been to the right schools from an early enough age and finished the process at one of the Oxbridge colleges, was a characteristically different British approach to the gradual widening of the political and social base of the political nation which became necessary in all European countries towards the close of the 19th century. In other countries which, like Britain but unlike France, had escaped a revolutionary termination of the ideal and practice of aristocratic government, such as Austria and in most of the states which came to form Germany, education was perceived in a different, a technocratic, sense. It was seen as a means for providing people (including members of the political ruling elite) with the technical knowledge required in an industrial economy, or the linguistic or legal or military training required by the modern state. Attendance at particular schools or the possession of 'academic qualifications' was neither here nor there as far as membership of that elite was concerned. 'Qualifications' gave membership to another elite, the intelligentsia, which was subordinate, and possibly parallel, to the elite by birth, but definitely not merged into it, or even a stepping stone into it. That very high expectation of what education can actually achieve in terms of fundamentally moulding character and personality which the British approach implied, and therefore that high status which educators at such schools and colleges had in Britain, was particular to Britain, perhaps even to England within it. And, it gave the word 'education' a particular meaning in English which underlay its use in contexts where the continentals would have used 'propaganda' or 'indoctrination' or some such word. Though, since the idea was itself sui generis there are no directly equivalent words in German or in other languages in that area of Europe which would lend themselves to the idea which such extensions of it as 're-education' implied. It does not of course mean that using schools for indoctrination was wholly unprecedented and unknown on the Continent. The Jesuits and the teaching orders, such as the Piarists and the Premonstratentians, which were founded to further the Counter-reformation, had sought to inculcate catholic ideals and outlook through education and other religions have copied their techniques for their own 'propaganda fidei'. Indeed, the secularisation of education has been a long-standing issue in continental politics for that very reason. It was the idea of 'education' in the British (ruling elite's) terms - with its concentration on 'character formation', 'values', 'soundness' and 'manners' instead of a mastery of scientific knowledge and intellectual skills - as a social and ideological education fitting and qualifying a person to be a member of the political ruling elite of Britain (and the extension of it to children of the elites of the subject-nations within the Empire), that was sui generis.

An elite formed by a particular kind of 'education' rather than by birth or wealth alone was also a British idea which having evolved as a result of specifically British conditions became part of a political philosophy on offer to other nations. Liberalism rested on the twin ideals of an ideologically ('morally') 'educated' elite and an 'educated electorate' - as distinct from a mass-electorate - who were to receive information and above all guidance from a 'responsible' Press in the hands of the 'educated' elite itself. The function of the 'responsible Press' was not to articulate the 'prejudices' of the people but to 'educate' them to see issues in a particular ideological, 'moral', light. Liberalism thus extended the particular British concept of 'education' to the media of communications and reinforced the belief that through the education of the elite and the control of the media of communications it was possible to generate major changes in the political, indeed ideological, outlook of a people. A part of that belief was the conviction that given such education of the elite and the people alike, it was not necessary in order to achieve desired changes also to force through extensive alterations to the social, economic or cultural structure: they would follow on in time by consensus, encouraged from above, without the need for the use of power. In the Imperial context this extended even to their religions, however disagreeable or even barbaric they might have struck British

Liberals. This approach had been the hallmark of the British approach to Empire in the later 19th century, and Lord Milner's work in South Africa after the Boer War contained practically all the basic ideas and techniques planned for the re-education of Germany. None of these deep-rooted beliefs in British political thinking and experience however made it inevitable that re-education should have emerged as the preferred policy for ensuring that the Germans would not again seek to resort to war against Britain. As the debate about what to do with Germany after victory in the first world war shows, it was however natural, in Britain, that the idea should arise during the Second World war and be at least seriously considered - and probably only in Britain amongst the nations of Europe.

As far as the Americans were concerned, in the United States there were both some ideas which they shared with their British cousins and some others derived from quite different historical experiences which however also provided a predisposition towards at least considering 're-education'. First, there was the Adams/Hamilton tradition of a patrician political elite. It was not a mere plutocracy despite the egalitarian constitution of the USA. Entry to it required not merely wealth, but also the possession of certain educational and manners attributes derived from an Ivy League education. As in Britain, it was only the sons, educated at the right places, of self-made millionaires, not themselves, who could aspire to become members of it. At the Ivy League universities - as at West Point - 'character-formation' and 'manners' were an avowed educational aim, though there was an also a greater emphasis on also acquiring applied intellectual skills and technical knowledge. In the United States too there was a tradition of a 'Liberal' press seeking to educate and lead opinion rather than merely reflect it, and also a belief in the power of such 'Liberal' newspapers, such as the Washington Post, to educate the electorate and mould its attitudes. These elements were less universal in the make up of the USA with its competing Jacksonian populist tradition alongside it, but they were certainly very much present and operative within the Roosevelt administration. Roosevelt himself (unlike Morgenthau) was a classic embodiment of this patrician-elite and 'Liberal' tradition. So were many of his closest associates and so were the officials of the State Department including both Cordell Hull and Stettinius, the two Secretaries of State during the planning period. Insofar as post-victory planning was essentially the job of officials, the background and ethos of the officials involved was of special importance, just as it was in Britain. Once the heat of the personal hatred which he felt, as much as a patrician as a democrat, for Hitler and the nation which provided him with the means to realise what he stood for begun to give way in Roosevelt to a cooler consideration of the issues, these shared elements of outlook provided a predispositon amongst this circle to give at least an increasingly favourable hearing to British ideas of 're-education' in place of, or at least in addition to, the punitive and physically pre-emptive notions of de-industrialisation and dismemberment.

Introduction

There were however also other elements, quite different from their British allies', in the American past and make up which gave their own impetus to the belief that an attempt to change forcibly the ideological, make up of the peoples of other nations was both legitimate and practicable. These derived from the experience of the 'melting pot' (or at least of what was then believed about it); the way in which the 'American Nation' had been created out of immigrants from widely different European states, cultures and political systems. The immigrant peoples of the United States were believed to have acquired a sense of national identity, and a remarkably strong one at that triumphantly demonstrated in the two world wars, through the insistent projection of a political ideology. It had been pressed on them by every means from childhood to old age. There was the Flag in the classroom, learned-by heart political credos, the placing of a mythologised and symbolicised history at the core of the educational system for the formative years. For the adult, there followed participatory affirmation and ritualised re-articulaion through a national calendar of celebrations of symbolised historical events as manifestations of various facets of the nation's ideology; and it was articulated and reitarated endlessly through the mass media, and principally in more recent times through the medium of film which was uniquely suited to inculcate ideology through mythologised history and national stereotyping alike. [7] Fundamental dissent - in the sense in which arguing for pluralist democracy in say Russia would be much the same as arguing for changing over to a totalitarian, or even to a non-democratic liberal system on the pre-1918 British pattern, would be in America - such fundamental dissent was deeply unacceptable and practically non-existent in the USA. The United States was an ideological nation, the world's first and most successful one, and like any other ideological state it had an almost total conviction about its moral right to project its ideology and to impose it by every available means on others: was democracy not 'the last best hope of mankind'? Thus, both parts of the historical tradition and experience of the United States, although different in some essentials from the British, also predisposed it to the belief that it was both legitimate and practicable to attempt the ideological conversion of peoples while under military occupation. In the case of the United States, this was coupled with the belief, in complete contrast with the British distillation of their own experience, that it was also both right and practicable to think of forcing through directly major structural changes in the social and political system, and to see re-education as 'democratisation' in a way in which the British emphatically did not. 'Mission on the Rhine' came to provide after 1945 as illuminating a phrase for the Americans as was 're-education' for the British. [8].

There were thus long-term elements in the past of both the British and the Americans which explain why such a radical idea as re-education could come to be widely considered rather than remain the property of some individual visionary or fringe group. It also helps to explain why there could be found the large numbers of

11

officials, teachers, academics and others who were capable and willing to work in the planning committees and who would serve in the field putting it into practice with a will, and why they could be left to operate it without the need for detailed directives: they shared a broad consensual understanding of what it was all about. Such long-term elements in the political culture and ideology do not however explain by themselves why it should come to be accepted as an actual policy by the political decision making groups during 1943-45 - and especially why such a radically new and untried approach would be formulated and approved within the Foreign Office, of all places.

For that we need to look to more immediate historical experiences and the lessons drawn from them. In this case that was the failure of 'peacemaking' in 1918-19. The most immediate conditioning factor for the generation of officials and politicians who had reached the senior level during the second world war was their awareness that the policies which had been adopted by their own seniors in 1918 had totally failed in their prime objective: to prevent the resurgence of Germany's power and her will to war. During the 1930s thus the debate within the Foreign Office - and that broader group formally outside it which together form in Britain what can fairly be called the 'policy making elite' - about which policies might be the most effective for dealing with the problem presented by a resurgent Germany, thus encompassed a running debate about what had been wrong with the policies adopted in 1918-19. After all, there ought not have been a German problem threatening another European war so soon after the crushing defeat inflicted on her, at such cost to British lives and treasure. These two elements, trying to find solutions to the immediate problems represented by resurgent Germany and a search for what had been the mistakes made in the post-victory policies of 1918, forward planning and post mortem examination, were linked in a way which was both poignant at the time and significantly conditioned the debate which was to take place during the second world war concerning the next set of post-victory policies. The debate polarised around those, such as Vansittart and his younger acolytes, who believed that, Germany being the same unchanged Germany in the 1930's as she had been before 1914, the Germans were simply on the march again. And that, having found another war-leader in their preferred image, the Germans, being the Germans, were once again as irreversibly set to launch a war the moment conditions seemed right, as they had been looking towards 'Der Tag' before 1914. Against them were those who disagreed on principle with such fundamentalism about another people, rejected the cultural-social evidence proffered by Vansittart and others as irrelevant, and rejected therefore both its premises and the conclusions to which they pointed: 'the bleak and barren policy of the inevitability of war'. [9] They believed that peace with Germany could be secured eventually through normal, pragmatic, policies seeking to settle by negotiation the particular grievances and claims of the German government, as with any other 'normal' country. At worst, that

Hitler personally constituted a special danger by being unreasonable if not downright mad.

What made this debate so poignant and so important for the eventual emergence of the policy of re-education was that there were two facts in the back of everybody's mind. First, the knowledge, that the same debate about Germany had taken place before the war, between those, such as Tyrrell and Eyre Crowe, who believed that there was an inner dynamic in Germany (the 'Prussian element') impelling in the long run whatever particular government may be in office in Germany towards war for world dominance in general and against Britain in particular, and those who had believed either that given a wise, sympathetic and pragmatic approach Germany would settle down to a modus vivendi like France, or that at worst the policies leading towards war were the work of just 'a small military aristocracy in Prussia' [10] or even of 'His Impetuous Majesty' personally. Second, the memory in the minds at least of an important group in the FO, that there had also been a debate during the closing stages of the Great War about what would be the appropriate policy to adopt towards Germany after capitulation – and that the idea of 're-education' in its ·essentials had in fact been put forward, debated and in the end rejected in favour of the 'normal' financial and territorial approach: the Great War Prelude.

That debate in the course of 1917 had been triggered by President Wilson's declarations about American war aims once the United States had entered the war. He accepted the view that although there were many stresses and strains in Eastern Europe making for a dangerous situation, the actual war was the responsibility of the ruling class of Germany, and therefore the ultimate peace aim of the United States was to secure that such a war should never again be launched on the world by Germany. Central to the realisation of this aim in Wilson's mind and statements at the time were the 'democratisation of Germany' and the establishment of an international League for Peace, jointly making the world safe for democracy and securing a lasting peace. The debate triggered in Britain by Wilson's belief in the need to reform Germany itself led to a revival of the passionate debate about Germany which had been going on in Britain at least since the 1890s and in some ways, as P.M. Kennedy has recently demonstrated, for even longer. [11] Therefore, whereas Wilson and his advisers were by and large little informed about the actual structure and development of Germany since it had played little part in the concerns of the American State Department until the war, there was a lot more intellectual ammunition in Britain with which the very large issues involved in trying to bring about internal changes in a defeated Great Power could be debated.

Thus the debate in Britain took on a more detailed and thorough form and led to the production of not only heated and heartfelt arguments in and out of Parliament but also to discussion papers and memoranda within the confines of the official and political circles. The simple notion that handing power to the people on the characteristically American assumption that the people, all people, were peaceable and therefore forcing Germany to change to a democratic constitution was essentially all that was required, dissolved in Britain into a larger debate about 'changing the heart of Germany' and led even to a discussion in terms of the 'education' of the German people. That widened the issue since it involved an even larger scale interference than forcing the adoption of a particular constitution in the internal affairs of another nation - and revived with a vengeance the long-running debate about the roots and long-term orientation of German policy which had been such a characteristic of the pre-war Foreign Office and of the political circles served by it.

For of course the idea of 're-education' presupposes the idea that there was something special about Germany, of the 'German mind'. It was the logical peace-making approach for those who held to the fundamentalist view about the dynamics of German policy, just as the rejection of the idea of a major interference in Germany's domestic affairs and educational or political system, and of the prolonged occupation and government of Germany which it entailed, was the logical approach for the others. Nevertheless, given the 19th century habits of thought in which they had all been brought up about the nature of international relations, according to which meddling in the internal politics of other countries in order to gain a diplomatic advantage was regarded as unacceptable on principle, to go the whole logical way to 're-education' was a very large step even for those who did hold to the former view. It would have been a quite horrifying departure from the norms of civilised diplomatic relations for the others. That nevertheless such a radically new idea as the 'education' of the people of Germany should have come up at all and to have been seriously discussed in the Foreign Office and its wartime subordinate organisations during 1918-19 was as much a demonstration of the corrosive impact of the first Total War on older modes of thought in general, as it was a demonstration that there were indeed long established and deep-seated elements in the political culture of Britain and the United States which gave an unconscious predisposition towards it.

When therefore minds were once again turning towards formulating a post-victory policy during the second world war, there was in the back of the mind of that generation of officials, journalists, academics and others forming part of the larger circle of foreign policy making elite also the memory that a radically new approach to peacemaking with Germany had in fact been put forward and extensively debated, only in the end to be jettisoned in favour of the orthodox approach. Whatever post-victory policy should eventually emerge, there was therefore a general feeling by 1939 that it would have to be something new and fundamental in approach. It was neatly symbolised in the foreword which one of that Chatham House circle, E.H. Carr, hastily wrote in September 1939 to a book about the twenty-years since 1918 which he had completed earlier in the year. E.H. Carr dedicated it to 'The Makers of the Next Peace' and wrote:'The next peace conference if it is not to repeat the fiasco of the last will have to concern itself with issues more fundamental than the drawing of frontiers'. [12] For once, it was the radical and the novel towards which there was a predisposition in the FO and the larger group around it when it came to thinking about peace-policies concerning Germany.

Although the idea itself had been both rejected in 1918 and had originated but from a small and junior group largely recruited from outside, the memory of it twenty years later was not quite as distant and uninfluential as it might have been. The idea of that radical approach of 'changing Germany' emerged from the Political Intelligence Department of the Foreign Office in the first world war. Together with the News Department it was a very new Department created in response to the change in the nature of warfare and the need to employ propaganda both as a new weapon of war and a means of wartime diplomacy. Since for many of the old school of diplomats that was in itself a grievous departure, from previous principles of the conduct of diplomacy and war alike, the PID, established in March 1918, came to be principally recruited from the young men who had been working together as the Intelligence Bureau of the (secret) War Propaganda Bureau, Wellington House. The new department was put under William Tyrrell, regarded as a non-orthodox official alike in his views and approach. The former placed him into the camp of those who had taken the fundamentalist view of Germany before 1914, and the latter logically extended to a belief in the essential importance of propaganda and news-management. The young officials themselves had originally been recruited from either academic life, such as Toynbee and Namier, or from education such as Percy Koppel and Headlam-Morley (who became Permanent Staff Inspector of the Board of Education in 1904 partly on the strength of a brilliant report on German secondary education), or from journalists such as George Saunders who had served as a resident correspondent for The Times in Germany for more than a decade before the war. They naturally continued to work in close co-operation with those colleagues of theirs who remained in the various propaganda agencies brought together into the Ministry of Information in 1918, such as Wickham Steed or Seton-Watson and with the members of the News Department of the Foreign Office itself which was similarly young in composition and also largely drawn from outside. [13]

When following the Peace Conference and the assumed return to normality, in a fit of parsimony the Treasury insisted on abolishing the PID, nicknamed 'the Ministry of Talents', some of its more junior members, such as Percy Koppel, Rex and Allen Leeper, were found a place in the FO, with several such as Koppel and eventually Rex Leeper in the reconstructed News (originally intended to be called 'Propaganda') Department. The first post-war head of which was Vansittart, who shared not only Tyrrell's fundamentalist views about the roots of German foreign policy but also Tyrrell's convictions about the essential importance of propaganda in every form and in every sense of the term. The more senior members of the PID, and their associates from the propaganda agencies which were also wound up in 1918, left the FO but continued to work together within the newly founded Royal Institute of International Affairs, 'Chatham House', which was de facto established in 1924 for the purpose of providing for the FO the functions of a political intelligence department, also engaging the services of some of the younger men also who had to leave the FO such as E.H. Carr. In turn during the inter-war years they brought in bright young men to work with them, such as Michael Balfour, and Rohan Butler. [14] Tyrrell and then Vansittart rose to be Permanent Under Secretaries of State and as such the head of the Foreign Office, while Headlam-Morley, until his untimely death in 1930, occupied a special position as its Historical Adviser. There thus remained a continuity in personnel and views both within the officials of the Foreign Office and of that larger group which in the British system plays a part in the debating process underlying the making of foreign policy. Both viewpoints about Germany formulated before the Great War continued and so did therefore the debates between the fundamentalists and the pragmatists about Germany itself, made perhaps unnecessarily heated by Vansittart's love for over-brilliant expression. [15] And so also did the debate continue between traditionalists seeking to return to the methods and concepts of the old world of diplomatic relations and the others who could perhaps be best described as the propagandists. In the case of the question what to do about Germany after victory the two aspects, fundamentalism in respect of the causes of the German propensity to war and acceptance of the need in modern times of appealing to the people of other countries over the heads of their government and diplomats, naturally coalesced.

In the interwar period both schools of thought continued to exist within the Foreign Office as well as in the broader advisory group. There was thus a deep split on both the question of what motivated Hitler's Germany and over the proper functions and methods of diplomacy. But while this unfortunately offered the politicians during the 1930s a choice in expert advice on how to respond to the rise of Germany under Hitler, the fact that Tyrrell and Vansittart had been in charge of the personnel of the Foreign Office for such a large part of the period inevitably led to growing strength for their school of thought and method amongst the generation rising to seniority during the inter-war period. Although Chamberlain - to whom the professional advice provided by the FO of Vansittart as Permanent Under-Secretary was advice which he did not want to hear - decided that Vansittart must go and the FO learn to believe and support his intuitive 'understanding' of Hitler and Germany and had him replaced in December 1937 with the impeccably pragmatist and traditionalist Cadogan, it came too late to make much of a change before war broke out. Some of 'Van's boys', such as Rex Leeper (made head of the News Department by Vansittart in 1934), begin to be shunted out by Cadogan after Munich, but the outbreak of war put an end to the attempt to shift the balance back to the traditionalists and pragmatists.

Moreover, during the last and earnest phase of rearmament the reconstitution of the wartime network of propaganda and political intelligence organisations proceeded under the guidance of Vansittart and his followers, first and foremost Rex Leeper. Thus it was Leeper who was in charge of rebuilding both the nucleus of the Political Intelligence Department and the new enemy propaganda organisation of the FO, both of which were proceeded with in secrecy, tucked away at Electra House on the Embankment, as much from the Germans as from too close a scrutiny from Halifax and Cadogan. [16] Nemesis in the shape of Cadogan and Sir Horace Wilson did catch up with Leeper after Munich and he was formally told that he had lost the confidence of his chiefs and would be posted overseas. However the outbreak of the very war which believed to be inevitable - 'with Germany there is nothing for us to negotiate, except our surrender' he wrote early in 1938 - came just in time to prevent his actual departure. [17] Instead he became Director of the PID itself when, on the outbreak of war, it was formally restored as a department of the Foreign Office. Subsequently his responsibilities were extended by also becoming Director for Subversive Propaganda (SOE 1 in the Ministry of Economic Warfare, dubbed by Churchill the 'Ministry of Ungentlemanly Warfare' and instructed to 'set Europe ablaze') and then going on to becoming H.Q. Director of the Political Warfare Executive under Bruce-Lockhart when subversive propaganda was raised into a separate organisation. [18] In a very real sense therefore Leeper was the father and creator of the PID of the second world war. [19] The change of name from 'Enemy Propaganda Department' in the first world war to the 'Political Warfare Executive' marked the culmination of the line of thinking which led from the first world war to the production of the plans for 're-education' and their realisation after the second world war. It represented the triumph eventually of the line of argument known as 'Vansittartism', however much that phrase is inappropriate since it preceded him. It was the line of those who saw the reason behind the invariable drift of German policies towards hostility and ultimately war against Britain and the rest of Europe in the mind of the German people - and therefore sought the ultimate solution to the German problem in changing it.

Changing minds is of course the particular business of propaganda. It was thus proper, as well as inevitable, that it would be in the community of the 'persuaders' and within their organisational framework, Enemy Propaganda Department in the first world war at Crewe House that the ideas of 'education' would first develop, and that in the second world war the planning of re-education would be located in the Political Warfare Executive at Woburn Abbey - 'PID', it should noted was merely the cover-name for 'PWE' which was a secret department. [20] Almost the first major policy paper submitted by the newly constituted Political Intelligence Department in 1918 argued that 'the CHANGING OF GERMANY (sic) was the primary war aim'. It had been submitted under the joint signatures of Headlam-Morley the newly appointed Assistant Director of PID and H.G. Wells the Director of Propaganda to Germany in Crewe House. The last memorandum from Crewe House before it was wound up, penned by Wickham Steed on behalf of Lord Northcliffe, proposed the continuation of Crewe House into an 'agency of enlightenment' for the purpose of 'enabling the German people gradually to see why Germany had lost the war, and to understand the force of the moral ideals which had ranged practically the whole world against her'. [21] It was equally natural, since it is a political warfare concept, that the planning process for re-education in the second world war should have began with a memorandum prepared in the Political Warfare Executive and signed by J.M. Troutbeck the Principal Assistant Secretary dealing with Subversive Propaganda operations at the Ministry of Economic Warfare and subsequently PWE It was equally natural that once the actual planning began the work was principally in charge of a Joint PWE/MOI/BBC Committee - a veritable 'Ministry of Propaganda Talents'. The Joint Committee was also under the chairmanship of Troutbeck, himself a 1920 Foreign Office entrant holding to the Tyrrell-Vansittart line throughout his career. who in December 1943 provided the final brief to which it worked 'What we are going to do is to stamp out the whole tradition on which the German nation has been built'. [22]

Thus, the historical background and explanation of the policy of re-education, as distinct from the general idea involved, lies first in the long-term continuity of this whole interlocking cluster of ideas which began to develop from before the first world war and were finally represented in the concept of 'Political Warfare'. Second, it is to be found in the overlapping and interwoven careers of people such as Tyrrell and Vansittart, Leeper and Troutbeck, and their institutional counterpart in the process of succession: Enemy Propaganda - PID - News Department/Chatham House - PID - PWE - and the circumstance that it took place within a short enough space of time to allow individuals, such as Rex Leeper, to span them all during their working career. This also helps to explain the speed with which such a radical idea entailing such a wide range of activities and mass of preparations could be worked up into a practical policy during just the closing months of the war, after it been adopted as the policy.

The third factor which also played a vital part in the acceptance of the idea of re-education was equally the result of a continuous development since the first world war. When in November 1917 Balfour turned on those in Parliament who pressed the Wilsonian call for 'democratising' Germany, he demanded to know how it could be done: 'How can we change the heart of Germany'? He recognised, as did others, that merely by compelling a defeated Germany to adopt an entirely new constitution would not achieve that end. But neither he nor anyone else in any position of political or official seniority in 1917 believed that there were any means in existence with which the German people's ideas could be brought to change. Even if he or the Prime Minister had not been totally out of sympathy with the very idea, regarding it as an utterly unacceptable departure from the old-world decencies of international conduct, there was a complete lack of means known to them for putting it into practice. Whatever the merits of the idea might have appeared in 1917, there was certainly a consensus that it was not practicable.

Twenty-five years later there was an equal consensus that changing people's ideas was a perfectly practical proposition. Propaganda had come to be believed to be a 'science', practical, well-proven, and virtually omni-competent in application. It remained fashionable to sadly deprecate that such a thing should have come into being - a sign of the times - and it was recognised that to admit using propaganda was counterproductive anyway. Nevertheless, by the outbreak of the second world war, there had come into being a belief in both the necessity and the practical effectiveness of propaganda so strong and so widely held as to be simply astonishing.

Equally remarkable was the speed with which that belief had developed. In 1917 at the time when the Parliamentary debate about 'how to change the heart of Germany' took place 'propaganda' was a word hardly used or seriously considered. In high places it was known that there were some small wartime agencies whose job was propaganda, a rather nebulous and underhand activity, in which Lloyd George seemed to have a personal interest - only to be expected. Apart from that it was known as the hobby-horse of that irrational baron of the gutter press, Lord Northcliffe, to keep urging it on the Government - and that too was only to be expected. Within less than a year members of parliament were asserting their belief, as a matter of fact, that 'propaganda probably more than any other single fact or factor brought about the disaster in Russia'. And that the defeat at Caporetto was 'almost entirely due to an extraordinarily successful propaganda...by the Austrians and the Germans'. [23] Even that model of staid conservatism, Stanley Baldwin, was telling the House that while 'Propaganda is a word which does not have a pleasant sound in English ears....Propaganda work is very like anti-submarine work. It is work which is necessary ....and it is work that can be and must be judged by results.' [24] By October 1919 The Times judged that 'Good propaganda probably saved a year of war and....at least a million lives'. [25] By the mid 1920s the Encyclopaedia Britannica and The Times History of The War joined in repeating with approval, and with additional 'evidence', the views expressed by Hindenburg, Ludendorff and other war-leaders of the Central Powers to the effect that: 'We were hypnotised by the enemy propaganda as a rabbit is by the snake.' [26] For good measure, by the beginning of the 1930s, wide currency in Britain was also given to the front-line soldier's view on the receiving end of British propaganda from one Adolf Hitler: 'Our soldiers learned to think the way the enemy wanted them to think.' [27]

Not only the peoples of the enemy were however increasingly thought of as capable of being made to think whatever way it might be desired through the science of propaganda. In fact more important in the long run was the process of belief-practice-belief in the use of propaganda at home which also followed the Great War and characterised, as much as any other single feature, the political scene in Britain between the wars. It provided pragmatic evidence, or what was believed to be pragmatic evidence, as to the powers of propaganda. The starting point in that process of self-education was the belief in the effectiveness of wartime propaganda combined with the belief in the effectiveness of newly invented 'mass-communication' technologies and the arrival of 'scientific' expertise in mass-persuasion. By March 1920 instructions to local Party organisations by the National Executive Committee (NEC) of the Labour Party stated as a fact that 'During the War the Cinematograph became a powerful instrument of propaganda in the hands of the Government', emphasised the importance of taking steps to 'counteract this new form of political warfare,' and concluded that the 'cinematograph is destined to play an ever dominating role in propaganda and educational work, hence no time should be lost in utilising such a powerful weapon in the cause of Labour.' [28] Party organisers and 'propaganda agents' were instructed that 'mass psychology must be scientifically studied', [29] and constant emphasis was placed on Ramsay MacDonald's long held view about the importance of 'putting into the field a body of men who recognise that their first duty is to educate the heart and the head of the people'. [30] When success first came in 1924, the Party Conference stated its belief: 'To have passed from the small beginnings ... to the formation of a Labour Ministry in so short a time is a remarkable testimony to the political education....and the effective character of the Party's propaganda'. [31] Looking back on winning the 1929 election and on the success of the Labour Government's first two years, the Party's Chairman (and Foreign Secretary) Arthur Henderson ascribed them to that: 'No Party has carried on such continuous and extensive propaganda during recent years as the Labour Party'. [32]

The same set of beliefs were shared by the Conservative leadership, if anything with an even greater sense of conviction and urgency. Immediately after the end of the war, the Party went out of its way to recruit leading figures of the secret propaganda war, such as Admiral Hall, the hero of the Zimmerman Telegram coup, who became its Chief Publicity Agent, and Joseph Ball who masterminded the Party's propaganda work from 1925. The Central Council of the National Union of Conservative and Unionist Associations passed resolutions such as: 'No time should be lost by Party experts in making close local studies of the mass-psychology of the electors' in preparation for 'intensified educational programmes of propaganda'. [33] Other Committees expressed their belief in the 'importance of national propaganda in all its forms.... since it is only by propaganda that the vast unorganised masses.... can be influenced'. [34] The dominant political figure of the period, Stanley Baldwin, Leader of the Party from 1923 to 1937, and three times Prime Minister between 1924-37, continued to avoid using the word in public and in fact asked his propagandists to come with a better word - 'political advertising' won by a short lead from 'political education' and 'information' - but this did not stop him from using the word in confidential papers or in meetings. He believed that '... faced with the intensive propaganda of socialism....The maintenance of an educated democracy depends on unceasing propaganda....' [35] and that 'Propaganda (is) now recognised as the world's most potent weapon....' expenditure on which '... should be regarded as an insurance premium'. [36]

On the institutional and government level too, the need for propaganda - which before the war was considered 'repellent ... the work of the vulgarian: it was also thought useless' - came to be accepted. [37] No less of a representative of the disdainful old-style aristocratic Foreign Secretary than Lord Curzon, felt it necessary to instruct all embassies (except Washington) on 19 May 1919 that 'British propaganda in foreign Countries shall, in future, be regarded as part of the(ir) regular work....I do not doubt that from the experience of the last four years you will have learned what forms of propaganda to encourage and what to avoid'. [38] Liberal traditions notwithstanding, censorship, negative propaganda, and and other forms of control over the new media of mass-communications also came to be accepted as necessary after the war. [39] Invented before the war and thus left free in the traditions of the press, 'this modern, up-to-date educational engine, the cinema....perhaps the most valuable means of propaganda' [40] was subjected to an increasingly sophisticated, effective and comprehensive censorship seeking to guide and mould films in the script stage rather than 'cut', though perfectly willing and able both to cut and to ban altogether. Film censorship was run from 1936 by Tyrrell himself after retiring from the Foreign Office as Lord Tyrrell of Avon. Radio reached the stage of technical development necessary for regular voice-transmissions only after the war. Hence, in the new atmosphere after 1918 - and traditions of the Free Press notwithstanding - radio was not allowed to operate as private enterprise like the Press, as in some other countries such as the USA and even France. The right to broadcast was confined to a Public Corporation with a complex and sophisticated relationship to Government, which became the powerhouse of equally complex and sophisticated ideas about how to fulfil its role as 'the integrator of Democracy' and the 'Voice of Britain'. [41] Its founder/creator John Reith, when Minister of Information during the war, coined that most illuminating of phrases for at least one of the ideas evolved there before the war: 'News is the shocktroops of propaganda'. [42] The British Council, a joint creation of Tyrrell, Vansittart and Leeper, was from 1934 increasingly evolving the techniques of 'cultural propaganda'. [43] All in all there is much truth in the view expressed by one observer, twenty years after the Great War and a year before the next: 'This generation is witnessing a boom in Propaganda.' [44]

It is therefore not surprising that Britain entered the second world war with large war-propaganda organisations in the process of being formed and ambitious plans for their use. The strategic assumption was that the war would settle down to a stalemate in front of the Maginot Line and would be determined by whichever side's morale could be broken first, under the combined assault of bombing and propaganda. Although the fall of France had disrupted the plans, after the defensive victory in the Blitz the stalemate did materialise. Anticipating Stalin's question as to how the British proposed to win the war after Dunkirk, Churchill instructed Lord Beaverbrook in September 1941 to answer: 'We shall undermine them by propaganda; depress them with the blockade; and, above all, bomb their homelands ceaselessly, ruthlessly, and with ever increasing weight of bombs.' [45] Both as a defensive and as an offensive weapon of the mind propaganda was believed to be of central importance. Accordingly it was endowed with an appropriately heavy investment of resources: which in this sphere meant people with high levels of intellectual and media talent: the PWE and the other propaganda organisations were assigned the cream of British intellectuals, second only to those working on code-breaking at Bletchley. Although the entry of the Soviet Union and the USA made psychological warfare essentially superfluous, the British persisted in the war on the mind by putting much of their resources into trying to break the German people's will to war through area bombing and propaganda and by trying to raise resistance movements. Despite the manifest failure to achieve anything at all significant as far as German morale was concerned and little beyond nuisance value by the resistance movements in Western Europe, there was no diminution in the faith in propaganda. On the contrary, the war ended with an even more general belief in the practicality, omnicompetence and overall importance of propaganda. Even such aristocratic Foreign Secretaries temperamentally out of tune with such things as Lord Halifax and Anthony Eden emerged from the war as converts. Eden for example, who began with a complete, and impatient, lack of interest in all matters of 'black' propaganda, by June 1944 declared : 'to give up control of Political Warfare would mean to cease being Foreign Secretary.' [46]

The culmination of it all was 're-education'; a conscious euphemism for the adaptation to post-victory conditions and needs of the concepts, techniques and personnel of what the British called 'Political Warfare' and the Americans called 'Psychological Warfare'. In either camp, 'propaganda' was the shorthand for it. There can be no doubt, incidentally, that the British and American officials and their political masters thought themselves in these terms. As the documents quoted in this volume show beyond a shadow of doubt, whenever the subject was discussed amongst themselves from 1943 to the end of the period, propaganda was the common shorthand for the whole exercise. From the title of the first major policy paper to emerge from the Committee established in the summer of 1943 'Lines for Emergency Plan, Propaganda to Germany After her Defeat' [47] to Sir William Strang's letter to Ernest Bevin asking for more newsprint in 1946 to ensure that 'the propaganda we try to put out' will in fact get through, the word was omnipresent. [48] Talking in 1978 and in suitably modest and self-deprecatory terms about it (he was talking to a German scholar) Sir Con O'Neill who played a central role in formulating British policy, said that 're-education was a kind of ambitious semi-propaganda concept'. [49] Others at times talked about it as a 'super-propaganda exercise'. In any case, as we

Introduction

have seen during the evolution of the belief in propaganda during the inter-war period in Britain, 'propaganda' subsumed 'political education' and 'education' in that concept. Born from the belief in the boundless powers of propaganda techniques, the post-victory policy of re-education was the most ambitious of all the propaganda projects of the first half of the twentieth century. It is possible that it also marked the high-water point of that belief.

*

The roots of the basic idea behind 're-education' went deep indeed into the culture and political experiences of the English speaking peoples. As an actual post-victory policy it was the offspring of a union between 'Vansittartism' and propaganda, two converging lines of thinking. The first was the Vansittartian analysis of what were the roots of foreign policy in the 20th century in general and of Germany's in particular. The belief that in the long run it was merely an external manifestation of the 'world-outlook' of the individual German (or Japanese) or at least of those of the dominant intellectual and social groups in the nation. The second was the belief that in propaganda - or psychological or political warfare if we prefer - there were now tools in existence, both conceptual and practical, for getting at people's perceptions, of making them see the world in a desired way. It was an Orwellian solution to a problem as defined by Vansittart: people who make war in their minds only wait for The Day when things seems propitious to make real war. It was the will to war, as Hitler insisted, which was the real, and the day-to-day twists of policy the apparent factors, which determined the course of the German foreign policies. Since effective mind-control techniques appear to have been developed, the road to lasting peace would be through disarming their minds.

Re-education was certainly not born of motives of charity, it was not the solution of those who felt more kindly towards the Germans than those in the FO who considered the various options for physical measures, such as dismemberment, and coolly discussed the prospects in Germany after 'several million Germans had disappeared into Siberia' by courtesy of 'Uncle Joe'. [50] A final solution to the German problem - the propensity for turning Europe into a charnelhouse - was going to be attempted at the end of this war by one means or another. The British may be 'slow to anger', but they, and their American cousins too, had had enough. The question was merely by what means that was to be achieved. Re-education was chosen as a policy because it was felt that it went to the root of the problem - and because it was thought to be more effective in the long run to go for minds rather than bodies.

If 're-education' was not a policy selected out of charity, nor were those who were in charge of carrying it out motivated by such sentiments. Evidence of feelings are rare to find for Englishmen seldom talk about that sort of thing and least of all when as in this case it may be counterproductive to the enterprise itself. But two examples might illustrate the point, coming from two of those who played a central part in the policy after 1945: Sir Hugh Greene, and Sir William Strang. Sir Hugh, remembered with respect in Germany as the father of the West German broadcasting system, had lived in Germany for some six years before the war as correspondent of Daily Telegraph, until expelled in the spring of 1939. He recently told the story of his departure. After a well lubricated round of farewells with fellow journalists and German acquaintances, he was escorted by them to the Railway station. A keen fencer he had his épée with him. Winding down the window he looked at the platform thick with uniforms. And then, in vino veritas, his feelings broke through. Brandishing the épée he shouted 'Ich komme als Gauleiter züruck'. Visiting the troops during the spring of 1945 he was amongst the first to enter Dachau: 'It was an experience which marks one for life'. Then, he did 'return' to Germany as Controller of Broadcasting in 1946. He had no compunction about the job being to set up a BBC model in Germany whether they liked it or not and of selecting suitable Germans and 'educating' them in how to operate that complex model, as his particular part in making Europe safe from them – nor of being driven about in a Maybach limousine the size of a locomotive which formerly belonged to an SS General. At the time a twenty-year occupation, one way or another, was talked of as the necessary period for the job to be finally completed. As far as he was concerned he hoped that his job would be over in more like two years, and he could then go home. [51] Sir William Strang was Political Adviser to the Military Government. In his memoirs he tells the story of how he went to see the Mayor of Hamburg whom 'I took to be a "good" German, if there were any such'. When the Mayor of that devastated city started to talk about the Germans' desire for friendship with Britain and suggested that a milder economic policy towards the suffering people might help to avoid the attractions of communism, the reserved and mild mannered Strang's feelings broke out.

> I interrupted this exercise in self-pity and covert blackmail to say that we were determined that there should be no repetition of the two world wars brought by Germany...the primary purpose of the occupation was to disarm and to demilitarise Germany and uproot the Nazi party, not to promote Anglo-German friendship...there was no reason why the German people should not in future take a worthy place among the peoples of Europe, but it would be for the Germans to deserve such a place, perhaps by long apprenticeship. [52]

These were indeed 'cold' motives. Nor is there any doubt that re-education was conceived as a continuation of psychological warfare into the occupation period designed to complete the job of physical defeat. As one of the leading figures in PWE wrote in his memoirs on reaching VE Day: 'The need for psychological propaganda did not however end; it was rather a question of replacing the undermining of German morale with the re-education of the German people, and the exposure of the real nature of Nazism.' [53] Looked at it in that light, re-education could be said to be open to the same sort of objections which psychological warfare, propaganda, had often had to encounter: that getting at people's minds was somehow a more insidious, sinister and less 'gentlemanly' kind of method for getting results than fighting with actual weapons or using economic measures. Certainly, a massive and in-depth indoctrination/ propaganda exercise extending into all spheres of publication, youth-training, education and so forth has an Orwellian flavour as against 'straightforward' military, diplomatic and economic measures proposed by others, but any comparison in such terms is pure political romanticism. It represents the same sort of 'argument' which opponents of propaganda in politics and warfare had always presented: that propaganda 'is a greater evil in wartime than the actual loss of life. The defilement of the human soul is worse than the destruction of the human body'. [54] The answer to this sort of gobbledegook was always the same. When Brigadier John Baker White, whose memoirs have been been quoted above, met a general in the club after VJ day, he was asked what he did in the war. 'Mostly psychological warfare, deception and kindred activities' he replied. 'Filthy game' grunted the general and started to walk away in disgust. 'You may call it a filthy game....but we were cutting down on the casualty lists and not piling them up' reposted the furious Baker White. [55] The classic answer had in fact already been given by Northcliffe, at the end of the Great War. He had had his proposal for using propaganda in 1915 rebuffed by one General with the words 'the thing was to kill Germans'. [56] So he was ready when 'propaganda is dirty business' was thrown at him by another. 'If we can persuade a German by propaganda to throw down his arms and come over we have deprived Germany of a soldier, without also having to kill a man.' [57] The same applies in this case: 're-education' was the most humane method for implementing a policy determined on a final solution to the German problem.

*

There was however another side to all this. Not only was re-education a humane approach in the sense that however dubious it might be to tamper with people's minds, it at least leaves them alive. It also left the door open to modifications, shifts of emphasis in response to changing circumstances without having to overtly change policy. Most importantly, it gave scope for different interpretations and allowed free rein to other deeply imbedded elements within the national culture to make their own kind of contribution. It gave scope to a particular kind of idealism - individualist and with its roots in the Non-conformist tradition and belonging to a lower social level than the political ruling elite - which was also a characteristic element in the make up of British 'weltanschauung'. It was Vansittart himself, always a more complex character than simply a product of his social class, who articulated the attitude of this element in Britain in those seminal 'Black

Record' broadcasts: 'By the Grace of God and for the salvation of man, we shall rescue the world from Germany, and Germany from herself.' Re-education was a policy which was also, as the Foreign Office put it, 'acceptable to the liberal sentiment'. Which, in Britain, was still alive and ready to be concerned over even Germany - at least in the longer run. It offered a way to obtain both an immediate and coldly practical political objective and a chance for working towards a longer term ideal in harmony with those sentiments.

In practice later on, re-education gave scope therefore to some other and equally characteristic products of the historical evolution of the English speaking peoples: those who are rather deprecatingly dubbed 'the do-gooders', representatives of the tradition that the individual should do whatever he perceives to be 'good' towards another human being, irrespective of any collective considerations or policy. As lower level officials working in the various branches and agencies required by the re-education policy, it gave them scope to practise the extension of that tradition evolved during the imperial experience: that whatever maybe the collective attitude or policy of the nation towards another nation, it was not to override the duty of the individual to behave in a humane and decent manner towards any particular individual of that nation. They acted in accordance with the humane m̲ores of their culture within which it was wholly unacceptable to de-personalise, de-humanise individuals on account of their collective being, the acceptability of which in the German culture was perhaps the basic cause of the extraordinary hatred left behind by the German occupation. These individual Britons and Americans, in Germany and in Japan, many of whom continued in fact to serve for many years after the formal end of the Occupation, softened and humanised and in a sense de-propagandised the policy in the practice of it. They helped it to go a long way towards the eventual i̲deal of the policy, to make the defeated Germans feel part of a European community of nations - a community based on a power-relationship of their country within it which totally denied their original aspirations. Perhaps, therefore, the most important aspect of the policy of re-education, with all its 'cold' motivation at the policy making and planning level, was that it allowed the installation of a large number of 'little people' - teachers, and others, ordinary, pragmatic people - in the community of their former enemies on a long term basis and in a shifting position in terms of authority. It thus provided, at any rate, the possibility for continuing contact and assimilation, which none of the other policy options would have offered. [58]

*

Whatever conclusions might arise from the evidence for the history of the years after 1951 concerning the rôle actually played by 're-education' as against the many other elements affecting the history of Germany and Japan, there is no doubt that in its aims and inception 're-education' was a singularly interesting and thought-provoking policy with some broad implications well beyond itself. 'To stamp out the whole tradition on which the German nation has been built' was a breathtaking brief: never before had a nation envisaged the wholesale political, ideological and psychological reconstruction of another equally advanced, populous and prosperous nation. It was certainly one of one of history's most imaginative, and perhaps humane, foreign policies. Intended to provide a 'final solution' by a Carthagenian pacification of the Germans' minds, it gave scope to interpreting it on the ground as if designed to 're-educate' the vanquished into feeling a common bond with their conquerors instead of dreaming of 'revanche'. In both ways, it represented an equally novel and imaginative approach to foreign policy.

Re-education also has a unique place in the history of the development of the techniques of government in the age of the 'communications revolution'. It unquestionably involved one of the most sophisticated deployments of the concepts and techniques of 'political' or 'psychological' warfare, of propaganda in every sense of that phrase. It was also a brief which Goebbels, the technician not the Nazi, would have relished. Whether that makes 're-education' all the more one of the most imaginative and humane policies of history or whether it makes it less so in our eyes depends on what view one holds about the legitimacy and effect of the use of modern persuasion techniques in the conduct of government. But that it gives it a special place in history for that reason too can scarcely be doubted.

NOTES

References and notes are confined to specific points which are either not common currency or are not dealt with in greater depth by the essays in this volume. As far as the interpretation of the roots of 'Prussian militarism' and the impact of the war on the Eastern front is concerned it would be impossible to provide detailed references in a brief general introduction such as this. My main debts are to the following: Karl Bracher, The German Dictatorship (London 1970); David Calleo, The German Problem Reconsidered: Germany and the World Order 1870-to the Present (Cambridge 1978); Klaus Hidebrand, Das Dritte Reich (München 1979); Herman Glaser, The Cultural Roots of National Socialism (London 1978); George L. Mosse, The Crisis of German Ideology, Intellectual Origins of the Third Reich (New York 1964); Louis L. snyder, Roots of German Nationalism (Indiana 1978).

1. For American ideas and plans from before and after the Morgenthau plan see The Memoirs of Cordell Hull (London 1948) vol. 2 esp. Ch.115: Plan for Germany. James F. Tent, Mission on the Rhine: Reeducation and Denazification in American-Occupied Germany (Chicago 1982); Edward N. Peterson The American Occupation of Germany: Retreat to Victory (Detroit 1979). For

Introduction

Soviet ideas and plans there is nothing available which is comparably authoritative. Stalin and the Soviet leadership played their cards close to the chest; such Soviet memoirs as are available are silent on such questions; Soviet archives are not open, and Soviet historical publications on the subject assume that 'contemporary history' has an active rôle to play in current policies. There certainly was an organisation for drawing up plans for Stalin on the post war treatment of Germany, which at the time of the Moscow Conference was headed by Maisky, but no reliable evidence has become available what they were. For a discussion of what little is known of Soviet plans see Adam B. Ulam, Expansion and Coexistence: the History of Soviet Foreign Policy from 1917-1967 (London 1968) and Wojtech Mastny, Russia's Road to the Cold War, Diplomacy, Warfare and the Politics of Communism, 1941-1945 (New York 1979). Perhaps the closest documentary evidence of what Soviet plans actually aimed at comes from the submission they made to the inter-allied Committee charged with co-ordinating surrender terms and organisation for the governing of Germany, rather grandiloquently called the European Advisory Commission. As there were certain things they needed to clear with their Western Allies of the moment they had to state some of what they intended actually to do, at least in the short period immediately after the joint occupation of Germany. The proposal asked the Allies to sanction (1) the right of the Soviet military authorities to transfer immediately all such research institutions and the like including those who worked in them to the Soviet Union and all such industrial plants which had been working for the German Armed Forces - which plants etc. did not work for the Armed forces in war? - ; (2) Allied sanction for declaring all members of the German armed forces whether captured or not to be prisoners of war and thus for placing under the 'immediate disposal of the Allies the most active, compact....and organised part of the German population'; (3) The right to use them as forced labour in the Soviet Union and agreement that the length of detention would be entirely at the victors' discretion; (4) that the Hague and Geneva conventions would not apply as far as their treatment was concerned. Mastny op.cit. pp. 150-151. British officials at the time had no doubt what this amounted to, see Victor Rothwell, Britain and the Cold War, 1941-1947 (London 1982) pp. 36-38. Equally revealing is what the Soviets did not want to be Allied policy. The Soviets were not keen at all to support the Western ideas about declaring all former Nazis prime facie criminals to be individually tried, partly because they did not want to have their hands tied as to which Germans they might employ most effectively for carrying out Soviet policies towards their fellow Germans and because they did not care for the implications of a formal policy of denazification trials, that Germans NOT tried would thus be exonerated from the 'war guilt' clause, which they also wished to write in as the general basis for dealing with the Germans. Apart from this one glimpse of what the Soviets were actually planning, there is some other evidence in some of the orders issued by the Red Army as it was approaching Germany. The Army Order of 2 February, on the eve of the entry of Soviet troops onto German soil, explicitly authorised each Soviet soldier to take revenge as he saw fit.

Although actual Soviet plans for Germany - as distinct from statements issued for propaganda and bargaining purposes - still remain 'a mystery wrapped in an enigma', the accounts and documents in British and American archives concerning actual Soviet proposals and accounts of what was said by Stalin and Maisky in discussions certainly disprove the claims made by Soviet historians to altruistic opposition to dismemberment and long-term occupation. As far as Soviet ideas about the human 'solution' was concerned, in addition to the right to transport and use at their discretion any able-bodied German male (for under the Total Mobilisation policy introduced in 1944 ALL able-bodied males would qualify as members of the Armed forces as the Russians well knew) as slave-labour under GULAG rather than Hague/Geneva rules, there is an authentic ring to Stalin's famous toast 'To the execution of at least 50,000 officers of the German Army', at Teheran, which so infuriated Churchill. They had done just that to the Polish officer class in 1939; to the White Officers and the Tsarist officers before them, as a matter of class-cadre policy. For official, and private, British attitudes to these proposals, as distinct from such public ones as Churchill's to the toast, see Rothwell, op.cit. Ch. 1.

2.   See John Erickson The Road to Berlin, Stalin's War With Germany, vol. 2, (London 1983). In the preface to this volume he points out that of the total 13,600,000 losses suffered by the Germans 'no less than 10,000,000 met their fate on the Eastern Front'.

3.   Figures obviously varied from time to time. In October 1942 Soviet tank production (of the vastly superior T34 and KV1 as against Mark IV Panzers and all other older types) run at close to 2000 while it stood at 100 in Germany. In the summer of 1944, at the height of German tank production the ratio was 5 to 1. for discussions of the relative strengths of the German and Russian armies, numerical and qualitative see Erickson op.cit. pp. 73-86; see also Albert Seaton, The Russo-German War 1941-1945 (London 1971); Figures for production and for the numbers of troops guns etc. at various times on the Eastern Front are conveniently provided in diagramatic tables in Purnell's History of the Second World War (London 1968). Amongst the various reasons why Germany was unable to match Soviet output were the deflection of resources into Hitler's pet 'miracle' weapon projects such as impractically large tanks, internal wrangling about design specifications in a desperate bid to overtake Soviet superiority by some technological leap, and the fact that Soviet production technology was in some crucial aspects ahead of the Germans. For example German tanks had to be built up by riveted or later welded plates rather than cast, essentially handcrafted as opposed to mass-produced - due to Germany lacking production technology for large-scale casting of steel unlike Soviet and American industry. Another area of technological falling behind was in production of high-velocity guns needed for tanks as well as anti-tank weaponry. From 1941 to 1945 Soviet tanks of comparable

vintage and size consistently out-gunned their German equivalents leading alike to the need for heroic tactics and unnecessarily heavy loss on the German side.

4. For the gradual impact of Soviet superiority in armour and weaponry see Erich von Manstein, Lost Victories (Chicago 1958), esp. pp 520-22 discussing the position in the spring of 1944 when numerical superiority also came to be established due to the reconquest of the Ukraine and other high population areas. Its immediate effect was to create a fatalistic warrior mentality stiffening the resistance of the troops and their willingness to accept virtually unlimited casualties: 'Will Over Matériel'. When that failed in the end, its effect boomeranged on the survivors. See also R.E.Herzstein, The War That Hitler Won (London 1979) pp. 399-401.

5. Lothar Kettenacker Grossbritannien und die zukünftige Kontrolle Deutschlands, in Josef Foschepoth and Rolf Steininger (eds), Die britische Deutschland - und Besatzungspolitik 1945-1949, Paderborn, 1984.

6. It certainly did not immediately (or even eventually) have that impact on at least some of the German Generals, as shown for example by von Manstein's Lost Victories published in 1958. Kesselring too still talked (to a BBC camera-team!!) in 1955 about former members of the Waffen SS as being 'the finest blood of the race' 'true soldiers born' and that now that the Russian menace was at last recognised by the Western Allies they would be of prime importance again. Film of this revealing interview is reproduced in N. Pronay/Howard Smith 'Have They Really Changed?' Pt. 4 Visions Of Change BBC TV Continuing Education Series.

7. See for example Michael Kammen's survey of the development and uses of the mythologisation of American history for creating a particular sense of national identity out of culturally and racially diverse people. Michael Kammen, The American Revolution in National Tradition in R. Maxwell Brown and Don E.Fehrenbacher (eds) Tradition, Conflict and Modernisation: Perspectives on the American Revolution (New York 1977) and see Ch. 4 Michael Kammen, A Season of Youth, The American Revolution and the Historical Imagination (New York 1977). I am grateful to my colleague David H. Murdoch for calling my attention to Kammen's work. For film, see in particular Robert Sklar, Movie Made America (New York 1978); and Pierre Sorlin, The Film in History (London 1978).

8. In General Douglas MacArthur these two traditions came together into a single personality and help to explain the total confidence and instinctive clarity with which he went about the changing of Japan - and the ease with which he assumed the style of an absolute monarch to carry through the 'democratisation of Japan'. See William Manchester, American Caesar, Douglas MacArthur, 1880-1964 (New York 1980).

9. Chamberlain in a rare moment of imaginative expression encapsulated the opposition to both in the course of the most-Munich debate on 3 October 1938. He quoted the elder Pitt 'To suppose that any nation can be unalterably the enemy of another is

weak and childish and has its foundations neither in the experience of nations nor in the history of man' and went on to coin the phrase about 'bleak and barren policy'. Printed in Neville Chamberlain, The Struggle for Peace (London 1939) p. 324. Within the Foreign Office, perhaps the best illustration of the intertwined nature of the debate is found in the Memorandum submitted by Cadogan on the occasion of Lord Lothian's interviews with Hitler and Goering, with a point--by-point commentary on it by Vansittart, substantially printed in the Introduction of D.N. Dilks, The Diaries of Sir Alexander Cadogan (London 1971) pp. 14-15. For example, Cadogan (arguing that when the Germans talk about German hegemony in Central Europe they mean that Germany is only seeking economic domination)'It can not surely be suggested that Germany could conquer and rule so many diverse elements' (Czechoslovakia, Hungary, Yugoslavia, Romania and Greece) - Vansittart: 'hegemony means... the conquest of Austria and Czechoslovakia...Danzig and Memel followed by the reduction of the other states to the condition of satellites - military satellites when required...We fought the last war largely to prevent this.' Cadogan on Vansittart's view: 'Even if all the Germans were mad....It's no good, as Van does, forming no policy and merely saying 'Rearm'. ibid.

10. Eric Drummond's phrase when Private Secretary to Balfour 23 May 1917, quoted V.H. Rothwell, British War Aims and Peace Diplomacy 1914-1918 (London 1971) p. 104. Professor Rothwell summarises the views of Tyrrell and Paget as expressed in a major memorandum on peace policy written in 1916: 'Germany...was suffering from a unique and dangerous political disease.' op.cit. p.45.

11. Paul M. Kennedy, The Rise of Anglo-German Antagonism, 1860-1914 (London 1980).

12. E.H. Carr essentially approved the anti-Vansittart line and argued for negotiations and settlement of German's reasonable grievances throughout the 1930's, as being both the rational and ethical approach. E.H. Carr, The Twenty Years Crisis (London 1939), pp. IX-X.

13. For the establishment of the PID and its relationship to the propaganda agencies see Michael Sanders and Philip M. Taylor, British Propaganda during the First World War 1914-1918 (London 1982) pp. 81-92, and Philip M. Taylor, The Foreign Office and British Propaganda during the First World War Historical Journal 23 (1980) 875-98.

14. For the disbanding of the PID and the inter-war replacement of its functions with Chatham House see Philip M. Taylor, The Projection of Britain, British Overseas Publicity and Propaganda 1919-1939 (London 1981) pp. 13-16, 55-6. For a self perception of its own functions see S. King-Hall, Chatham House (London 1937) and Arnold Toynbee's own affectionate account in Experiences (Oxford 1969). Rohan Butler produced a very influential presentation of the case for the Vansittartian analysis of the motivation of German foreign policy in the same year as Vansittart's seminal broadcasts, Rohan Butler, The Roots of National Socialism, 1783-1933 (London 1941).

15. As Cadogan put it, 'dancing literary hornpipes'. Cadogan Diaries op.cit. p. 13.

16. Philip M. Taylor Projection op.cit. 285-7. See also Michael Balfour, Propaganda in War 1939-1945 (London 1979) pp. 89-94. Electra House was one of the centres where propaganda and intelligence organisation interlocked. See Nicholas Pronay and Philip M. Taylor 'An Improper Use of Broadcasting' The British Government and Clandestine Radio Operations against Germany During the Munich Crisis and After, Journal of Contemporary History Vol. 19 (1984), 370-373.

17. Letter to his sister, quoted in P.M. Taylor, Projection op.cit. p.35.

18. For the development of the Political Warfare Executive from Electra House onward see Balfour Propaganda in War op.cit. pp. 55-57, 88-94 correcting some errors in Charles Cruikshank, The Fourth Arm, Psychological Warfare 1938-1945 (London 1977) but it needs to be read in connection with P.M. Taylor's account in "If War Should Come"; Preparing the Fifth Arm for Total War, 1935-1939, JCH 16 (1981) pp. 27-51 for the earlier period and Cruikshank for the broader subversive context within which 'black' propaganda was designed to operate.

19. In a paper delivered at a Conference on Propaganda in the Second World War at Bellagio, Italy 1982, Personalities and Organisation of British Propaganda 1936-1945, Michael Balfour, who worked with him in PWE described him in this period as 'Certainly his best work was done before the war...But in the controversies over the creation of PWE in August 1941, he was the only one of the Executive Committee whom the staff at Woburn were prepared to trust.'

20. There is much room for confusion over the interchangeable appellation of PID and PWE in the memoranda and papers of this period. Michael Balfour's cautionary footnote is worth repeating here 'PWE as a secret department used as cover, and communicated with the outside world on the notepaper of, the Political Intelligence Department which continued until April 1943 to lead a quiet existence of its own alongside the propagandists at Woburn. It was then absorbed into a new FO Research Department but PWE went on using the title PID as a cover and, after warfare ended and the need for secrecy disappeared, emerged openly for some months as PID. This proved a trap for uninitiated writers!' Balfour op.cit. p. 92.

21. For the earliest PID memorandum see Ch.1 - Great War Prologue, below. For the final memorandum from Crewe House see H. Wickham Steed, Through Thirty Years (London 1924) vol. 2 p. 248. The memorandum does not seem to have survived, but its existence is confirmed by Lloyd George who rejected it. See Philip M. Taylor, 'British Official Attitudes Towards Propaganda Abroad' in N.Pronay and D.W. Spring, eds. Propaganda, Politics and Film, 1918-1945 (London 1982) p. 27.

22. The Troutbeck definition is in PRO FO 371/390.93, quoted in Kurt Jürgensen, British Occupation Policy and the Problem of the Reeducation of Germany, History 68 (1983) p. 229. For Troutbeck's

views about Germany, which included considerations of methods for reducing the German birthrate by a combination of feminist propaganda (to get them to want other things); abolishing family allowances and liberal supplies of contraceptives, see Rothwell, Cold War op.cit. pp. 31-48 et seq. He acted on orders from above to look into the matter, it should be added, as these were typical rather than a-typical of FO attitudes by 1943 - which he shared .

23. House of Commons Debates vol. 109 col. 1009 5 Aug. 1918.

24. H.C. Debates vol. 1000, 5 Aug. 1918.

25. The article in The Times provided a wide-ranging survey of German and other newspapers and memoirs on the occasion of the appearance of Ludendorff's own. It concluded that 'It is quite certain in view of this evidence from the most important German leaders that the British enemy propaganda hit the German Armies very hard and that, even if we heavily discount Ludendorff's statements, it greatly accelerated the Allies victory. The Times, 31 October 1918.

26. The article in the Encyclopaedia Britannica, 1923 Edition, was written by Lord Riddell, Chapter CCCXIV, 'British Propaganda In Enemy Countries' of The Times History of the War (London 1920) began: 'Before 1914 the function of propaganda in war was little understood. In operation during the war under skilful direction it achieved marvellous results.' (p. 325) The article reproduced copious extracts from German Army Orders, from the reports and editorials of some eight German newspapers and quoted in extenso both Hindenburg and Ludendorff, whose memoirs appeared in the previous year, pp. 349-357. Ludendorff's memoirs were translated into English and appeared in 1920, and went through several reprints within the next decade. The striking phrase about being hypnotised as rabbit by the snake, appears on p. 362 of the first English edition, Erich Ludendorff, My War Memories 1914-1918 (London 1920). Highly influential was also the 'unofficial' history of the Enemy Propaganda Department written by its former Deputy Director; Sir Campbell Stuart, The Secrets of Crewe House (London 1920). It contained a great volume of documentation manifestly from official sources and gave an air of professionalism and indeed of a science about the techniques of propaganda. It proved an instant bestseller and went through five reprints in three years. Its penultimate Chapter, From War Propaganda to Peace Propaganda described the formation of Joint Committee including representatives of the Cabinet, Admiralty, War Office, Foreign Office, Treasury, MOI, Air Ministry ang four other organisations which was to consider a new extension to the work of propaganda to secure peace, and lasting peace. The last of the five areas of new activity which were to be planned was 'Special consideration of the reception to be given to German statements as to the course of democratisation in Germany'. Campbell's account of the decision not to proceed with monitoring 'democratisation' as a precondition, and instead adopt the policy that given 'sufficient (military) guarantees there need be no waiting to see whether the transformation of the German Government from irresponsible autocracy to responsible democracy is...genuine...or

whether...represent a change of heart' must have posed its own question in the reader's mind as the 1930's progressed. op.cit. pp. 209-10, and 222.

27. Adolf Hitler, Mein Kampf (James Murphy's translation of the unexpurgated edition) (London 1939) p. 164.

28. N.E.C. Circular on Labour Cinema Propaganda, March 1920, quoted in T.J. Hollins, The Presentation of Politics, The Place of Party Publicity, Broadcasting and Film in British Politics, 1918-1939. Unpublished PhD thesis, University of Leeds, 1981, pp. 186-187.

29. Labour Organiser, December 1931, quoted in Hollins op.cit. p. 211.

30. Ramsay MacDonald writing in 1900, quoted in Hollins op.cit. p. 123.

31. Labour Party Annual Report, 1924, quoted in Hollins op.cit. p. 117.

32. Labour Magazine, November 1931, p. 292, quoted in Hollins op.cit. p. 141. For Labour's attitude to 'political education' and 'propaganda' and changes to it after 1918, see also H.C.G. Matthew, R.I. McKibbin, J.A. Kay, 'The Franchise Factor in the Rise of the Labour Party' English Historical Review 91 (1976) and R.I. McKibbin, The Evolution of the Labour Party (Oxford 1974). Dr. McKibbin's view was that the Labour party was 'almost obsessed by the needs of propaganda' op.cit. p. 222.

33. August 1929. Quoted in Hollins, op.cit. p. 62.

34. Finance Committee Report, 1943. Quoted in Hollins, op.cit. p. 108.

35. Politics in Review, 1934, p.3. Quoted in Hollins op.cit. p. 80.

36. Notes for a speech delivered at a meeting, held at Lord Tredegar's home in March 1927, with businessmen for the purpose of collecting funds for a propaganda campaign for fighting socialism. Quoted in Hollins, op.cit. p. 39. The meeting was presented with a detailed analysis of left-wing propaganda operations in Britain and the organisations and methods employed, as well as plans to combat it, by J.C.C. Davidson, the Party Chairman and Joseph Ball its Director of Publicity, soon to become Head of the Research Department. See also R.R. James, Memoirs of a Conservative, J.C.C. Davidson's Memoirs and Papers (London 1969) pp. 288-290. See also J. Ramsden The Age of Balfour and Baldwin, 1902-1940 (London 1978) for a discussion of the development of Conservative attitudes to propaganda and its rôle and organisation under the impact of the post-1918 conditions and beliefs. For a contemporary viewpoint see P. Cambray, The Game of Politics (London 1932). This was written by a former Deputy Head of the Conservative Central Office Publicity Department. A striking feature of it is that it is written in military terms with chapter headings such as 'Propaganda Offensives', 'The Value of Surprise, Weapons and Machinery in relation to Political Strategy' etc. On Cambray, see Hollins, op.cit. pp. 14-16.

37. H.O. Lee's memorandum on the work of British propaganda during the war, describing the attitudes before the war, written in 1919. Quoted in P.M. Taylor, Official Attitudes, in Pronay and Spring op.cit. p. 32.

38. Circular dispatch signed by Curzon, 19 May 1919. Quoted in P.M. Taylor Official Attitudes, in Pronay and Spring op.cit. p. 30.

39. For a discussion of the reasons why censorship, practically unthinkable in peacetime before 1914, came to be accepted by a political establishment devoted to Liberal principles, see Nicholas Pronay The First Reality, Film-Censorship in Liberal England in K.R.M. Short, ed., Feature Films as History (London 1982) and for its subsequent development before and during the second world war, see The Political Censorship of Films in Britain Between the Wars, and The Newsmedia At War, by the same author, both in Pronay and Spring op.cit.

40. H.C. Debates Vol. 109 col. 1009, 5 August 1918.

41. For the development of that system of political control and ideas on the subject, see Chapters 3-8 of Hollins op.cit. which now makes Asa Briggs History of Broadcasting in the United Kingdom vols. 1-2, published before the Thirty Year Rule took effect out of date on this aspect of the history of radio in Britain.

42. J.C.W. Reith, Into the Wind (London 1949) p. 341.

43. For the evolution of the British Council and its ideas and techniques concerning cultural propaganda see Diana J. Eastment, The Policies and Position of the British Council from the Outbreak of War to 1950. Unpublished Ph.D. thesis, University of Leeds 1982. Philip M. Taylor, Cultural Diplomacy and the British Council 1934-1939, British Journal of International Studies 4 (1978) and David Ellwood, Showing the World What It Owed to Britain: Foreign Policy and 'Cultural Propaganda' 1935-1945, in Pronay and Spring op.cit.

44. A.J. Mackenzie, Propaganda Boom (London 1938) p. 7.

45. L. Woodward, British Foreign Policy in the Second World War (London 1971) vol. 2 p. 28.

46. The Diaries of Bruce Lockhart, quoted by Michael Balfour, Personalities and Organisation, Conference Papers, op.cit. p. 12; Lord Halifax lectured the Foreign Office in June 1945 on the importance of propaganda: 'Abraham Lincoln once said..."he who moulds public opinion goes deeper than he who enacts statutes or pronounces decisions". This' - he added - 'is still profoundly true.' Halifax to FO 15 June 1945 FO 371/44599 AN 1961/84/45,. I am grateful to Caroline Anstey-Johnson for this information.

47. 6 July 1943 FO 898/370.

48. 12 May 1946 FO 945/533.

49. To Professor Kurt Koszyk, see p. 130, n.7, below.

50. See Rothwell Cold War, op.cit. p.37 et seq. for other examples. Also Michael Balfour's contribution below. It is sometimes implied that those who fashioned the re-education approach to making the world safe from the resurgence of Germany were taking a softer line, were the doves to the hawk Vansittart. Michael Balfour suggests this in Propaganda in War, op.cit. p. 312 and so

does Lothar Kettenacker in this volume, suggesting that Vansittart's deservedly famous and indeed seminal 'Black Record' broadcasts in 1940 pushed the idea that the Germans were 'incorrigible'. On the contrary. In the preface to the printed version he wrote in response to those who thought that he did not 'believe in the possibility of conversion. I have said nothing of the kind. I explicitly do not discard the possibility of a change of heart - though it must be utter and therefore not easy - provided that it is not impeded by indulgence and wishful thinking.' Sir Robert Vansittart, Black Record (London 1941) p. V. He concluded the first broadcast: 'By the Grace of God and for the salvation of man, we shall rescue the world from Germany, and Germany from herself.' (p.13) And the second: 'It is time that change began. The capacity to change is the very essence of man: and a nation that should lack it would be less than human.' (p. 20) He concluded the series: 'I end as I began. The regeneration of the Brazen Horde is not impossible. Nothing in History is impossible. The soul of a people can be changed...the effort can be made, but it will have to be a very big effort.' (p. 87) The cover for the first edition said 'He looks forward to a real and profound change of heart in the German people. But this will be a slow process.' The planners of re-education thought so too: they expected something like 20 years for it to be completed during which some kind of Allied presence in Germany would be needed.

51. He told the story of his departure in an interview on Radio 4, 7 January 1984. His feelings on visiting Dachau he told the Conference in the course of his talk 'The Rebuilding of German Broadcasting', and also the story of the Maybach limousine. See also Michael Tracey, A Variety of Lives, A Biography of Sir Hugh Greene (London 1983) p. 58.

52. Lord Strang, Home and Abroad (London 1956) p. 234-235.

53. John Baker White, The Big Lie (London 1955) p. 210-211.

54. Arthur Ponsonby, Falsehood in Wartime. (London 1925) p.18. see Sanders and Taylor, op.cit. p. 250.

55. John Baker White, op.cit. p.211.

56. General Henry Wilson gave that reply. Reginald Pound and Geoffrey Harmsworth Northcliffe (London 1959) p. 468.

57. John Charteris, At G.H.Q. (London 1931) p. 98.

58. The personalities of some of those who carried on this work in Germany long after the 'stars' such as Michael Balfour or Sir Hugh Greene had returned, and the effect which they had on German people who came into contact with them, was captured in the collection of papers and the discussion which followed them printed in Arthur Hearnden (ed.) The British in Germany, Educational Reconstruction After 1945 (London 1978).

Chapter One

GREAT WAR PROLOGUE

KEITH WILSON

On May 1918 Mr J.W. Headlam-Morley, Assistant-Director of
the Foreign Office's Department of Political Intelligence, and Mr
H.G. Wells, who on 14 May had agreed to direct propaganda against
Germany, submitted a memorandum for discussion by the Enemy
Propaganda Committee. They wrote:

> It should be pointed out that nothing stands between
> enemy peoples and a lasting peace except the predatory
> designs of their ruling dynasties and military and economic
> castes; that the design of the Allies is not to crush any
> people, but to assure the freedom of all on a basis of
> self-determination to be exercised under definite
> guarantees of justice and fair-play; that, unless enemy
> peoples accept the Allied conception of a world peace
> settlement, it will be impossible for them to repair the
> havoc of the present war, to avert utter financial ruin,
> and to save themselves from prolonged misery; and that
> the longer the struggle lasts the deeper will become the
> hatred of everything German in the non-German world,
> and the heavier the social and economic handicap under
> which the enemy peoples will labour, even after their
> admission into a League of Nations.
> The primary war aim of the Allies thus becomes the
> changing of Germany...

The authors of this document went on to note that the financial
transactions of the last few years had created a monetary inflation
which 'without the concerted action of all the Powers, may mean a
collapse of world credit':

> Add now the plain necessity for continued armament if
> any League of Nations is not attained. Without any
> exaggeration, the prospect of the nations facing these
> economic difficulties in an atmosphere of continuing
> hostility, intrigue, and with a continuing distrust, is a
> hopeless one. The consequences stare us in the face;

Russia is only the first instance of what must happen generally. The alternative to a real League of Nations is the steady descent of our civilisation towards a condition of political and social fragmentation such as the world has not seen since the fall of the Roman Empire. The honest cooperation of Germany in the League of Nations, in disarmament, and in world reconstruction is, therefore, fundamentally necessary. There is now no other rational policy. And since it is impossible to hope for any such help or cooperation from the Germany of the Belgian outrage, the Brest-Litovsk Treaty, the betrayal of Ukrania, THE CHANGING OF GERMANY becomes a primary war aim, the primary war aim for the Allies. How Germany is to be changed is a complex question. The word Revolution is, perhaps, to be deprecated. We do not, for instance, desire a Bolshevik breakdown in Germany, which would make her economically useless to mankind. We look, therefore, not so much to the German peasant and labourer as to the ordinary, fairly well-educated mediocre German for cooperation in the reinstatement of civilisation. Change there must be in Germany; in the spirit in which the Government is conducted, in the persons who exercise the control, and in the relative influence of different classes in the country. The sharpest distinction, therefore, has to be drawn between Germany and its present Government in all our propaganda and public utterances; and a constant appeal has to be made by the statesmen of the Alliance, and by a frank and open propaganda through the Germans of the United States of America and of Switzerland, through neutral countries, and by every possible means, from Germany junker to Germany sober. We may be inclined to believe that every German is something of a Junker, we have to remember he is also potentially a reasonable man. [1]

*

On 4 October 1918 Sir Campbell Stuart, Deputy Chairman of the British War Mission, addressing the first meeting of a Policy Committee composed of representatives of all government departments concerned in any way with propaganda, defined the latter as meaning 'the education of the enemy to a knowledge of what kind of world the allies mean to create, and of the place reserved in it for enemy peoples according as they assist in, or continue to resist, its creation'. Despite the 'fundamental necessity' of Germany to civilisation as it was known to Headlam-Morley and Wells, it is clear that their idea of 'educative efforts' consisted of threats of physical violence rather than of appeals to reason, of the stick rather than the carrot. Campbell Stuart, however, on 4 October, looked forward to the end of the war, and the passing of propaganda into peace offensives and counter-offences:

Our Mission, therefore, has already in existence an organisation to collect and collate various suggestions, territorial, political, economic, and so forth, that have been made by the different sections and parties in Allied, neutral, and enemy countries. A step in this direction was the report on the Propaganda Library issued by the War Office early in 1917 by Captain Chalmers Mitchell, who is the liaison officer between the British War Mission and the War Office, and whom we have asked to act as Secretary of this Committee. Captain Chalmers Mitchell is in charge of the aforesaid organisation at Crewe House, and although its immediate function is to collect information useful for propaganda, it is clear that it will also obtain materials useful to those who have to shape peace policy. For propaganda to the enemy is in a sense a forecast of policy; it must be inspired by policy, but at the same time its varying needs also suggest policy.

It is hoped, therefore, that this Policy Committee may assist in furnishing materials for the compilation of the various peace proposals, in revising the collation of them, in drawing inferences from them, and discussing the action and reaction of peace propaganda and peace policy that the inferences suggest. [2]

That means were to hand was also recognised in the House of Commons on 7 November 1918. Booth MP claimed that 'the Ministry of Information has not been able to do much in the way of educating the Czecho-Slovaks, Jugo-Slavs or even the Hungarians with regard to this great Empire in the past few years'. Ignoring Hazleton, who rose against the prospect 'of a sort of current history of England or a history of current events in England in practically all foreign countries, particularly among the new nationalities', and who would rather they were told about Ireland, Booth maintained that the Ministry of Information's chance had now come. [3]

*

Five days later, on the day following the Armistice, Lord Northcliffe's resignation as Minister for Propaganda in Enemy Countries was accepted by the Prime Minister. On 15 November Northcliffe wrote to all the members of the Policy Committee telling them that, as there was 'no immediate sphere for our action', their services were no longer required; Sir Campbell Stuart would stay on to wind up the activities of the British War Mission by 31 December. [4] On 22 December the editor of the Daily Mail, one of the organs of Northcliffe's newspaper empire, declared: 'We are not the schoolmasters of Russia or of other nations.' [5] Inasmuch, however, as the claim made in his memoirs by Sir George Cockerill is correct, that the War Office and in particular the Department of Special Intelligence of which he was Director from March 1915, had had more experience in propaganda and therefore by Campbell Stuart's definition in 'education' than either the Ministry of Information or Crewe House (to which organisation the responsibility for propaganda in Germany was transferred only on 1 September 1918), machinery remained in being. [6] Moreover, the Political Intelligence Department of the Foreign Office remained in being. It was to this Department that a copy of a memorandum prepared in M.I.6b and dated 22 January 1919 found its way. This memorandum, called 'Some Fundamental Problems Presented by the German Revolution', was a condensation of a more detailed attempt to examine the questions posed by current events in Germany. Under the heading 'The Task of Reconstruction' there were three sub-divisions: Political, Economic, and Social. Under the sub-division 'Political' the memorandum reads as follows:

> (a) The maintenance of German unity.
> At present, the separist tendencies which appeared at the beginning of the revolution have, apparently, diminished. The principal difficulties to national unity, which existed in 1848, have been done away with....
> (b) The reconstruction of an orderly and disciplined national life on a new basis other than that of the Army. This is implied in the collapse of Prussia and Prussian predominance. Such a change would affect Germany more fundamentally than any other change.
> (c) The reorganisation of the army, on a national and not a dynastic and Prussian system, and its complete subordination to the civil authorities...
> (e) The reconstruction of the civil service and police in such a fashion as to replace the dynastic and bureaucratic spirit by a national and liberal spirit...
> (f) Foreign Policy. The new Germany has to shape its policy to a resettlement of the map of the world, in which she has no voice and which is likely to be supported by guarantees of so formidable a character that she cannot venture to upset them by force, except in the case of war between the guarantors, supposing she has the sufficient forces to do so...

Under the heading 'Social', the memorandum went on:

> (b) Education. The national ideal in education needs a complete revision in view of the facts, and the change in outlook. This is also a matter of very fundamental importance in view of the immense influence which public education has played in German national life since the days of Stein, Fichte and Humboldt, and of the great resistance from the reactionary and conservative elements, especially the Church, with which new theories must meet.

(c) The absorption in or readjustment to their new environment of a large privileged caste, both civil and military...

The memorandum concluded with a paragraph entitled 'The Outlook'. This read:

> It is obvious that the solution of these problems must take some considerable time and be a difficult process.The most disquieting feature of the situation is psychological. Exhaustion, apathy and fear appear to be the prevailing moods of Germany in her defeat. But no revolution or reform or successful reconstruction can be carried out under such conditions. Germany needs a leader and an inspiration before she can undertake the very heavy task which lies before her and before the great masses of the population can recover the hope and energy necessary to secure their willing cooperation in the self-denial, hard and concentrated work, patriotism, and self-sacrifice which alone can save the country from anarchy, with its concomitants of famine and pestilence, and ultimately give it a chance of recovery... It may be that the Constituent Assembly will give Germany the leaders she needs, but, in view of the general lack of political experience of the German people, it is evident that such leaders will have a hard task in framing a policy and in securing the necessary support to make it a political reality. [7]

That there was a void in Germany, and that 'the kind of ideas' that prevailed would determine her future, was recognised by the PID in productions of its own on German matters for its political masters. [8]

II

Early in October 1918 the War Cabinet had received from the PID a memorandum called 'The Situation in Germany and Peace Overtures'. Taking the fall of Hertling as recognising that some form of parliamentary government would be established in Germany, the writer maintained that

> Ever since the beginning of the war, not only public opinion, but repeated utterances of responsible statesmen – especially in this country – have again and again insisted upon the point that we were at war not so much with the German people as with the German Government, and that one of the main objects was to bring about a change both in the system and in the spirit. It has moreover again and again been suggested that the attitude of the Allies, and especially of this country and America, towards Germany,

would be very different if we had to deal with a new form of Government... In its most extreme form this view has been expressed under the formula 'No peace with the Hohenzollerns'. Our Government, however, have never committed themselves to this, but have confined themselves to vaguer expressions. [9]

This impression was not universally held. At a meeting of the National War Aims Committee on 10 October 1917, for instance, it was reported that 'organised labour in nearly every constituency declines to cooperate in forming a War Aims Committee on the grounds that our Aims are not defined'. Whilst in a report asked for on 5 December 1917 into public opinion and the Lansdowne letter of the previous month the same body concluded that the country was 'as resolved as ever to achieve victory and to smash Prussian militarism', a memorandum produced on Christmas Day 1917 after a visit to England by the British agent for propaganda purposes in Denmark claimed that amongst the mistakes being made was the failure to offer any encouragement to the liberal forces in Germany which had produced the Reichstag resolution of July 1917, and the need for every statement of Allied war aims to contain some suggestion of an alternative - 'that is of milder conditions which might be obtained by a non-militarist Germany'. [10]

In support of the disputed impression a number of items can be adduced. Shortly after becoming Prime Minister Lloyd George told the House of Commons that 'The Allies entered this war to defend Europe against the aggression of Prussian military domination, and, having begun it, they must insist that the only end is the most complete and effective guarantee against the possibility of that caste ever again disturbing the peace of Europe. [11] In January 1917 the Entente Powers officially announced:

It goes without saying that if the Allies wish to liberate Europe from the brutal covetousness of Prussian militarism, it has never been their design, as has been alleged, to encompass the extermination of the German peoples and their political disappearance. [12]

One year later Lloyd George stated:

Our point of view is that the adoption of a really democratic constitution by Germany would be the most convincing evidence that in her the old spirit of military domination has indeed died in this war, and would make it much easier for us to conclude a broad democratic peace with her. [13]

On the other hand, contradicting the impression given by this particular PID memo is a long series of public declarations by Lloyd

George's Secretary of State for Foreign Affairs, A.J. Balfour. On 30 July 1917 he told the House of Commons:

> One word let me say as to the democratisation of Germany. We all hope that autocracy in Germany will give place to free government as we understand it and to parliamentary institutions as we understand them. As has been said by high authorities, it is hard to see how you can negotiate a stable peace except you find a community to deal with based upon a popular will, and a popular will not corrupted by sinister designs of universal domination. But that does not mean that anybody is fool enough to suppose that he can impose upon Germany a constitution made outside Germany. Germany must work out her own salvation. You do not mend matters by imposing a constitution even if you have the power to impose it. [14]

On November 6 he chided Ramsay MacDonald in the House for having given the impression that Britain ought to fight on until every country in Europe was democratised. Balfour himself, though always 'one of those who passionately desire that free institutions should be extended throughout Europe', had 'never thought it would be a wise or a possible thing for one country to dictate to another country under what form of government it should live'. He went on to ask, despairingly: 'How can we change the heart of Germany? That is the point - that is the difficulty. How can we approach those great classes which I am sure must exist, in potentiality if not in actuality, which will understand the ideas that commend themselves to the American, British, French, and Italian nations?' [15] This is the same message which he delivered at the Mansion House ten days later - 'We recognise fully that each nation should be allowed to make for itself the government which suits its history, its character, and its ideals'; and to which he referred Lord Lansdowne on 22 November 1917: 'I certainly do not...desire to compel Germany to adopt full-blown Parliamentary institutions.' [16]

This series of public statements, it seems to me, considerably outweighs in significance the first set of items. It is as well to recall here that no one considered himself less bound by a speech than Lloyd George. Indeed, he made the remark, 'Nobody was bound by a speech' to the Supreme War Council at Versailles less than a month after his statement of war aims of 5 January 1918. [17] In secret, moreover, Balfour had been even more categorical, denying what he had allowed himself only to be highly sceptical about on 30 July 1917. [18] As First Lord of the Admiralty in Asquith's Coalition Government he produced a memorandum on the Peace Settlement in Europe to which he was later to stick very closely. He wrote:

> If I had my way, I should rule out any attempt to touch the internal affairs either of Germany or Austria. It may be that, under the stress of defeat, ancient jealousies ...will revive. South may be divided from North, Roman

43

Catholic from Protestant, Wurtemburg, Bavaria, and Saxony from Prussia, or from each other. A revolution may upset the Hohenzollerns, and a new Germany may arise on the ruins of militarism.

Any or all of these changes are possible, but I would certainly deprecate any attempt on the part of a victorious enemy to bring them about. One of the few recorded attempts to crush militarism in a defeated State was Napoleon's attempt to destroy the Prussian army after Jena. No attempt was ever less successful...I hope no attempt will be made to control or modify her internal policy. The motto of the Allies should be 'Germany for the Germans - but only Germany'.

He went on even further to doubt that Germany would undergo 'a spiritual conversion':

Those who think the future must necessarily resemble the past may perhaps be disposed to remind us that for the five centuries preceding the Bismarckian era the political tendencies prevailing in Germany have been, on the whole, centrifugal and separatist. They will argue that this inveterate tradition, interrupted though it has been by forty-five years of a united and triumphant Germany, nevertheless represents the real tendencies of the race; and that to this tradition it will revert after a war for which Prussian policy and a Prussian dynasty have been responsible.

Personally, I am inclined to doubt this conclusion... [19]

The distinction between the German people and the German Government, as Balfour's predecessor Sir Edward Grey made clear in a most judicious preface written in September 1917 to Gilbert Murray's essays The Way Forward, was much more an American than a British strain. [20] At the Foreign Office, in the summer and autumn of 1918, Balfour simply 'took note' of the information which reached him as to developments of a democratic nature within Germany. [21] The receipt in England on 15 October 1918 of President Wilson's reply to the German request for an armistice, reiterating as it did the language of his Mount Vernon address of 4 July to the effect that the destruction of the arbitrary power that had hitherto controlled the German nation constituted 'a condition precedent to peace' [22] , created consternation in both the Cabinet and the Foreign Office.

At the former, Austen Chamberlain said that there was nothing so humiliating for the Germans as to be told to alter their government at the order of the President, and insisted that 'we should say we are not prepared to go on to fight to get rid of (the) Hohenzollerns'; Balfour stated: 'I don't want to go beyond making Germany impotent to renew the war, and obtaining compensation. I don't want to trample her in the mud.' [23] The War Minister, Lord

Milner, who in March 1917 had not been able to see 'what direct steps we might take' for the destruction of Prussian militarism [24]; who on his return from a mission to Russia in the autumn of 1917 had been reported to be 'hankering for peace by agreement lest worse befall the British and German Junker class alike' [25]; who in November 1917 had told Buckler of the US Embassy in London that he was one of those who would have preferred that 'the President had not insisted so strongly upon what amounted to a revolution in Germany...' [26]; gave an interview the following day (16 October 1918) to Arthur Mann of the Evening Standard in which he said that he was 'inclined to think that if the Allies...attempt to dictate to Germany certain drastic changes in their own government both as regards constitution and personnel, the resistance of the German armies and people...may be stiffened'. This, for being 'a slap in the face to President Wilson', and for being an appeal 'to save the Hohenzollerns and the autocratic power of Germany', incurred the wrath of John Dillon in the House of Commons. It also led to a campaign against Milner in the Evening News and the Daily Mail, in which Sir Edward Carson intervened on Milner's side. [27]

At the Foreign Office Sir Eyre Crowe, Assistant Under-Secretary, recorded on 16 October that he did 'not share President Wilson's apparent illusion that the disappearance of the Hohenzollern dynasty would be equivalent to a regenerated Germany' [28]. Lord Robert Cecil, Balfour's relative and Deputy from 19 July 1918, who in August had said 'Nothing would please me more or be more wholesome than to secure the dethronement and if possible the execution of the Kaiser and Crown Prince', put his personal behind his official self to the extent of falling into the following line: 'I cannot imagine any conditions in which our interference in the internal affairs of Germany would be wise'. [29] Wilson's line was so lost on Balfour that another American note refusing to make peace with a disunited and unrepresentative German Government because this would be 'a violation of democratic principles and a dangerous attitude to adopt' was actually lost by the Foreign Office. [30]

III

The principle of non-interference in the internal affairs of other states had been well put, and àpropos Germany, on one particular occasion before the outbreak of war in 1914. In a long despatch of 12 January 1907 Mr Fairfax Cartwright, the British Minister in Munich, had considered the political situation in Germany, and made certain suggestions as to policy. Starting from the position that whilst the Kaiser was haunted by an idea of worldly grandeur the mass of the population asked only for peace and quiet; and helped by his own location to observe that public opinion in Germany, and especially in South Germany, was beginning to pronounce itself with much more freedom as the Emperor sought to assume greater personal authority in the management of public affairs, Cartwright believed that 'this awakening of the forces of democracy should not be lost sight of...'. He suggested that two points should be borne in mind:

> - namely the attitude which should be assumed by His Majesty's Government towards the Imperial authorities at Berlin, and the attitude they should assume towards the German nation as a whole. The first should be governed by business considerations alone: no concession should be given without an equivalent...As regards the second point, it seems to me that it would be a wise policy for the British Government to do all that lies in their power to conciliate and to pacify German public opinion and to encourage the development of that natural sympathy which exists between an Englishman and a German when not of the official class.

Cartwright's conclusions, dubbed 'excellent' by Sir Charles Hardinge the Permanent Under-Secretary, were heavily criticised by Eyre Crowe, recently promoted to Senior Clerk. In minutes printed before it was decided not, after all, to circulate them to certain Cabinet ministers, Crowe disputed Cartwright's claim that Germany was crushed by militarism: 'The whole nation is genuinely proud of its army (not to speak of the navy), and feels convinced that its possession and maintenance confers the greatest possible advantages from an economical as well as a political point of view.' He also took issue with Cartwright's view that anti-English feeling in Germany and particularly in the German press, was artificial: '... there is in the minds of most German people an innate disposition to that feeling, due to historical causes... the rivalry between Prussia and Hanover, and...the attitude of Frederick the Great after the lapse of the Treaty of Westminster in 1762.'

In particular, Crowe pronounced:

> The suggestion that the British Government should adopt a separate policy towards the German nation as a whole, apart from its Government, would, if practicable, involve very serious dangers. The British Government cannot properly have relations with anybody in Germany except the Emperor and his Government. If His Majesty's Government were to embark on the perilous course of 'influencing' or 'pacifying', as Mr Cartwright says, German public opinion, they would almost inevitably lay themselves open to the reproach of carrying on intrigues with Germans not in agreement with the policy of their own Government. We should and do resent any such proceedings on the part of foreign Governments in this country, and we should be careful not to fall into the same error ourselves. [31]

*

The PID memorandum of 3 October 1918 concluded:

> The truth is that by demanding 'the democratisation of Germany' we may easily get into a very awkward and delicate position. The whole idea originally arose naturally from the circumstances of the origin of the war and was merely a war measure against a specific tendency in a single country. There are many who are attempting to invert it into a general principle and are anxious to lay down the maxim that none but democratic states should be admitted to the League of Nations. Against this we cannot be too carefully on our guard. At this moment we are chiefly occupied with the German Government, but the weapon is one which might be used also by others and we may easily find that we are playing into the hands of international socialism or international labour. We do not wish to have the discussion on changes in our own constitution carried on under external pressure. It may be suggested that it would be wise as quickly as possible to get back to the old and sound principle that the internal forms of government in any one nation are not the concern of other nations. [32]

It was not simply the 'awkward and delicate position' that would be produced if any encouragement was given to generalise from the particular that caused the British leadership to remain more loyal than some of their officials were prepared to be [33] to the principle of non-interference. (Chicherin, the Soviet commissar for Foreign Affairs, did offer in February 1919 to pledge his country not to intervene in the internal affairs of other powers. [34]) It was not simply that embarrassing questions about British rule in India and Ireland might be provoked. Lord Robert Cecil had drawn attention to this in his contribution to the composite speech which Lloyd George had delivered on 5 January 1918. [35] (A motion for the granting of self-determination to Ireland was defeated in the House of Commons on 5 November 1918. [36]) It was not simply that the British might first have to democratise themselves. At the end of 1917 Wade had written, from Denmark:

> It is inevitable that neutrals should feel some scepticism when we stand up as champions of democracy under leaders, some of whom have not, in the past, shown much enthusiasm for democracy, and are supported by newspapers which have been its determined opponents. Indeed the northern neutrals have gone so far beyond us in the path of democracy that some of our institutions appear to them hardly less feudal than those of Germany. The attitude of a part of our Press towards the Russian Revolution has been watched in Scandinavia with surprise and curiosity. Our ability to regain the sympathy of

Ireland and of the new Eastern democracies will be
regarded by many as the touchstone of our sincerity. [37]

It was not the realisation of the existence of this sort of anomaly
and incongruity that caused Lord Robert Cecil, who had already
interfered in German domestic affairs to the extent of making, in
August 1918, 'a statement to the German people' in which he altered
a draft given him by the Crewe House organisation so as to describe
the current holders of power in Germany as 'medievalists', to draw
the line where he drew it in October 1918. [38] It was not the fact
that the British were not without sin that caused them to be
reluctant to cast, as it were, the first stone. They did not limit
their hypocrisy on this occasion because they had doubts as to its
plausibility. (One member of the PID wrote, in February 1919,
'Hypocrisy, to be plausible, implies the real existence somewhere of
the type which it counterfeits.' [39]) Their hypocrisy, as the
preceding section was designed to show, was not without
qualification. But it was not 'the old and sound principle' of
non-interference that caused them not to pursue the democratisation
of Germany. The principle was being ignored, throughout the whole
period of the peacemaking, in relation to Russia. It was being
ignored even as Lloyd George re-iterated it in the House of
Commons on 16 April 1919. [40] Chicherin's offer of February 1919
was conditional upon the cessation of interference in his own
country's internal affairs.

Nor was it that the Napoleonic precedents already cited were
deemed to have proved counter-productive. Nor was it that the
British leadership was bearing in mind the perceptive point made by
one member of the PID, namely that if President Wilson's programme
of refusing to negotiate with the former holders of power in
Germany were carried out completely, 'the full responsibility for
accepting terms of peace, which will undoubtedly be very
humiliating to Germany, would attach to the Liberals and Socialists.
This would therefore enable the Conservative and Military elements
to wash their hands of the whole thing.' [41] Nor was it simply that a
democratic German Government might offer a peace which, in the
words of another PID memorandum, 'would not concede all our
points'; that unless treated leniently by the Allies, which would
involve the sacrifice of certain of their war aims, and in particular
of the German colonies, the charge would be made by a democratic
Germany 'that all our talk about the democratisation of Germany
was mere war propaganda and hypocrisy'. [42]

Nor did the American strain not prevail because the Allies were
the victims of 'The Physical Force Fallacy'. This was defined by
Wade as the belief that militarism could only be destroyed by the
overthrow of its exponents on the battlefield. On the contrary, the
British leadership, like Wade, took the position that

To argue that (a belief in physical force as the <u>ultima
ratio</u>) can be destroyed by arraying greater physical forces
against it is illogical. Under such conditions the belief in

physical force would be not destroyed but vindicated, and the obvious conclusion to be drawn from an Allied victory would be, <u>not</u> that physical force was a false god, but that the Germans had not enough of it on their side. [43]

No chances were taken with Germany in this respect. Not only was a dutch auction conducted on the military terms of peace which reduced the size of the German army to 100,000 volunteers [44]; but on 3 March 1919 a discussion took place at the Peace Conference which clearly revealed that the meaning which attached to the word 'final' in the phrase 'final military conditions' presented to the Supreme War Council on 12 February by Foch was 'in perpetuity'. As Clemenceau said: 'President Wilson in that very room had declared that Germany must be disarmed. He did not say that Germany must be temporarily disarmed. Other countries might perhaps be content with transitory Naval Terms, but he himself was not prepared to sign an invitation to Germany to prepare for another attack by land after an interval of three, ten, or even forty years. He would not be prepared to sign a Peace in those conditions.' Although Balfour proposed the formula that 'the limitation on German armaments, whether military, or naval, or aerial, should last until Germany has fulfilled all the obligations imposed on her by the Peace Terms, and thereafter for as long as, and with such modifications as, the League of Nations may determine' [45], the effect was the same. Lloyd George said that Germany had been reduced, militarily, to the state of Greece, and, navally, to that of the republic of Argentina. [46] The intention was to keep her that way.

In the end, the lesson taught to Germany was in the outcome of the fighting (as Lloyd George put it: 'L'Allemagne à reçu une leçon telle qu'il n'en est de plus grande dans l'histoire') and in the terms of what the disenchanted Smuts, the only British war leader to have believed the sentiments he expressed publicly in the course of it, described as 'the last shot of the war' (as Lloyd George put it again: 'Il faut que ce que nous ferons soit une leçon pour les rois et pour tous ceux qui ont la responsibilité du gouvernement'). [47] This was signed, on 28 June 1919, with a state whose constitution was still to be settled, but which was already in several respects, including those of 'universal suffrage and proportional representation [48], more democratic than that of Great Britain at least. The lesson was that not war, but defeat, did not pay; that defeat would be paid for; that might was might. This, supplemented by what she received at the hands of the supervisory commissions and the French forces of occupation, was the only 'education' of Germany that took place.

*

The reason for this resides in the fact, if it is a fact (as Balfour not only might have said but did say) that two factors much more fundamental than the self-serving British principle of non-interference were governing the thinking and outlook of the Allied statesmen. These two factors were encapsulated in one sentence of the PID memorandum of 3 October 1918 already much drawn upon. The sentence runs: 'Even as regards Germany, it is not so much the forms of the constitution as the spirit of the nation with which we are at issue.' As another PID memorandum of February 1919 recognised, carrying coals to Newcastle, forms of government were immaterial:

> All that democracy means is that the Government is controlled by the will of the majority of the nation. There is nothing in the nature of things to guarantee that the will of the majority of a nation in regard to its dealings with other nations will be morally good. Narrow nationalism, aggressive imperialism, vindictiveness, pride, suspicion, may sway the great mass of a nation, just as they may sway a militarist clique. [49]

The idea of the spirit of the nation was all too material. On 6 November 1917 Balfour, allowing that there had been occasions in the past in which the belligerents had made peace and forgotten their differences, said: 'That is not the case in this war. You must consider the psychology of the German people, and it really is not prejudice to say that the German people have an entirely different view of international morality and of the rights and duties of a powerful state from any other community in the world.' [50] This was echoed by Clemenceau at the Peace Conference. He told President Wilson:

> ne croyez pas que les principes de justice qui nous satisferont satisfassant les Allemands. Je les connais: je me suis imposé, depuis 1871, d'aller presque chaque année en Allemagne; je voulais connaître les Allemands... . Je puis vous dire que leur idée de la justice n'est pas la nôtre. [51]

Again, on the following day, again to President Wilson:

> Vous cherchez à faire justice aux Allemands. Ne croyez pas qu'ils nous pardonneront jamais; ils ne chercheront que l'occasion d'un révanche; rien ne détruira la rage de ceux qui ont voulu établir sur le monde leur domination et qui se sont crus si près de réussir. [53]

Balfour echoed himself when pressing for the destruction of the German naval base at Heligoland, on the grounds that there was no certainty that Germany would stay as desired navally and militarily. Faced yet again with Clemenceau's support for Balfour ('Je connais les Allemands depuis bien des années' [53]) President Wilson conceded that if one didn't believe in the permanency of treaty arrangements by which the naval and military force of Germany must be reduced to limited size, one was right to take 'd'autres précautions'. In the Cabinet on 1 June 1919 Balfour had echoed

Clemenceau: 'If the Germans were to be given an army tomorrow, he thought that they would immediately begin a war of revenge.' [54] Before this, Lloyd George had issued his own indictment of the German nation:

> Throughout the war, as before the war, the German people and their representatives supported the war, voted the credits, subscribed to the war loans, obeyed every order, however savage, of their Government. They shared the responsibility for the policy of their Government, for at any moment, had they willed it, they could have reversed it. Had that policy succeeded they would have acclaimed it with the same enthusiasm with which they welcomed the outbreak of war. They cannot now pretend, having changed their rulers after the war was lost, that it is justice that they should escape the consequences of their deeds. [55]

That the Germans were regarded as incorrigible largely accounts for the extent to which the next war was being prepared for throughout the actual hostilities - why as the editor of the only English newspaper to be exempted from the censorship of the Press Bureau during the war put it to Asquith 'those who think that this is a war against war and who hope that with it all war will end, are living in false security'. [56] There can be no mistaking the pessimism of Asquith's Lord Chancellor (and former War Minister) Haldane, who knew Germany probably better than any contemporary politician, when outlining the need for something in the nature of a League of Nations in 1915:

> ...the most crushing defeat will not prevent Germany from setting herself to work, with her population and national spirit and her great powers of scientific and industrial organisation, to accumulate wealth and diplomatic influence. The sequel may, if no counter-step is taken, be a still greater military power than that which she now possesses. The task of rendering the success of (such an effort) so unlikely as not to seem to Germany worth attempting, and of thus instilling into the German mind the desire for a government with other than warlike ideas can only...be successfully accomplished if the cooperation of all the Great Powers of the world is secured. [57]

Lord Kitchener was a little more direct. To his mind, 'even if the arrogant despotism of the Prussian race were chastened...the danger in the future is that Germany will never rest satisfied until Great Britain has been reduced to impotence, and...Great Britain will inevitably have to face the consequences of German determination to take revenge upon us for having upset the calculations on which she commenced this war'. [58] Lord Robert Cecil, in a memorandum on Proposals for Diminishing the Occasion of Future Wars written in

October 1916, began: 'Even if we succeed in destroying German militarism, that will not be enough...'. [59] Balfour at the same time clearly contemplated another German war, even if the German power base was reduced:

> ...it seems to me quite clear that, measured by population, Germany – and still more, Germany in alliance with Austria – will be more than a match for France alone, however much we give to France, and however much we take from the Central States. If, therefore, Europe after the war, like Europe before the war, is to be an armed camp, the peace of the world will depend, as heretofore, on defensive alliances...In that event the Entente is likely to be maintained. Germany will still be the enemy, and an enemy strong enough to be dangerous. [60]

'Nations work out their own schemes of liberty for themselves according to their own ideals and on the basis of their own history and character...', Balfour had told the House of Commons on 30 July 1917. His, and Lloyd George's, and Clemenceau's, ideas of what were German ideals and of what the German 'history and character' required, overwhelmed at Versailles Wilson's American strain, such as it was, for despite the President's diplomatic Notes his advisers had devised no schemes of reforms that might be implemented and had studied hardly at all the question of the governance of Germany. [61] In The Truth about the Peace Treaties Lloyd George retails how the German delegation, led by Brockdorff-Rantzau, received the terms of peace at the Hotel Trianon:

> Clemenceau, opening the proceedings, stood up and in a few short but perfectly courteous sentences addressed the German delegates and said that the representatives of the Allied and Associated Powers had assembled to hear their reply to our peace terms. When he sat down it was expected that Count Brockdorff-Rantzau would follow the President's example and rise in his place to reply. Instead of which he leisurely or morosely unfolded a manuscript document and, after a painful interval of strained silence, proceeded from his seat to read it page by page in a loud, harsh and defiant voice...
> The effect on President Wilson's mind was to close it with a snap. He turned to me and said: 'Isn't it just like them?'. [62]

*

At the outbreak of the Great War George Saunders, who had spent twenty years in Germany working for the Morning Post and The Times before being transferred to Paris in 1908, wrote to his sister Margaret: 'the reason why the German Emperor, German Kings, statesmen and men of letters let loose this hell is to be sought in the experiences through which the German peoples themselves came in former centuries. They themselves had been harried, hunted, sacked and tortured by invaders. They find the only defence of their hearths and homes in a war of aggression in order to strike down the growing strength of dreaded neighbours...'. In connection with taming and cowing 'the German spirit', his first thought was that if the Germans were defeated 'they must be divided up and treated so that they cannot again organise their vast system of domination'. He did not conceal the difficulty of achieving this: so far as he was concerned, the legitimate desire for national unity had been implanted in the minds of all the German tribes, and 'if the German-speaking peoples want to be united, it is hopeless to try to prevent them'. [63] At Christmas 1918, whilst working for the PID, Saunders met Clemenceau in London and asked him 'what was going to be done with Germany - was she to be dismembered?'. The reply was: 'No, not quite that. We are going to treat the German States as Caesar treated the Aeduan prisoners - send them back with a leg or an arm cut off.' On special assignment for The Times in Germany in the spring of 1920 he reflected that this treatment would have been far more appropriate than what had been, and was still being, meted out. At pains to convince his editor, Wickham Steed, that the Germany that the Allies and particularly the French, were continuing to 'squeeze' was in no sense - financially, economically, politically - 'the old Germany', he wrote:

> I am steadily coming to the conviction that the whole Treaty and the whole spirit in which it was conceived was one vast error. If our policy was to reform Germany and to mould it to our own views, we ought to have struck while the iron was hot - i.e. at the moment of the Armistice. We could then have asked what we liked, and the Germans were so utterly beaten on the front and at home that they would have accepted any terms. We had the right, after Germany's madness and crime, to impose just terms in the hour of victory. But, even then, they ought to have been terms which involved no protracted period of internal supervision.

Steed, who had been a member of the Enemy Propaganda Committee in the closing stages of the war, replied:

> It may be natural for the Germans to wish to recover their self-respect, police themselves and get rid of foreign control. But it is not natural for us and the French to connive at this German naturalness until we have made sure as sure can be that the Germans will not be in a position to resume their other sort of naturalness, which is to make war upon us as soon as they get the chance. The root of the trouble is that the Germans do not yet seem to know that they have been beaten and still less that they themselves are responsible for the beating they

got...the only means of getting rid of foreign
supervision...is for them to comply as rapidly as possible
with the disarmament conditions and thus prove that they
do not contemplate any further military ventures. [64]

As the 1920s and 1930s wore on they seemed to demonstrate the
correctness of the stereotype of the German held by Steed, the more
distant observer. [65] This was not a case, however, where the
spectator saw more of the game. The prevalence, during the war and
at the peace, of the conviction that the Germans were incorrigible,
that their mentality was in some sense fixed, set, by definition had
excluded attempts at correcting, altering, moulding. With another
opportunity in sight Sir George Cockerill, former Director of Special
Intelligence at the War Office, in a bid to redress the balance of
attention given by Campbell Stuart's book about it to the Crewe
House organisation and to thwart the damage that would in his view
be done if those who were anxious to repeat that operation were
indulged, delivered himself of the view that it was a 'fantastic
theory' 'that the vice of international aggression on the grand scale
is no more endemic in the German nation than in others, and that if
only we relate our propaganda to policy and produce a sufficiently
attractive policy to set before the German people, we may ensure
permanent world peace by negotiation and appeasement without
destroying finally her military power and (a more difficult and
perduring task) exorcising her lust for world domination and
spoliation'. He, for one, was in no doubt that Germany's alcoholism
was, pace Wells and Headlam-Morley, chronic, and that its only cure
was likely to be found 'in a prolonged period under observation and
restraint'. [66)

NOTES

1. Report on the work of The Department of Propaganda in
Enemy Countries, GT 6839 pp. 19-23, CAB 24/75. All italics and
capitals are in the original. This Report was transmuted by Sir
Campbell Stuart into Secrets of Crewe House: the story of a famous
campaign (London 1920).
2. ibid. pp.58-9.
3. Hansard 5th series vol 110 cols 2401-3.
4. GT 6839 pp. 71-2.
5. A.Rothstein The Soldiers' Strikes of 1919 (London 1980) p. 32.
6. Sir G. Cockerill What Fools We Were (London 1944) pp.66-79.
7. FO 371/4375 ff. 113-6.
8. FO 371/4374, memo on The Inner Change in Germany, 4 Feb
1919, PID, G/033: memo on Germany Forecasts, 20 Feb 1919,
PID,G/036.
9. 3 Oct 1918, PID, G/016, CAB 24/65.
10. T 102/16, /18: memo by Wade 25 Dec 1917 on War Aims and
Publicity, FO 371/3435/16409 paras 20, 22, 24.

11. 19 Dec 1916, in James Brown Scott Official Statements of War Aims and Peace Proposals December 1916 to November 1918 (Washington 1921) p.19.

12. 10 Jan 1917, ibid. p.37.

13. 5 Jan 1918, ibid. p. 227. Wade's memorandum was not distributed outside the Department of Information until 25 Jan 1918.

14. ibid.p.127.

15. ibid.pp.175-86.

1 6. The Times 17 Nov 1917; Balfour to Lansdowne 22 Nov 1917, in Lansdowne 'The "Peace Letter" of 1917' The Nineteenth Century and After, 1934, 370-94.

17. 2 Feb 1918, CAB 25/120.

18. Scott op.cit. pp. 127-8, from 'But if it be true...'.

19. 4 Oct 1916, CAB 37/157/7, all italics mine.

20. Grey clearly found it difficult to endorse Burke's remark, which he cited, that he did not know how to draw up an indictment against a nation. He merely said, of President Wilson's declarations, that 'great consequences depend upon whether these statements are true or whether they are not'. See Wilson's statement to Congress 2 April 1917, recording the Declaration of a State of War between the United States and the Imperial German Government: 'We are, let me say again, sincere friends of the German people...'. Scott op.cit. pp.89-92.

21. Rumbold (Berne) to Balfour 20 Aug 1918 FO 371/3223/144814; same to same 14 Sept 1918 ibid./157365; Findlay (Christiania) to Balfour 11 Oct 1918 ibid./3444/171468; Robertson (The Hague) to Balfour 14 Oct 1918 ibid./172383.

22. Scott op.cit. pp.349-52, 421-2. This was repeated on 23 October 1918, ibid.pp.434-6.

23. T.Jones Whitehall Diary vol i (London 1969) 67-70.

24. D. Chapman-Huston The Lost Historian - a memoir of Sir Sidney Low (London 1936) pp.267-8.

25. M. Cole (ed.) Beatrice Webb's Diaries 1912-24 (London 1952) pp.96-7.

26. A.J.Mayer Political Origins of the New Diplomacy 1917-1918 (Vintage books edn. New York 1970) p.334. On 2 January 1918 Haig told the King: 'Few of us (soldiers) feel that the "democratising of Germany" is worth the loss of a single Englishman.' He also pointed out 'that the removal of the Hohenzollerns from Germany is likely to result in anarchy just as was the case in Russia'. R.Blake (ed.) The Private Papers of Douglas Haig (London 1952) p.277.

27. A.Gollin Proconsul in Politics (London 1964) pp.568-74.

28. Minute by Crowe 16 Oct 1918, FO 371/3444/172800.

29. Minute by Cecil ibid.; and of 23 Aug 1918 ibid./4367/339.

30. ibid./3227/199100.

31. Cartwright to Grey no. 2, 12 Jan 1907, minutes by Crowe 21 Jan., ibid./257/2390. For another occasion when the unconventional Cartwright was brought back into line see K.M.Wilson, 'Isolating the the Isolator: Grey, Cartwright and the seduction of Austria-Hungary 1908-12', Mitteilungen des Österreichisches Staatsarchiv (35) 1982.

32. CAB 24/65.

33. Headlam-Morley, distinguishing between a political change in Germany, which 'every one wants', and a social revolution which 'would be disastrous not only to Germany, but to the world as a whole, for it would only too probably spread to other countries', advised that Allied troops should with the greatest rapidity occupy German territory with the object of maintaining order, following the military defeat of Germany; he contemplated Britain and America 'policing nearly the whole of Europe'. Though not prepared to make such a 'spontaneous offer... to assist any German party ("bourgeoisie", or conservative, or monarchist) against a social revolution', Crowe did allow himself to say 'But let us by all means be prepared with a policy in case a reasonably constituted government in Germany... ready to accept our demands, asks us for armed assistance in keeping order and preventing a regime of "terror".' Memo by Headlam-Morley 12 Oct. minute by Crowe 16 Oct. 1918, FO 371/3444/172800. Lloyd George on 10 November 1918 stated his unwillingness to have British troops garrisoning areas in Germany where 'the virus of Bolshevism' was rampant. W.C. 500, CAB 23/8.

34. L.Kochan The Struggle for Germany 1914-45 (Chicago 1963) p.7.

35. See draft memos by Smuts and Cecil 3 Jan 1918, GT 3180-1, CAB 24/37.

36. Hansard 5th Series cx col.1962.

37. FO 371/3435/16409.

38. FO 371/4367/339. The interview given to Henricksson for publication in the Swedish press backfired: ibid./386.

39. FO 371/4374/97.

40. '...there is the fundamental principle of all foreign policy in this country - a very sound principle - that you should never interfere in the internal affairs of another country, however badly governed; and whether Russia is Menshevik or Bolshevik, whather it is reactionary or revolutionary, whether it follows one set of men or another, that is a matter for the Russian people themselves'. Quoted in D.Lloyd George The Truth about the Peace Treaties (London 1938) i.569.

41. Memo by Saunders 22 Oct 1918, FO 371/4369/503.

42. 3 Oct 1918, GT 5883, CAB 24/65.

43. FO 371/3435/16409, para 10. He spoiled his case by going on to say that belief in force could be discredited by failure.

44. In a memorandum On Conscription and Militarism of January 1919 Headlam-Morley pointed to the historical evidence that made it 'very difficult to support the view that the introduction of universal compulsory service has made wars more common'. He also pointed out 'that it is quite true, as it has often been pointed out by German apologists, that Prussia, the home of this system, has been one of the most peaceful States on the Continent'. Lord Robert Cecil minuted that the paper 'omits one consideration, Universal military service gradually becomes so onerous that war tends to be welcomed as a relief.' FO 371/4356 ff. 252-4.

45. Minutes of 16th session, Supreme War Council, 3 Mar 1919, I.C.153 (SWC 381) FO 371/4376; see also minutes of 7 Mar 1919 I.C.156.
46. P.Mantoux Les Délibérations du Conseil Des Quatre (Paris 1955) i.46, 27 Mar 1919.
47. ibid.pp.42, 187-8; W.K.Hancock and J. van der Poel Selections from the Smuts Papers (Cambridge 1966) vols 3, 4; Smuts to Gillett 24 June 1919 ibid. iv. 247.
48. PID memo on The German Constitution 7 Feb 1919, FO 371/4374/124 (G/034): and PID memo 4 Feb 1919 ibid./97 (G/033), para 9: '....by the revolution Germany has set about establishing popular assemblies which, in virtue of Proportional Representation, will represent the people more truly than the British Parliament represents the people...'.
49. ibid. para 10. Not all the staff of the PID were of this opinion: see J. Headlam-Morley A Memoir of the Paris Peace Conference 1919 (London 1972) xxvii, pp.51-2.
50. Scott op.cit. p.181.
51. Mantoux op.cit. i.44-5, 27 Mar 1919.
52. ibid. i.70, 28 Mar 1919.
53. ibid. i.253-5, 15 Apr 1919. On 27 March Clemenceau had stated: 'Nous avons appris malheureusement à connaître les Allemands à nos dépens et nous savons que c'est un peuple qui se soumet à la force pour imposer lui-même la force au monde.' ibid. i.42. See also Foch ibid. i.94 and Clemenceau ibid. i.287: Clemenceau was against the inclusion of the Germans in what in French was La Société des Nations.
54. Lloyd George op.cit. i. 699.
55. ibid. i.685-6. This was as ludicrous as Grey's statement in his preface to Murray that 'At the outset the war was popular and was hailed with popular enthusiasm in Germany, and in no other country'. One should not presume that the point made by Saunders of the PID on 24 October 1918 that 'The present majority (of the German press) calling for an Armistice would not be so large unless it had the authority of the military leaders for the view that armistice is a matter of extreme urgency' did not reach the Prime Minister: FO 371/3444/173397. On Rumbold's despatch of 14 September to the effect that the democratisation of Germany would not begin until Ludendorff quit office, Oliphant at the Foreign Office had minuted: 'There is a lot of truth in this.': ibid.3223/157365.
56. H.A.Gwynne to Asquith 22 Apr 1915, Gwynne MSS 14.
57. Haldane memo 'The Future Relations of the Great Powers' 8 Apr 1915, CAB 37/127/17.
58. Kitchener memo 'The Future Relations of the Great Powers', 21 Apr 1915, ibid./34.
59. October 1916, GT 484, FO 371/3082/103293, my italics.
60. 4 October 1916, CAB 37/157/7.
61. L.Gelfand The Inquiry: American preparations for peace, 1917-19 (London 1963) pp.198-9.
62. Lloyd George op.cit.i.675-7.

63. Saunders to his sister 20, 29 Aug. 1914 Saunders MSS GS/2/50, 51. It is of interest that he does not distinguish between Prussia and Germany in these letters.

64. Saunders to Steed 13, 23 Apr.; Steed to Saunders 19, 23 Apr. 1920: The Times MSS.

65. Chapman-Huston op.cit. p.257.

66. Cockerill op.cit. pp.75 (my italics), 69.

Chapter Two

THE PLANNING OF 'RE-EDUCATION' DURING THE SECOND WORLD WAR

LOTHAR KETTENACKER

The term 're-education' and what it implies have become so controversial over the years that it might be assumed that it must have figured prominently in British war-time planning for post-war Germany. However, this was by no means the case: officials were rather sceptical about its likely results and the Cabinet discussed the matter only once or twice in connection with the question of what to do about the political attitudes of German prisoners of war in British hands. Nevertheless, it is equally true to say that public opinion was indeed obsessed with what seemed to be the distorted character of the German nation which required to be thoroughly expurgated at the end of the war. To a large extent, this was a reflection on, if not a rationalization of, the lack of comprehension in Britain of what it meant to live in a totalitarian society constantly manipulated by indoctrination and terror.

There was a widespread feeling in Britain that the solemn declaration of war by the Prime Minister and the Dominions, in other words by the mighty British Empire, would shake the National Socialist regime to its foundations and would convince both the German masses and the conservative elites, who had supported it while 'the going was good', that Hitler had pushed them over the brink and that it was high time to get rid of him and his system of government. [1] Through their correspondents, Western capitals were well aware that the Polish campaign was by no means a popular event comparable to August 1914.[2] Most of the pronouncements of the Government and the Press seemed to suggest that it was Hitler's war and that it was his evil spirit that Britain was fighting, not the German army. No doubt, this was Chamberlain's strongly held view. It was also good propaganda during what was to be called the 'phoney war'. Last but not least, it was a convenient rationalization on the part of the Government for the lack of action during a period of military build-up. Chamberlain had given the lead with his indictment of the German Chancellor in his speech on 1 September which contained the famous words borrowed from a message of the Labour Party to the 'German people': 'We have no quarrel with the German people except that they allow themselves to be governed by a Nazi Government'.[3] It was a formula which was meant to exonerate the German people and which implied nevertheless that they had some influence on the course of events after all. In this respect, Chamberlain and the left were not at issue. For the Manchester Guardian there was no doubt what the British war aims were: 'the overthrow of this dictator and his system of Government' [4]. Even more categorically Stafford Cripps stated: 'Our enemy is Hitler and the Nazi system and not the German people'.[5] The left was, naturally, hoping for some sign of resistance from the working class, whereas Chamberlain and Halifax were more inclined to bank on the so-called 'moderates' around Göring and Schacht who, with the backing of the Wehrmacht, might be induced to remove Hitler from power. [6]

It is to the ensuing debate, at first within the Government, about the character of the war and the nature of British war aims that the origins of the concept of 're-education' has to be traced. The Foreign Office did not object to the public opinion campaign against Hitler as the chief perpetrator of the war but only as a means of psychological warfare, of strengthening the home-front and undermining enemy morale. While Chamberlain was quite genuine about the removal of Hitler and his system as the pre-requisite of peace, the Foreign Office warned against the illusion that a change of regime in Germany would redress the balance of power in Europe. Commenting on a passage in Nevile Henderson's draft for his Final Report [7] which pointed to the error of confusing the virtues of a whole people with the vices of a system and its rulers, Orme Sargent wrote:

> To contrast the virtues of the people with the vices of their rulers at once leads to the counter-assertion that whatever their virtues may be the German people have a very definite vice of choosing vicious leaders and of following them both willingly and blindly. It is really impossible to maintain that the German people are being governed by a small minority against their will.[8]

The objectionable passage was scrapped. More fundamental still was the criticism which Robert Vansittart, Chief Diplomatic Adviser to the Government, levelled against the woolly liberalism of his countrymen who did not grasp the 'German danger'. In his memorandum of 8 November 1939 headed 'The Origins of Germany's Fifth War' [9] he also attacked Nevile Henderson who was reported to have said 'the megalomania of one man defeated the Prime Minister and me'. Vansittart called this the 'theory of accident' which in his view was 'inherent in the doctrine of appeasement'. He argued instead that three generations of Germans had striven hard to dominate the world and that it was therefore an illusion to think that Britain was only fighting 'Hitlerism'. 'We are fighting the Old Adam, plus Hitlerism'. To him, Stresemann and Brüning were also expansionists, though of a different style:

Let us make no further mistake about it, we are fighting the German Army, and the German people on whom the Army is based. We are fighting the real and not the 'accidental' Germany. That the real Germany contains many good individual Germans is, of course, incontestable. The trouble is that they are never there on The Day.

Vansittart's colleagues did not subscribe to his indiscriminate condemnation of the German 'race', but they agreed with his criticisms of appeasement, believing strongly that Britain had to recover a position of strength, so as not to be forced into meeting Germany half-way. They felt the real task was not to find a face-saving formula for Britain, but to drive home to the German people, not only the German government, that their whole venture had utterly failed. Cadogan summarised the debate by concluding:

The first essential ingredient is a complete defeat of Germany, or a complete collapse, which may bring home to yet one more generation of Germans, that Prussianism or Hitlerism organising for periodical war is neither a pleasant nor a profitable system.[10]

Since all other methods had failed, the Germans now had to learn by force that aggression did not pay, and that the age of unrestricted imperialism had gone forever.

During the first months of the war, the advice of the Foreign Office mainly served to accelerate the process of the 'unwinding of appeasement'. [11] Certain suspicions still lingered on as to the hopes and intentions of the former appeasers, and therefore one might argue that the policy of 're-education' began with the attempt to re-educate the former appeasers at home, teaching them the hard lessons of power politics; that the balance of power had already been disturbed by Germany before Hitler provoked the outbreak of war. Consequently, the war should not be allowed to end before Germany's potential as a troublemaker had been destroyed. A compromise peace with the army generals who were supposed to be unhappy about the state of affairs was no solution. 'Without Hitler', William Strang observed, 'Germany might be less evil, but not necessarily less dangerous. Unless German military power were first broken, peace would be a brief and uneasy respite.' [12] Nor were there any signs that the Germans were anxious to part with their leadership, nor that a collapse of the German home-front was in the offing. Together with the advice of the FO experts, the reports of the PID served as a warning to the Government to brace themselves, and to prepare the general public for the long, bloody days ahead. [13]

As the war showed no signs of ending, and especially as the first reports of large-scale atrocities in Poland seeped through, the distinction between 'Nazi' and 'German' became increasingly blurred in the public mind. Again, the Government had given the lead, when, instead of specifying their war aims, they had simply stated their resolve 'to redeem Europe from the perpetual and recurring fear of German aggression'. [14] The German people were warned, both by the P.M. and the Leader of the Opposition, that they would not be absolved from their share of responsibility for the continuation of the war. From February 1940 onwards voices were heard stressing the necessity of bringing about a 're-orientation' of the German nation. Elizabeth Wiskeman called for 'education to re-humanize', [15] Lord Sankey demanded the 'uneducating of the youth of Germany'. [16] After the Norwegian campaign, the BBC was instructed to abandon the distinction between Nazis and Germans altogether. 'At present, events show that the German people is in fact identifying itself with its Government and it is therefore useless to try to make a non-existent distinction.' [17]

*

By the time of the Battle of Britain, supervised, incidentally, by Hermann Göring, once the great white hope of the appeasers, the Foreign Office's view of the war had been generally acccepted. To a large extent, this was due to the personal impact of Churchill on the public mind; any idea of a negotiated peace appeared to be out of the question. [18] However, a military solution implied and required a different, more comprehensive concept of who 'the enemy' was, for to be fighting only Nazis did not make sense when in actual fact the bombs which destroyed British homes were dropped by ordinary Germans.

Broadcast two months after the worst of the Blitz, Vansittart's <u>Black Record</u> fell on fertile ground, not only among the population at large, but also among intellectuals who ought to have known better. The BBC failed to tone down even the more vulgar of his generalisations. Vansittart struck a chord even among those who rejected his denunciation of the German character, for it was due to the controversy he unleashed that the idea of 're-educating' the Germans received so much public attention. Vansittart was no racist, however, though his opponents labelled him as such, nor did he exclude the possibility of a radical change in the historically distorted character of the Germans. 'Without a fundamental change of soul', he wrote, 'no other cure, no mere administrative or technical tinkering can be permanent.' [19] Nor, indeed, were his suggestions for the treatment of Germany after the war particularly outrageous or unorthodox. Basically he tried to unite public opinion against a compromise peace and to prepare the ground for a thorough-going de-militarisation as well as de-nazification of Germany; in this respect he was not at issue with his former colleagues, and when Germany, in the end, was forced to accept unconditional surrender, including total occupation, he felt that he had achieved his aim: 'the perdition of Germany, not as a people but as a power.' [20]

One of Vansittart's former colleagues, E.H.Carr, who had become an academic, was soon to publish a less controversial and more respectable book, <u>Conditions of Peace,</u> in which he rejected the 'thesis of German wickedness'; he strongly objected to 'the proposed policy of penalisation, dismemberment and permanent coercion of Germany' by saying that 'such a policy would prove in the long run morally repugnant, physically impossible and economically retrograde'. [21] Nevertheless, he too believed that, before eventual reconciliation, a strong dose of coercion, and above all, military defeat and total occupation of the country was essential. He was one of the first to realise that military defeat would be accompanied by a kind of spiritual collapse, 'a state of moral and intellectual exhaustion and chaos' [22] and that a new European perspective had to be opened up to the young Germans, compensating for the misled idealism of the past. In this, of course, the British were only partially successful; they did not wish to enter into any European commitment themselves, preferring to be left in peace with the crumbling remains of their Empire. One is impressed by Carr's vision, and at the same time, depressed by the lack of positive response to his ideas, when he writes:

> It will be necessary to give the German people, not only a common interest in the building of the new Europe, but also the sense of a common moral purpose; and before we can hope to inspire this sense, we must first acquire it ourselves. The problem is sometimes described as that of the 're-education' of Germany; and the description is not a bad one if we realise the importance of applying the results of modern psychological science, which shows that neither penalty nor precept, but example and confidence are the most potent instruments of education. We can 're-educate' the Germans only if we are prepared, in the course of the same process, to re-educate ourselves. [23]

In many respects, Carr's approach came close to the official line as it evolved during the war, a policy of reconciliation, following a short, sharp shock. As a consequence, however, the impression prevails that the priorities of British policy remained essentially negative, as the favoured prefix 'de-' symbolises, in de-militarization, de-nazification etc.; even re-education was predominantly negative inasmuch as it emphasised the necessity of defeat as the primary lesson, and the obligation on the Germans to work out their own salvation. This liberal consensus, subscribed to by both informed public opinion and official thinking, is demonstrated in an Interim Report by a Chatham House Study Group dated Summer 1943, namely, that the Germans should be offered a helping hand but there should be no interference with Germany's social and political renaissance. [24]

While the public concern for the 're-orientation of the German mind' was inspired by the controversy sparked off by Vansittart, official planning for German education progressed on an altogether different plane. Suspicious of the advice given by well meaning educationalists working with German emigrants, the Central Department of the Foreign Office usually consulted the German

63

section of the Foreign Research and Press Service (FRPS) first set up at Balliol College Oxford and later taken over by the Foreign Office as its own Research Department (FORD). When in the summer of 1942, on a visit to this country, Lord Halifax, the then Ambassador to the United States, required further information on plans regarding the post-war treatment of Germany, it was to the FRPS that he turned. Among his concerns was planning for re-education. 'Could any international action be taken in connection with education in the technical sense?' [25] he asked. T.H.Marshall, head of the German Section, felt that nothing very definite could be done from outside which would have any chance of success. He stressed that what mattered was not the imposition of new text-books, but the political and social environment in which young Germans would grow up. [26] In his 'Speakers Notes' for the discussion with Halifax, Marshall was more explicit: 'Re-education is one aspect of reconstruction, not a thing apart.' [27] It was an almost Marxist approach: no matter what the Allies poured into Germany in terms of teaching aids, only the overall environment would determine the outcome. Marshall, for one, believed in and wanted a socialist future for Germany, but this view was not shared by most of the officials of the Central Department, who, however, assumed that since the Germans were by nature collectivist they would anyway end up with their own new brand of socialism. Marshall was typical of many liberal intellectuals in Government service in feeling that the experience of what they called 'war-time socialism', was the answer for the future. The Germans should be allowed to develop their own social order based on their own specific experience. It might then turn out that Germany had learned a lesson which could even be an example to her conquerors!

In the concluding paragraph of Marshall's paper on 'What to do with Germany', he writes:

> We cannot re-educate Germany...The Germans have their own problems to solve, born of their own historic experience. We have ours; they are different and we cannot claim we know the solutions. Still less can we know how to solve Germany's problems. We are liberals by tradition seeking how to strengthen the community without sacrificing the essentials of individual liberty. Germany has tried varieties of socialism, democratic and national, and will emerge from totalitarianism seeking how to restore individual liberty without sacrificing the essentials of socialism. For I believe that the new Germany must be built on socialism. The anti-capitalist urge of recent times, the development of state socialism by the Nazis, and the general belief that Germany cannot become a good neighbour until the power of the big industrialists and the big landowners is broken, all point that way. The Western democracies can contribute much to the re-education of Germany in social and political morality,

but they cannot shape its social and political structure.[28]

Marshall's paper marked the beginning of a systematic, conceptual, approach within the Government to the problem of post-war Germany. Even though most of the FO officials were less attracted than Marshall by the prospect of a socialist Germany, they tended to agree with him that it was none of Britain's business to encourage this development or prevent it, and, moreover, that if she tried she was bound to fail. It was one of the most important underlying assumptions of post-war planning that legitimate British interests vis-à-vis Germany were confined to security in the narrowest sense, disarmament and demilitarization, and did not extent to interference in Germany's social and economic affairs.

Attlee and the Labour Party followed a different line, but without much success; they failed to achieve much more than drawing up manifestos for party consumption. [29] When it came to the application of specific measures inside Germany, the liberal consensus, reinforced by the dictates of economic necessity, prevailed. John Troutbeck, the Government's Adviser on Germany (within the Foreign Office) was not at all convinced that a German government in control of industry was per se sufficient safeguard against future German aggression. When, after the failed coup of 20 July 1944, the question was raised as to whether Germany would 'go Communist' or not, the official response was one of indifference. What was worrying, however, was 'Germany going over to Russian Communism (i.e. taking orders from Moscow), or a non-Communist Germany run by a clandestine party of revenge, leaning on Russia'. [30]

Since most of the members of the FRPS were academics, it is not surprising that German secondary and higher education received particular attention. A critical assessment of the Weimar education system led to the conclusion that the authorities had failed to carry out a thorough reconstruction on democratic lines, leaving the strong class structure within the education system as intact as it had been since the 19th century. It was recognised that the Hitler regime had tried to pull down the class barriers and that efforts had been made to curb the extreme academic bias in German education in favour of character training. [31] If it had not been for the indoctrination of a perverse ideology, and for the formation of a new, arrogant elite, the principles of Hitler's Social Revolution [32] would have found favour with British educational reformers. The German universities, however, came in for particular criticism. That the 'decay of the traditional universities was one of the causes of National Socialism' [33] was a central premise for the reformers. A purge of the universities was not regarded as sufficient, even the dismissal of (a) all pre-1933 National Socialist activists, (b) all the leading personnel, such as Dozentenführer, Rectors etc., and (c) professors of Rassenbiologie and similar bogus sciences would not suffice. [34] What was called for was a thorough-going reform, bringing the universities into line with a democratic society, with entrance based on a system of scholarships to ensure fair representation of all classes. Universities should no longer be allowed to remain ivory towers of pure scholarship; availability of higher education was to be adjusted to meet society's needs, in order to avoid the re-emergence of an academic proletariat, as had occurred between 1928 and 1933 with such disastrous consequences. As to the necessary political education, the old mould would have to be broken by a new, international, outlook. 'The best hope may lie in international exchanges of teachers and students; but to be effective such exchanges would have to be organised (preferably by an international authority) on a scale hitherto undreamt of.' [35] Before the gloomy realities of the post-war era and the new political climate descended on Germany, schemes for reconstruction which would bring about a social revolution by democratic means were pursued with the same fervour as similar plans for Britain which was by no means seen as the model for Germany.

The Central Department of the Foreign Office, in charge of post-war planning in conjunction with the Reconstruction Department, shared the academic planners' deep-rooted scepticism as to the likely success of any educational reforms imposed from outside. The crucial prerequisite before any specific measures could be successfully launched, beyond the de-nazification of the system, was a 'change of heart' among the German people, a phrase which constantly crops up in official papers. No conquering missionary zeal would help, quite likely it would be counter-productive. Various unofficial bodies, such as the <u>German Educational Reconstruction</u> committee, set up in 1941 by S.H.Wood, a Whitehall civil servant, were engaged in drawing up curricula, schemes for text-books and the like; they received no official encouragement. [36] Nor did English publishers, hoping for a profitable market. 'They may lose interest', remarked Con O'Neill, 'when they come to enquire how they are to receive the proceeds of sales in Germany!' [37] The Germans would only be receptive to Western values as a consequence of their new material existence, and through making comparisons with their previous experiences. This feeling is expressed in the first Cabinet Paper on 'The Future of Germany', prepared by the Foreign Office in consultation with their Oxford-based FRPS colleagues, which refers to 're-education' only briefly in its revised form of August 1943:

> It must be understood that any scheme for the re-education of Germans, young or old, by means of text-books, teachers, censors or advisers supplied by the United Nations may be ruled out as futile. It may indeed be necessary to exercise a negative censorship of some kind, but the days of St. Boniface are passed and any hortatory efforts from without to 'convert' the Germans will merely harden their unrepentant hearts. Germans alone can re-educate their fellow countrymen, and Germans will make the attempt only if they themselves

are convinced that the future of their country lies in co-operation with her neighbours. [38]

Sensible as these views were, and they are a fine example of British common-sense - and its limitations - they tended to emphasise the repressive, though not vindictive, measures 'necessary in the interests of safety'. Education was low down on the list of British priorities in post-war planning, because it contributed little of any consequence to British security, unlike, for example, the territorial settlement, the balance of power between central and local, or rather regional, government or the organisation of the German economy, all questions which were debated at length. If one were to examine only the topics of public concern, then no doubt re-education would rank much higher on the scale of importance. [39] However, public opinion, at least as judged from Whitehall, was not expected to contribute much to the highly complex, and largely technical, questions facing the Allies at the end of hostilities.

In the context of these concrete issues, all requiring debate and agreement amongst the Allies, censorship of the media was seen as more pressing than educational reconstruction. Censorship fitted very well into the overall concept of Imperial rule abroad. The first Cabinet Paper to deal specifically with Re-education contains a sentence bearing all the hallmarks of a classic quotation:

> In order to achieve our object, control of German education should aim, on the whole, at being as indirect, invisible and remote as is compatible with its being effective. We should appear to guide rather than lead, to influence rather than to initiate. [40]

Rarely have the principles of indirect rule been formulated with more precision. The liberal concept of democracy, which concerns itself as much with the ritual structure of politics as with the achievement of practical goals, was ideally suited to the management of an already overstretched Empire. It made practical sense 'to insist that certain things shall not be done, rather than that other things shall be, i.e. lay down what the Germans must not do, but otherwise leave them to do what they like'. [41] It goes without saying that this, admittedly sensible, advice was not conducive to the achievement of far-reaching reform.

Apart from the genuine aversion of British officials to the methods of 'Dr. Eisenbart', there were then three basic objections to any policy which called for closer involvement: administrative inconvenience, particularly with regard to the additional demands on manpower, the incompatibility of liberal democracy with indoctrination; and the likely resentment of the Germans - following the post-Versailles experience.

The first guidelines on 're-education' submitted by the Foreign Office to the Cabinet Committee on Armistice and Civil Affairs (ACA) were discussed by Ministers on 24 February 1944; they found themselves in broad agreement with them. [42] The Labour representatives welcomed the fact that the problem of 're-education' was taken at all seriously by the Foreign Office. Attlee suggested that broadcasting might be a suitable means for the furtherance of 're-education' during the occupation (it later turned out that this idea did not appeal to the media experts on Eisenhower's SHAEF staff); the Labour leader was also in favour of making a start with 're-educating' German prisoners of war.

Unlike US planning which suffered from the rivalry between the various government departments and the consequent lack of co-ordination, the British had established an effective machinery, which provided for speedy agreement in Whitehall of most of the politically less controversial plans for Germany. However, civil servants were generally left without much guidance from the Cabinet, until the planning had already reached a fairly advanced stage. Hence most decisions, regardless of their potential importance, were based on certain underlying assumptions, which did not allow for quick readjustments to changing events. One of these assumptions was that the war-time alliance would continue unchanged into the post-war period of joint occupation of Germany [43] The original guidelines on 're-education' were returned to the official A.C.A.Committee (consisting of civil servants representing the various Whitehall departments involved) on the understanding that a final and detailed Draft Directive was to be prepared for submission to the European Advisory Commission, the only permanent inter-allied co-ordinating machinery. The intention was that once approved by the EAC, plans would only require the formal assent of the Allied Governments before being issued by the Control Commission to the Commanders-in-Chief.

The Draft Directive on the Re-education of Germany was circulated to the Armistice and Post-War Committee of the Cabinet on 3rd July 1944 and formed the basic British blueprint for German education during the occupation period. Since it was also necessary to plan for the pre-surrender period, and since it was thought desirable to co-ordinate pre- and post-surrender planning as far as possible, it was thought sensible to consult the Americans at an early stage in preparing the Directive, so that it could be used as guidance for Eisenhower's HQ staff (SHAEF),of which the British were part who were responsible for preparing for Military Government in the eventuality of an advance by the Allied armies into Germany. Therefore, in the course of preparing the Directive an informal working party under the chairmanship of Professor Dodds of FORD was set up which consisted of representatives from the Foreign Office, the War Office, the PID, and the Board of Trade, together with experts from SHAEF and, later, Dr Kefauver, Consultant to the US State Department on educational reconstruction. [44] Some of the groundwork had already been covered by PID, namely the preparation of alternative text-books, pamphlets, teacher's guides and broadcasts, etc. The new working party also concerned itself with the purge of educational personnel, for which 'Black', 'Grey', and 'White' lists were drawn up. Those on the 'Black List' were to be dismissed without notice or compensation at the earliest possible date after occupation; they included, inter alia, war criminals, all members of the SS, and all administrative officials of the various Party organisations in the field of education. The 'Grey List' covered the remaining categories of personnel 'against whom there are reasonable positive grounds of suspicion'[45], such as school inspectors, headmasters and headmistresses of all kinds of schools and heads of Institutes of Adult Education, who were to be automatically suspended during investigation. University professors, however, together with primary schoolteachers, were allowed to remain in their posts during investigation, unless 'the prima facie grounds of suspicion appear strong'. The 'White List' consisted of all those who could be readily employed to fill the gaps. However, it is worth noting that German emigrés with a record of strong opposition to the Hitler regime were not included, since the list was tò contain 'the names of persons inside Germany, whose [and note the order] character, professional standing, experience and political reliability render them especially suitable to be placed in positions of special responsibility'. German emigre teachers were referred to in connection with foreign visiting teachers and lecturers who should only be invited 'to the extent that there exists a genuine demand in Germany for their presence and services'. [46]

The Draft Directive distinguishes between the period immediately following the close of hostilities, during which the tasks to be achieved were identical with those in the pre-surrender period, and 'later stages'. It was only in this second, later period, that it was thought desirable, as one of the 'long-term' objects of the Allies, 'to foster in Germany education interest in the ideas of popular democracy, such as freedom of opinion, speech, the press and religion'. [47] The coercive and repressive measures, as the purge of personnel and the 'de-nazification of teaching', enjoyed clear priority. The two major requirements of British education planning were thus conceived as separate issues, and not as part and parcel of the same process. To some degree this may have been for the sake of planning, but there were more fundamental reasons, for example the expectation of fierce resistance on the part of German fanatics. Further, concern about the possible reactions of Britain's most sensitive ally was uppermost in the Foreign Office mind. In this regard, it was clearly prudent of the British planners to concentrate in the initial stages on those measures for which the Soviet government's agreement could be taken for granted, namely on that purpose which united this most heterogeneous alliance - the fight against fascism - and not on potentially disruptive matters such as the notion of democracy. The Russians could not possible object to a joint proclamation, as was suggested, which proscribed all teaching which

(i) glorifies militarism;
(ii) seeks to propagate, revive or justify the doctrines of National Socialism...

(iii) favours a policy of discrimmination on grounds of race
or religion;
(iv) is hostile to, or seeks to disturb the relations
between, any of the United Nations;
(v) expounds the practice of war... [48]

Furthermore, according to information received through Dr
Kefauver, planning within SHAEF was going in the same direction.
The general view among Eisenhower's staff was 'that steps shall not
be taken by the occupying authorities to bring about the
development of education to support democratic values'. [49] The
reason for this requires explanation. SHAEF was concerned only with
the pre-surrender period, and until surrender the elimination of the
National Socialist regime was more important than democratic
self-determination, which might indeed complicate the process of
'de-nazification'. However, in Washington, the Post-War Committee
of the State Department was developing plans which strongly
emphasised the more positive objects of 're-education', 'as a first
step in the revival of self-government'. [50] Seen from Washington,
the problem was 'how to foster the development of a positive
programme and how to assist the Germans in affecting the change'.
[51] For SHAEF, faced with the more pressing task of establishing
Military Government behind the front lines, this must have sounded
like so much idealistic eyewash. They understandably preferred the
more sober wording of the British Draft Directive which, together
with the Directive on German Church Affairs, with few alterations
became Eisenhower's instructions to his field commanders on 10
February 1945. [52] Importantly for the British, SHAEF agreed to
provide the necessary facilities for the printing of text-books etc.;
but in return the British had to accept the temporary closure of all
schools, and the licensing of text-books, which went further than
they had originally intended. They did not like disruption of the
education system, nor the increase in Allied manpower which
inevitably followed; but the Americans, regardless of cost or
inconvenience, had come prepared for a much more thorough-going
reform, which went far beyond the British concept of fingertip
control.

Following the eradication of National Socialist ideology, the
next stated object in the Draft Directive was 'to avoid as far as
possible any increase of administrative difficulties in Germany'. [53]
Indeed administrative inconvenience, or more precisely, concern
about manpower, pervaded all aspects of British post-war planning.
It is, therefore, not surprising that the Directive specifically refrains
from dealing with the machinery required for the control of German
education. This task was left to one of the sub-commissions of the
International Affairs Section of the Control Commission - later
upgraded to the Education Branch.

Because of the damage done by Goebbels' Ministry of
Propaganda [54], it was not thought advisable to maintain Central
Government control over education and propaganda; nor was it
thought necessary. As in the field of health, it was felt that

education should be left to the regional authorities. [55] It was therefore all the more important to reach prior agreement with the Russians, who left to themselves, and without a central German authority in administrative control, might well establish a separate education policy in the Russian Zone. Furthermore, the more the German administrative infrastructure was left intact, the less likely it was that the Russians would feel the need to set up authorities of their own.

*

On the whole it can be said that there was great reluctance in official quarters to draw up detailed plans for re-education. Again and again it was pointed out that the task of 're-education' or 're-orientation' was best left to the Germans themselves and all the Allies could hope to achieve was to create favourable conditions: total defeat and complete demilitarization but no territorial or economic settlement which would prejudice the future. It was stressed, especially by those in high office, that in the first instance the realization of utter defeat brought about by unconditional surrender was all that mattered. No room was to be left for another stab-in-the-back legend which would allow the myth of military invincibility to linger on. The lesson of defeat was supposed to be more salutary that any other for the purpose of teaching the Germans that war does not pay. Churchill was not alone in believing that the Prussian spirit of militarism was more deeply-rooted than any of Hitler's more vulgar ideas. If Churchill kept referring to the twin aim of destroying 'Nazi tyranny and Prussian militarism' [56] it was clearly the latter which was regarded as the greater threat for the future. It was Prussianism which provided the link between the First and Second World War and which, especially for one who had witnessed Imperial Army manoeuvres as the Kaiser's guest, contained the potential for future trouble if not curbed once and for all. Indeed Churchill was so convinced that Germany had to be defeated by military means that he was accused of distorted priorities. [57] However, even for members of the Government like R.A. Butler, who tended to take a more positive line, military defeat of the most uncompromising kind was regarded as the essential prerequisite [58] for what was to be termed in later years 'educational reconstruction'. [59] While the disappearance of Hitler and his regime at the end of the war could be taken for granted, the much hoped for 'change of heart' on the part of the German people could not be predicted with the same certainty. This is also borne out by a Cabinet paper about the 'German Reaction to Defeat' which warns:

> It would be superficial to regard Hitlerism as likely to remain a menace of the same order as German nationalism and German militarism. These two evils may unite again under a new totalitarian cloak. [60]

One method of dispelling the 'evil spirit' of Prussia and what it stood for in British eyes was to eliminate this entity within the Reich rather than, as recommended in various quarters including the 'Big Three', to dismember the whole of Gemany. In order to weaken central authority and to strengthen the sound traditions of German federalism Prussia was to be divided into its provinces which were to be accorded equal status with the non-Prussian Länder. [61] A Cabinet paper submitted by the Foreign Office outlining this idea states: 'Prussia has undeniably been the focus of German militarism since the days of Frederick the Great. The elimination of Prussia would be a strong and symbolic action, clear to all'. [62] While a federal reconstitution of the Reich might be welcomed by the Germans who had after all made unsuccessful efforts in this direction, the policy of outright dismemberment was assumed to be detrimental to Allied aims inasmuch as it would rekindle nationalism and the desire for reunification.

There was broad agreement that once Germany was thoroughly purged and demilitarized it should be readmitted into the family of Europe. [63] Churchill for one did not believe in pariah nations. [64] Consequently, no long-term policies were to be adopted which stood in the way of eventual reconciliation. This applied to the territorial as well as economic set-up. Demilitarization went further than demobilising the armed forces and closing down armament factories; it required sophisticated methods of controlling the German industrial potential. However, British planners were equally concerned that the German economy should not be tampered with to such an extent that the country would be in danger of going bankrupt and becoming a burden to its neighbours instead of, as it was hoped, yielding reparations in kind for the benefit of European reconstruction. [65] They therefore insisted that reparations, too, should not exceed certain limits and should not be allowed to trigger off the same development as after the First World War. [66] Whatever the theories put forward to explain the rise of Fascism there was a general consensus that without the economic turmoil of the Great Depression the Hitler movement would not have gathered enough momentum to bring down democracy in Germany.

Until the middle of 1944, planning was based on German experience gained during the inter-war period. This experience seemed to suggest that history might well repeat itself if no adequate precautions were taken in advance to prevent it; at least one was well advised to brace oneself for the worst. After all, Hitler was a far greater fanatic than the Kaiser, and so might be his people. However, following the capture of large numbers of German soldiers after D-Day the 'Weimar terms of reference' as one might call them, could be called into question, and checked against new evidence. At last it was possible to glean a sufficient amount of information from them about the attitudes of the younger generation of Germans, whose active co-operation was to be crucial for the democratic reconstruction of Germany. Assessments of the results of extensive interviewing and screening was not shocking, simply rather depressing. What was disturbing was not the fanaticism of the hard core, but the apathy and indifference of the vast majority who had no constructive ideas about their future. A report on 'Mind of the German Army' sums it all up:

It is the absence of any feeling for individual or communal initiative and responsibility which is the most startling and depressing symptom. There exists among these young men, who should be looking forward to a life of activity, no civic sense at all. They have no constructive conceptions of their own and profess, to all intents and purposes, a complete bankruptcy of political ideas. [67]

When asked what they expected from the future these young prisoners wanted to resume their normal peaceful life as though nothing much had happened in the meantime except for a change of leadership. Now it was up to the Allies to make plans and issue orders and to take it on themselves to fight the Russians. A special place in the prisoners' mind was reserved for the person of the Führer who was much more important to them than National Socialism as a set of ideas:

Hitler, in their view, continues the war because he knows that he can win it. If he knew he couldn't win it, he would call it off at once because it would then injure 'his people'. Hitler, in fact, is the one and only stable factor in their whole political outlook. He provides the continuity, and many of these men are quite incapable of visualising any future of Germany without him. If you remove Hitler from their mental picture, it does not disintegrate, but simply fades out, and behind it is nothing. [68]

In some POW camps elaborate celebrations were staged to mark Hitler's birthday. There was a high percentage of fanatics among the non-commissioned officers who continued to indoctrinate their comrades. Some of those suspected of defeatism were murdered under the eyes of the British guards. [69] This prompted the authorities to do something about the 're-education' of prisoners of war as suggested by the Deputy Prime Minister. On 18 September 1944 the Cabinet requested Political Warfare Executive (PWE) to undertake this task. By late autumn PWE was in charge of some 120,000 POW's in Britain and 30,000 in the Middle East. [70] The screening and subsequent segregation of POW's was seen as the most urgent step which in itself would be conducive to further re-education. Prisoners were divided into three categories (extended to eight after the war): A: reliable opponents; B: the majority of non-political followers; and C: faithful National Socialists. [71] Even though camps contained prisoners of all shades one category usually dominated so that they were commonly referred to as 'white', 'grey' and 'black camps'. During the last months of the war more than 50%

of all prisoners were transferred to 'black' camps in order to facilitate the 're-education' of the politically more promising. It is to the credit of the educational work carried out in this field that one of the British officers chiefly responsible for it was subsequently invited to contribute the relevant volume to the German official history of the prisoners of war in Allied hands. [72]

Henry Faulk was far ahead of the ordinary camp commander inasmuch as he perceived the need for a social-psychological approach rather than seeing his task purely in political terms. He recalls that the whole idea of 're-education' was fairly unpopular with the majority of British officials as well as the bulk of German POWs who disliked intensely the notion of 'Umerziehung'. Constant reference to 'democracy' was equally resented amongst the German prisoners because it seemed to imply that one ideology and one form of government was being substituted for another by virtue of military victory alone. Let down by the Nazi regime they were tired of every kind of political propaganda and indoctrination. The situation was made worse by the fact that many camp commanders unknowingly supported Nazi officers because they could be handled more easily as spokesmen for their camp and were prepared to acknowledge the code of military discipline. Apparently the British never attempted to explain to their German POWs what the concept of 're-education' really implied. Officially the aims of 're-education' as applicable to German POWs were:

> 1) to eradicate from the minds of the prisoners belief in the military tradition and the Nationalist ideology, of which the basis is that might is right and that the necessity of the state knows no law;

> 2) to impart to the prisoners an accurate understanding and a just appreciation of the principles of democratic government and their implication for the conduct of men and nations... [73]

Even though these aims were of a predominantly political nature Henry Faulk emphasises that the actual attempts at 're-education' were directed towards changing ethical norms and values rather than towards straightforward political conversion. [74] The means employed were lectures, films, discussion groups and the like on a voluntary basis except for a short film on the concentration camps at Belsen and Buchenwald at which attendance was obligatory. The results of all these efforts were, of course, difficult to assess. What could be ascertained was a dwindling in the number of Nazi fanatics and a corresponding increase in the number of non-political prisoners (category B) with only a marginal growth in the 'whites'. To a large extent this was no doubt due to the traumatic experience of defeat and occupation which took some time to work its way through to the minds of the German prisoners and which, as anticipated, seemed to be a crucial element in the whole process of coming to terms with the past. However, it would be unfair to minimize the impact of the deliberate and conscientious efforts made by the British to instil a new outlook in their German captives. The screening of prisoners from Canada and the United States who had not undergone the same kind of treatment when they arrived in June 1946 showed considerable improvement after a period of six months. [75] Similar results were gained from 're-education' courses in Camp 180, where the youngest prisoners, those most affected by Nazi indoctrination, were gathered.

In a category of its own was the training centre at Wilton Park (Camp 300) which was set up in November/December 1945 as a kind of POW staff college or university headed by a naturalized German academic, Dr Heinz Koeppler. [76] The basic approach was not altogether different from what was practised in other camps, except that the whole atmosphere was much more liberal and enlightened setting an example of what 're-education' at its best could mean. For British public opinion Wilton Park and 're-education' were almost synonymous; former students, both POWs and civilians from the British Zone, came to look upon themselves as a special fraternity ('Wiltonians'). Facilities did not allow for more than 1% of all German prisoners in British hands to attend Wilton Park's six to eight weeks' courses. The unashamed appeal to elitism was more than making a virtue out of necessity: it also struck a familiar note in many prisoners, something with which they could identify and which forged a link between past and future. The main idea behind Wilton Park was to have a training centre for (a) German POWs, generally of anti-Nazi persuasion (category A) - early attempts to work with young Nazis proved to be a failure - who could be trusted to carry on the work of influencing their comrades in ordinary camps; (b) to recruit professionals and specialists of all kinds to fill the many vacancies in the British Zone, mainly in the administrative machine; 53% of the students came from the British Zone, most of them (45%) were between 25 and 40 years of age. According to Faulk, cooperation between Wilton Park and the Training Advisers in ordinary camps left something to be desired: there was the charge of recruiting 'opportunists', 'anglophiles' and 'academics' who would not cut much ice with their comrades. Apparently, what mattered above all for the dispirited German POWs, whose belief in one sort of leadership was shattered, was personality and character which applied both to British officers and German camp leaders.

*

It would be faint-hearted to shrink from making certain generalisations when discussing a subject riddled, as it were, with national prejudice. It would appear that Britain was most confused about the future development of Germany, whether she would turn East rather than West, whether 'the claws of militarism (would) become rudimentary, and finally drop off' [77] or whether later generations would only remember how narrowly final victory had slipped from Germany's grasp. What is even more remarkable is that in spite of all preventive planning the British Government were not at all sure to what extent they would in fact be able to determine the outcome. The anxiety was never far from their mind that they might be defeated by yet another erruption of fanaticism. No doubt the fear of German nationalism bent on militarizing society for expansionist aims was much greater than that of a re-emergence of National Socialism. In view of these uncertainties and of the fact that her resources were clearly overstretched, it is perhaps not surprising that Britain should have adopted a rather reluctant and non-commital approach to Germany. The result was by no means p u r e l y n e g a t i v e as evidenced by the following FO recommendation:

> We should concentrate on what is necessary for our own security remembering that the purpose of peace, as of the war, is not to punish the Germans but to secure our own safety and advantage. [78]

What mattered in the end was primarily how to secure peace most effectively and not how to make Germany safe for democracy or how to tame her through a socialist economic order or any other far-reaching involvement. Not to be discounted are, furthermore, the liberal inhibitions of British officials who disliked forcing their own concept of democracy on unwilling foreigners. As they saw it the very essence of democracy was self-determination, especially in the field of education which was so much tied up with a nation's cultural heritage. Later on one of them justified this approach by saying: 'It would be the height of arrogance to assume that victory somehow gave us the moral right to impose our way of life'. [79] It is most significant that Robert Birley, who was to become Britain's most successful educational adviser in Germany, should have reminded his countrymen in a letter to The Times on the very day of the Wehrmacht's general surrender that Germany had admirable humanist traditions of her own which could guide her into the future. [80]

Once the war was over and the Germans had turned out to be much more manageable than anticipated, efforts like these towards achieving a more positive approach to the German problem were not lacking. [81] This was due to the unexpected Labour victory which unleashed the educational zeal of the British Left onto Germany, as well as to the emergence of the Cold War which turned Germany into a battlefield of competing ideologies. Text-books, educational visits and the like were now shown to be no less important than measures concerning 'economic security'. What only a few months before appeared to be naive, at best well-meaning, suddenly gained the stamp of approval from Whitehall realists. Times changed quickly in 1945.

NOTES

1. This was certainly true of Chamberlain. See Maurice Cowling,The Impact of Hitler. British Politics and British Policy 1933-1940 (Cambridge,1975),pp. 355-59.

2. Cf. Marlis Steinert, Hitler's War and the Germans. Public Mood and Attitude during the Second World War (Athens/Ohio 1977) pp.50-59; also William L. Shirer, The Rise and the Fall of the Third Reich (London, 1964), p. 721-22.

3. Hansard vol. 351, col. 132. Greenwood replied for Labour (col.135): 'We shall enter this struggle without passion against people. I was glad when the Prime Minister used words which we had used in our official declaration.' Cf. also T.D.Burridge, British Labour and Hitler's War (London, 1976), pp. 17-24.

4. Manchester Guardian, 2 Sept. 1939.

5. Tribune, 15 Sept. 1939. •

6. Cf. Peter W. Ludlow, 'The Unwinding of Appeasement', in Lothar Kettenacker (ed.), The 'Other Germany' in the Second World War. Emigration and Resistance in International Perspective (Stuttgart, 1977),pp. 9-48; also Bernd Martin, Friedensinitiativen und Machtpolitik im Zweiten Weltkrieg 1939-1942 (Düsseldorf, 1974), pp. 82-117.

7. Nevile Henderson, Final Report on the Circumstances leading to the Termination of his Mission to Berlin, 1939 (Cmd. 6115). The passage in question was eventually scrapped; for the draft see FO 371/22984/C15195.

8. Ibid., C15195.

9. FO 371/22986/C19495, all further quotations ibid.

10. Ibid. The same idea was phrased more succinctly by Eden in his broadcast of 11 Sept. 1939: We have decided to fight to show that aggression does not pay. Louise Holborn (ed.), War and Peace Aims of the United Nations, vol. 1 (Boston, 1943), p. 159.

11. See note 6.

12. Minute by William Strang, 8 Nov. 1939, FO 371/22985/C16404.

13. Cf. Memorandum on the First Two Months of the War, 27 Oct. 1939 FO 371/22986/C18065.

14. Chamberlain's reply to Hitler's so-called peace offer of 6 Oct. 1939: Hansard vol. 351, col. 978. See also the Government's reply to the peace initiatives of Belgium and the Netherlands: The Times, 13 Nov. 1939.

15. Spectator, 23 Feb. 1940.

16. 'Britain's Job After the War - Un-educating Young Nazis', Daily Herald, 11 April 1940.

17. Wellington to Nicholls, BBC Archives: Acc. No. 46235/2; See also Hermann Fromm, Deutschland in der öffentlichen Kriegszieldiskussion Grossbritanniens 1939-1945 (Frankfurt am Main, 1982),pp. 45-50.

18. Cf. Martin Gilbert, Winston S. Churchill, vol. 6: Finest Hour 1939-1941 (London, 1983) pp. 402-36. Churchill's difficult position in Cabinet around the time of Dunkirk is also well documented in John Grenville, A World History of the 20th Century 1900-1945 (Brighton, 1980), pp. 473-79.

19. Robert Vansittart, Black Record. Germans Past and Present (London, 1941) p. 54.

20. Hansard vol. 136, col. 82 (1 May 1945).

21. E.H.Carr, Conditions of Peace (London, 1942), p. 224.

22. Ibid., p. 234.

23. Ibid., p. 233.

24. Cf. Chatham House, The Problem of Germany. An Interim Report by a Chatham House Study Group (London, 1943), pp. 65-67.

25. Report of the discussion at a meeting held at Balliol College (Oxford), on the 13th July 1942, FO 371/31500/U276.

26. Ibid.

27. Speakers Notes, Question 8, A. What is the Future of Germany?, 29 June 1942, FO 371/31500/U306.

28. What to do with Germany? (T.H.Marshall), 9 July 1942, ibid.

29. See Burridge, op. cit pp. 59-68.

30. Will Germany "go Communist" after the War? (G.W.Harrison), 11 Sept. 1944, FO /30.With G/371/39211/C14245; also Kettenacker (ed.), p. 217. Reference is made to the result of a discussion within the FO in response to the above mentioned memorandum.

31. The German Schools (RB VI/4/ii), 14 Sept. 1942 FO 371/30951/C8907.

32. Cf. David Schoenbaum, Hitler's Social Revolution (New York/London, 1967).

33. The German Universities (RB VI/2/iii), 10 Dec. 1942, ibid., C12454.

34. Some Thoughts on the Future of the Universities, 25 May 1942, ibid. C5903.

35. Ibid.

36. Cf. Jane Anderson, '"GER": A Voluntary Anglo-German contribution', in Arthur Hearnden (ed.), The British in Germany. Educational Reconstruction after 1945 (London, 1978), pp. 253-67; also Gunter Pakschies, Umerziehung in der Britischen Zone 1945-1949 (Weinheim, 1979) and Maria Halbritter, Schulreformpolitik in der Britischen Zone 1945-1949 (Weinheim, 1979).

37. Draft Memorandum: The Re-education of Germany, 17 Nov. 1943, FO 371/34462/C14087.

38. The Future of Germany, PS (43) 2, 8 Aug. 1943, FO 371/34459/C9516.

39. Cf. Fromm, op.cit., pp. 211-21.

40. The Re-education of Germany, ACA (44) 5, 27 Jan. 1944, CAB 87/84.

41. Ibid.

42. Minutes of the Meeting of 24 Feb. 1944 regarding ACA (44) 5, ibid.

43. Cf. Lothar Kettenacker, 'The Anglo-Soviet Alliance and the Problem of Germany, 1941-1945', Journal of Contemporary History, 17 (1982), pp. 435-58.

44. Re-education of Germany. Report by the Chairman of the ACAO Committee, APW (44) 37, 3 July 1944, CAB 87/67.

45. Purge of German Educational Personnel, Appendix A to Draft Directive on the Re-education of Germany, ibid.

46. Draft Directive on the Re-education of Germany, ibid. See also Lothar Kettenacker, 'Der Einfluss der deutschen Emigranten auf die britische Kriegszielpolitik', in Gerhard Hirschfeld (ed.), Exil in Grossbritannien. Zur Emigration aus dem nationalsozialistischen Deutschland (Stuttgart, 1983), pp. 80-105. A translation of this volume from the publication series of the German Historical Institute London into English is in preparation (Leamington Spa 1984).

47. Ibid.

48. Ibid.

49. Post-Surrender Policy for Schools in Germany, enclosure to letter from Winant to Hull, 8 Aug. 1944, National Archives Washington: Mosely File (EAC) RG 43/8/VII.

50. Germany: Pre- and Post Surrender Policy with Respect to Schools (PWC-164b), 18 July 1944, Notter File RG 59/18.

51. Ibid.

52. Directive for Military Government of Germany Prior to Defeat or Surrender: Education and Religious Section (APO 757), 10 Feb. 1945, RG 59/C119/740.00119 Control (Germany) 3-1045. About planning for 're-education' in Washington see James F. Tent, Mission on the Rhine. Re-education and Denazification in American-Occupied Germany. (Chicago/London, 1982), pp. 13-39.

53. See note 46.

54. Cf. Michael Balfour, Propaganda in War, 1939-1945 (London, 1979).

55. Effect of Disintegration of Central German Administration, APW (44) 105, 20 Oct. 1944, FO 371/40672/U8025.

56. See for instance his speech to the House of Commons, 21 Sept. 1943: Nazi tyranny and Prussian militarism are two main elements in German life which must be absolutely destroyed. They must be absolutely rooted out if Europe and the world are to be spared a third and still more frightful conflict. Charles Eade (ed.), The War Speeches of Winston Churchill (London, 1952), vol. 3, p. 18.

57. 'Soviet Victories and allied Plans', New Statesman, 19 Nov. 1943: We wish that Mr. Churchill could become as enthusiastic about the exciting task of reconstruction as he is about the planning of destruction.

58. See his speech in the House of Commons on 27 May 1943, Hansard vol. 389, col. 1856.

59. Cf. Hearnden (ed.), note 36.

60. WP (45) 18, 10 Jan. 1945, FO 371/46791/C150.

61. For details of these plans see Lothar Kettenacker, 'Preussen in der alliierten Kriegszielplanung, 1939-1947', in Lothar Kettenacker et al. (eds.), Studien zur Geschichte Englands und der

deutsch-britischen Beziehungen, Festschrift für Paul Kluke (Munich, 1981), pp. 312-40.

62. Confederation, Federation and the Decentralisation of the German State and the Dismemberment of Prussia, APW (44) 118, 27 Nov. 1944, FO 371/39080/C16550.

63. This is explicitly stated in Eden's last Cabinet paper before setting off to the Moscow Conference of Foreign Ministers in the autumn of 1943: 'I suggest the only policy holding out any real hope for the future is one which, while taking all necessary safeguards, aims ultimately at the re-admittance of a reformed Germany into the life of Europe', WP (43) 421, 27 Sept. 1943, FO 371/34460/C11296.

64. Cf. Gilbert, Churchill, vol.6, 1031.

65. See Report of the Interdepartmental Committee on Reparation and Economic Security, 31 Aug. 1943, FO 371/35305/U4079. The Committee is usually referred to as the Malkin Committee by virtue of its FO chairman. See also E.F.Penrose, Economic Planning for Peace (Princeton, 1953) and Friedrich Jerchow, Deutschland in der Weltwirtschaft 1944-1947. Alliierte Deutschland und Reparationspolitik und die Anfange der westdeutschen Ausenwirtschaft (Düsseldorf, 1978), pp. 61-63.

66. For British reparation policies see also Josef Foschepoth, 'Britische Deutschlandpolitik zwischen Yalta und Potsdam', in Vierteljahrshefte für Zeitgeschichte 30 (1980), pp. 675-714.

67. The Mind of the German Army, 21 Sept. 1944, FO 371/40666/U7549.

68. Ibid.

69. See Matthew Barry Sullivan, Thresholds of Peace. German Prisoners and the People of Britain 1944-1948 (London, 1979) pp. 86-112; also Herbert Sulzbach, 'Inside Featherstone Park', In Rolf Breitenstein (ed.), Total War to Total Trust (London, 1976), pp. 10-32. Herbert Sulzbach 'commissioned both in the German Imperial Army in 1916 and by King George VI in 1945' was another of those few influential personalities who knew how to approach the difficult task of 're-education' in the right spirit.

70. Progress Report on the Re-education of German Prisoners of War, APW (44) 113, 16 Nov. 1944, CAB 87/68.

71. Helmut Wolff, Die deutschen Kriegsgefangenen in britischer Hand. Ein Überblick (Munich, 1974), pp. 46-50.

72. Henry Faulk, Die deutschen Kriegsgefangenen in Grossbritannien. Re-education (Munich, 1970). This volume of 783 pages is by far the most detailed account of British 're-education' efforts with regard to German prisoners of war. Most information given in this paper is, if not otherwise specified, derived from this source. About Faulk's personality see Sullivan, op. cit., pp. 66-74.

73. The Re-education of German Prisoners of War, ed. Pristoners of War Division, Political Intelligence Department of the Foreign Office (London, 1945), p. 4; see also Faulk, p. 63.

74. Faulk, p. 681.

75. For figures and percentages see ibid., p. 702; also Sullivan, pp. 113-33.

76. Faulk, pp. 186-225 and the more popularly written chapter 'Koeppler's College' in Sullivan, pp. 240-57.

77. See note 60.

78. Ibid.

79. George Murray, 'The British Contribution', in Hearnden (ed.),p. 66.

80. Robert Birley, letter to The Times, 8 May 1945: 'It is no use hoping to build anything except on some foundation of national tradition. Germany will not be a tabula rasa. Every means should be taken to persuade the Germans that they themselves have such a tradition, however completely forgotten now, on which a decent society can be based. There was once a Germany of Goethe...'.

81. See Kurt Jürgensen, 'British Occupation Policy after 1945 and the problem of "Re-educating Germany"' in History 68 (1983), pp. 225-44.

Chapter Three

THE CONCEPT AND PRACTICE OF 'RE-EDUCATION' IN GERMANY
1945-50

KURT JÜRGENSEN

Before and after the collapse of Germany 're-education' expressed
British policy. On 8 May 1945 (Victory in Europe Day) The Times
published a letter from Robert Birley, then Headmaster of
Charterhouse, under the title 'Re-educating Germany'. [1] Birley
pointed out that the '"re-education" of Germany by the Allies' had
become an unavoidable duty. He deplored the lack of consensus on
what was meant by the term. This problem was to be solved by
considering what kind of country the British expected a
're-educated' Germany to be. Birley made three suggestions. The
first task was to teach the Germans to accept political
responsibility. The second was to turn the German people towards
their liberal traditions. The third was the acid one: the Germans had
to learn to respect other peoples and especially the Slavs; the
Germans must be prepared 'to accept the Czechs and the Poles as
peoples with cultures and traditions of their own'. On 8 September
1945, the leading article in the British Zone Review dealt with the
question 'Can we Re-educate Germany?'. [2] The answer to this, as
a result of the Germans' complete disillusionment and their desire
for serious information and intellectual instruction after a long
period of isolation, was in the affirmative.

In April 1948, the question was discussed whether the Wilton
Park Educational Centre, administered until that time as a Prisoner
of War camp, was to be closed after the last course attended by
Prisoners of War in June 1948. Lord Pakenham, then Chancellor of
the Duchy of Lancaster and as such politically responsible for the
German Section in the Foreign Office, pleaded successfully for the
continuation of Wilton Park as a civilian establishment. He argued in
a letter to an important Member of Parliament: 'To close the centre
down in June...would constitute a serious blow to our plans for the
re-education of the Germans. This task remains of the utmost
importance.' [3] In this view Lord Pakenham was entirely supported
by Mr Crawford, head of the German Education Department (which
was far and away the biggest Department in the German Section).

Even after the 26 July 1948, when the three Western Military
Governors and the West German Minister Presidents agreed upon the
way to create the West German Federal Republic, re-education was

one element (and an important element) of British policy towards Germany. The first regular Conference of the Regional Commissioners after this vital decision took place in Lübbecke on 13 August 1948. General Sir Brian Robertson, Commander-in-Chief and Military Governor, was in the chair, and he was accompanied by his Deputy, Major General Brownjohn, and by his advisers, among them Robert Birley. The conference had to deal with a submission obviously prepared by the Head of the German Education Department, Mr Crawford. This submission (which forms an Appendix to the minutes of the Conference) was called: 'Educational policy in relation to numbers of personnel in regional Education Branches'[4]. The content of the Submission was summarised in four points: (1) on financial resources, (2) on contracts given to the education officers, (3) on 're-education', (4) on general Allied policy. Points (3) and (4) read:

> We are all agreed that re-education is one of the chief objects of our Occupation. It must be remembered however, that there is no word the Germans, even the most friendly Germans, detest so much and none which is liable to call forth such powerful reactions, as this word 're-education'.
> 'Re-education' depends on the general Allied policy towards Germany. If this policy is wrong, no amount of inspection or control or suggestion will ensure the adoption of democratic methods or prevent the revival of nationalistic teaching.

The conference held by the Military Governor with the Regional Commissioners discussed mostly the policy of recruiting first-class people to go to Germany, while the policy of Re-education was a matter dealt with in a memorandum sent by the Deputy Director of Education Branch, Mr Herbert Walker, to the Foreign Office. Education Branch was in general agreement with the Foreign Office's German Educational Department; but Education Branch protested emphatically against the use of the term 're-education'. Mr Walker said: 'We detest the word "re-education" as much as the Germans. This is an Education Branch, not a "Re-education" Branch, and the word has never been used in our directives.' [5] This was correct. So was the reference to the reaction of the Germans. Members of the Education Branch must have felt that the use of the term 'Re-education' would make their task of co-operating with the Germans and making democratic ideas acceptable to their mind even more difficult.

In an article which appeared in Brunswick in March 1947 in a German journal on adult education, the well-known educationalist Georg Alexander argued against the policy of re-education, as it made self-appraisal/self-education (Selbstbesinnung) impossible; re-education was likely to exclude joint responsibility in a field where co-operation was needed. A schoolmaster-like behaviour on

84

the side of the victors was apt to prevent the Germans from reflecting on the reasons for their disaster [6]. When this article was published in March 1947, Robert Birley had just arrived in the British Zone of Occupation as Educational Adviser to the Military Governor. What was Birley's position at that time on re-education, for which he had pleaded so fervently two years earlier? Birley had visited the British Zone in the meanwhile, for four weeks, from early November to early December 1946. About Christmas-time, he sent a long report to the Control Office in London. Birley's general impression was summarised in this sentence: 'The general picture one obtains of the British Zone today is of a country intellectually and culturally starved.' But what about 're-education'? Having reported on his visit to two Civil Internment Camps and having explained the fact that - owing to 'the necessary policy of Denazification' - 16,000 teachers had been dismissed or forbidden to teach, Birley pointed out that a certain 'scheme of Informal Education...might become a means of doing something to re-educate the many thousands deeply tainted with Nazi ideology for whom we are not yet doing anything'. [7]

What Birley had in mind was well prepared discussions with well-trained discussion group leaders under the control of the Education Branch. This scheme became part of adult education in adult colleges like Göhrde in Lower Saxony. [8] I doubt, however, if this scheme did have a broad participation, and I doubt especially if it had a broad participation of former Nazis.

But this is not the point now. We should take notice of the fact that in contrast to what Birley wrote to the Editor of The Times in May 1945, he limited re-education in December 1946 to those who were 'deeply tainted with Nazi ideology'. What is even more striking than this, is the fact that Birley - after having taken over the function of Educational Adviser to the Military Governor, in April 1947 - never used the term 're-education', not even when he addressed a solely British audience and did not have to consider the feelings of the Germans. [9] When he described British policy in retrospect (the title of his contribution to Hearnden's book The British in Germany, 1978) he dissociated himself entirely from that term. Birley relates that many people in Britain immediately after the war believed that it was possible to teach the German nation to be democratic through its schools and universities. He continues: 'For this reason there was coined the horrible word "re-education" to express our policy in Germany. What is more, two of the occupying powers, the French and the Russians, also believed it. But the British Education Branch did not. Its approach was very different.' [10]

The approach employed by Birley and the British Education Branch is indicated in Birley's Burge Memorial Lecture of 3 December 1947. It was one of open-mindedness, of getting into touch with the Germans, of calling upon them to co-operate in the difficult task of rebuilding a community. This educational task required knowledge and discernment. These would help (as Birley put it) the realisation 'that much that is wrong in Germany is part of what is wrong with our civilisation as a whole'. Birley described the most obvious symptom of the 'spiritual disease of our civilisation' as the 'widespread feeling among men that they had lost all control of their own destinies'. His emphasis was on the promotion of common educational efforts on the part of Germans, British and others, in order to awaken a sense of moral and social responsibility within a free and democratic community.

II

Insofar as a political aim underlay the terms 're-education', 'education', and 'educational reconstruction', it was the regeneration of Germany. When Germany could be described as free and democratic her regeneration would be considered to have taken place.

On 21 May 1942 in the House of Lords Nathan quoted a phrase from the Observer: 'I believe indeed that that is the task to which we must set ourselves - to make Germans real Europeans, make them co-operators in the building up of the new society'. Another speaker, Lord Rankeillor, quoted from The Times of 8 May the idea of a 'Civilian Germany'. [11] The Earl of Mansfield concluded this most revealing debate with the following statement:

> Individual Germans should be treated with every consideration so that they may be re-educated - or rather educated, I do not think the 're' is required - to take his part as a European citizen. [12]

At that time, the emphasis was upon the re-education of individual Germans, and breaking up Germany into its component parts for the sake of permanent peace in the world. At least, this was the idea of Mansfield, amongst others. So far as the policy of the British Government was concerned, however, there was from this point a clear tendency towards the regeneration of Germany as a whole. 'The Regeneration of Germany' was the title of a memorandum by Troutbeck, German Adviser in the Foreign Office, of December 1943. [13] After hostilities, Germany was treated as an entirety according to the political and economic principles laid down in the Potsdam Agreement of August 1945. According to the Potsdam Agreement, the task of the Education Branch, which started its activities in the British Zone in July 1945 under the Directorship of Donald Riddy, was that 'German education shall be so controlled as completely to eliminate Nazi and militaristic tendencies and to make possible the successful development of democratic ideas'. [14] Birley thought that this was 'a reasonable and sensible statement' and a good ground to work on. [15] Even in January 1950, Mr Warner, Head of the German General Department, Foreign Office, reminded Birley's successor as Educational Adviser, Professor Tom Marshall, of the Potsdam Agreement and emphasised the validity of its educational principle. Warner said in his letter to Marshall: 'The work on education appears to me to be the same, namely to continue to keep anti-democratic philosophers out of German education and to help the Germans to develop a spirit and method of education which can strengthen the growth of democratic ideas and practice.' [16]

The plan for a federalised Germany presented by Bevin at the Conference of Foreign Ministers in Moscow and London early and late in 1947 came to nothing. Instead, West Germany was set up, in September 1949, as a Federal Republic, and the Soviet Zone became the German Democratic Republic. [17] The political aim behind the policy of re-education or educational reconstruction could only be applied to Western Germany.

When the process of establishing the Federal Republic of Germany began, Birley warned that the process of democratisation had not gone far enough: 'the democratic forces are very weak'. [18] He wanted educational work to be continued. Before General Robertson left Germany in June 1950 as the first British High Commissioner in the Federal Republic, he sent a final report to the Foreign Secretary, and admitted in his conclusions: 'One cannot eradicate all the evil habits and practices of the past in such a time.' [19]

The task was, in Robertson's words, 'the progressive integration of Germany into the Western World...There must be an integration of mind'. He went on:

This does not mean that individual Germans will be expected to see all things just as they are seen by Englishmen and Frenchmen. It does however mean that they must have the same attitude towards the fundamental principles of Freedom and Democracy.

He admitted: 'We know very well that (the Germans) have not got this attitude of mind today, although some progress has been made during the period of occupation.' He thought 'Our best achievements have concerned those matters which are generally referred to as measures to promote democracy'. Nevertheless, Sir Ivone Kirkpatrick, his successor, concluded in November 1951: 'The battle for the German mind is still in full swing, and our educational work has its part to play.' [20]

There were shifts of emphasis. What Birley had stressed in May 1945 was that a liberal and democratic Germany would be reconciled with her own liberal traditions: 'Every means should be taken to persuade the Germans that they themselves have such a tradition, however completely forgotten...Germany was a land of liberal thinkers.' [21] He had the advantage of having heard of Wilhelm von Humboldt, and the liberal revolution in Germany in 1848. He said in December 1947: 'We must be ready to learn about the history and traditions of Germany before we can usefully speak.' [22] So far as reconciling the Germans with their own liberal traditions (I am inclined to say Western traditions) the British had much co-operation from the Germans. Germany's Basic Law is deeply rooted in her nineteenth-century liberalism.

A leitmotiv that ran from the period of the war through to the present day was that only a freedom and peace-loving Germany was capable of supporting a peaceful world. Only a Germany so re-educated would cease to be a threat to the rest of the world. The British Zone Review pointed out in December 1945 that efforts were to be made 'to effect a radical and lasting change of heart in the hard-working, efficient, inflammable, ruthless and war-loving German people...The spiritual regeneration of the German people would...be the greatest and most durable guarantee of the peace of Europe that we could hope to attain'. [23] On 27 February 1951 Kirkpatrick wrote to Bevin:

> The maintenance and development of educational work in Germany have always been accepted, both at home and here, as representing not just cultural embellishment, but an essential feature of our political work as an Occupying Power...If it was true in May 1950, to quote my predecessor (Robertson) that the motive behind our policy for the integration of Germany into the Western World is primarily that of our own security, it is more than ever true today. [24]

Robertson himself had said in May 1950 that if the British Government had to choose between the Educational Division and the Military Security Board (both were parts of the British High Commission in Germany) he would unhesitatingly choose the Educational Division in the interests of security. The Commander-in-Chief of the British Forces in Germany, then, rated the security value of the Military Security Board 'below that of our work in the field of education'. [25]

With the onset of the Cold War that the re-educated Germany should become an ally against the Soviet Union became more prominent. In the conclusions he sent to Bevin in June 1950 after five years in Germany Robertson wrote: 'Western Europe cannot be defended against Russia without the inclusion of Western Germany in the defensive arrangements...Germany must be re-armed.' [26] This prospect of German re-armament made the following aspects even more important: the regeneration of Germany, her integration of mind into the Western principles of freedom and democracy, and her inclusion into the various formal arrangements of political, economic and military co-operation. This policy however was also dictated by the concern that, in the long run, Germany might swing to the East and co-operate with Russia. This idea became an even bigger concern in 1952, because on the one side were signed the so-called 'Contractual Agreements' providing for the European Community of Defence with West German participation, and on the other side

Russia tried to interfere with the prospect of a reunited independent Germany. Chaput de Saintonge who was then Head of the German Education and Information Department, reacted to the Soviet interference and gave utterance in May and in September 1952, to the British concern: 'For the effective defence of Western Europe, Germany must be given those weapons of war which will increase her power and independence and make her potentially an even greater menace, should she choose to desert the Western Community' [27] and - so I may add - wish to co-operate with Russia. This concern was the greater as in the very early Fifties German society temporarily showed signs of a nationalistic revival of the extreme right wing, especially in Lower Saxony where the German Reichs Party (of Major Remer) was rather popular. And even the Christian Democratic and Liberal Parties in Lower Saxony in the very early Fifties contained reactionary elements. [28] What was to be done? The risks of the new Western policy towards Germany were to be met - in the British view - by increasing for the Germans - through educational means - the attraction of Western ideas, Western civilisation, Western prosperity and Western strength. Adenauer's visit to London in late 1951 had put the new Conservative Government under Winston Churchill in an optimistic mood as to the Chancellor's intentions. Chaput de Saintonge commented: 'Adenauer is pledged to the creation of a democratic community...tied to the West.' [29] He added that all the challenges could only be met 'by linking the interests of Federal Germany as closely as possible to the fate of the West'. With regard to the educational task which was the same in 1952 as in the years before the educational work had to aim at the integration of the German mind into the Western Community for the sake of security and lasting peace.

III

We have now to consider the Methods of how the educational work was to be carried out. What about the concept of educational reconstruction in this respect? This is no easy question. We are challenged by the fact that in early 1950 the Educational Adviser - that was then Professor Marshall - declared 'the absence of a clear statement of policy'. General Robertson wrote for that reason to the Minister of State, Mr Younger, in the Foreign Office, on the 4th of May 1950: 'You will, I am sure, agree that if the Educational Adviser and his staff feel that they are lacking guidance on policy, that is a situation which must be remedied immediately'. [30] Younger did not respond to Professor Marshall's and General Robertson's reproach. The former University Officers who were present at a Conference at Oxford in July 1982 agreed upon the fact that for their specific task, they had no briefing. [31] They must have seen, however, the Handbook for Military Government drawn up in late 1944 and revised in 1945. They must have seen the technical Manual for Education

Officers. [32] But these publications were on general lines and the University Officers had no specific instruction for their specific task. But if my impression is right, they generally did not feel the need for such a briefing (some of them, perhaps, but certainly not all of them). Why not? Dr Beckhough, one of the University Officers (in Cologne), said it was really sufficient to have very general guidelines: 'You have to allow the man on the spot, or the woman on the spot, to make the final decision... The situation on the ground... is always different.' [33]

When Birley was Educational Adviser, he never complained about the lack of detailed instruction, nor did Professor Marshall's successor, Professor George Allen. Both Birley and Allen appreciated the pragmatic approach, which, however, was carried out in different stages. Following a Report on the Present Work and Future Task of the British Education Service in Germany - this report was worked out in the Educational Adviser's Office in 1950 [34] - British education work in Germany fell 'naturally' into three phases, each with its distinctive character because of the different circumstances and the different methods.

Phase One ran from the beginning of the occupation to the issue of Ordinance No.57 under which education became a subject within the German sphere of responsibility from January 1947. During Phase One control was complete. The main task was to get the Schools and Colleges and Universities going. To do this, the teaching and administrative staffs had to be purged of Nazi elements, and they had to be replaced, if possible, by new people who could be trusted to bring education on democratic lines. Phase One was mostly a period of material reconstruction, and teachers and students worked mostly under very hard conditions. They worked in overcrowded classrooms, without textbooks (those were scrutinised by the Textbook Section of Education Branch), and they were often on the starvation level. The school system was under strong supervision of the British authorities who issued the Education Instructions to German Authorities. These instructions did not alter the German school system. The problem of school reform was left to the Germans during Phase Two.

Phase Two ran from the issue of Ordinance 57 to the coming into force of the Occupation Statute in September 1949, when the Federal Republic of Germany came into being. The British authorities did not want to interfere in the educational legislation and did not impose any alteration of the existing school system. The British authorities had, however, made plain that they wanted to have four principles respected: (1) a raised academic status for Teacher's Training Colleges, (2) no fees to be paid for secondary education, (3) the possibility of the six-year primary school, (4) the preservation of private schools. For the rest, it was less important to change the schools, than to know - as Robert Birley, Educational Adviser during Phase Two, said - 'what is taught in them and how it is taught'. [35] Phase Two was a period of moral reconstruction during which a lot of personal contacts between the British

Educational Officers and the German educationalists were established or intensified: the British acted by advice and recommendations in conformity with the basic idea of education which requires free persuasion and understanding, not orders or impositions. During Phase Two, educational efforts were multiplied, especially in the wide field of adult education. In order to show the Germans a living democratic tradition in Britain, and in order to have the stimulus of mind on mind, a broad scheme of exchange-courses with a mixed attendance were organised. Wilton Park, which started in January 1946 as a re-education camp for German prisoners of war, was opened during Phase Two to civilians, and it became a fascinating and in general highly appreciated experience which was continued (though the Treasury wanted its closure) during Phase Three. [36]

In Phase Two, in July 1948, the decision to set up the Federal Republic of Germany did have an impact on British educational policy. To give an example which is related to Wilton Park: on the 20th of July 1948 Mr Crawford, then head of the German Education Department in the Foreign Office, advised Dr Koeppler, Warden of Wilton Park, to raise the morale of the Germans who attended Wilton Park's six-week courses. Mr Crawford said:

> We must avoid doing anything which suggests that we think the Germans unready to set up an independent democratic government and we must make it clear that our aim is to help them to do so. Therefore, in all discussions and lectures (in Wilton Park) we should not probe for the weak points in German history or in the German character, but for the strong points. The aim should be to encourage the Germans to build on the good elements in themselves and in the country as a whole and to develop a well founded self-confidence in their ability to conduct a democratic state. [37]

It is possible that the German Education Department acted under the pressure of the German Political Department. Crawford's utterances are in striking contrast to what members of the German Education Department and of the Education Branch said. Even Robert Birley said in a memorandum to the Secretary of State, four days after Mr Crawford had written his letter to Dr Koeppler: 'I do not consider that a democratic order in Germany, in political life, social relations or education is in any way assured...the democratic forces are still very weak'. [38] General Robertson commented on Birley's memorandum. He made plain in a letter to Sir William Strang that Birley's memorandum did not represent his (Robertson's) opinions. [39] Robertson certainly did not believe that the process of democratisation in Germany had gone far enough. In his later conclusions, he described the Germans as an exasperating people with an emotional character and difficult to handle. [40] But how to do this; under what conditions? Robertson answered in August 1948: 'The democratisation of Germany will not be achieved by means of a

protracted and delayed tutelage'. [41] The next stage in the political
and educational efforts deployed in Germany was imminent.

Phase Three started with the Occupation Statute in September
1949 and ended in May 1955, when the Federal Republic of Germany
became a sovereign State. During this Phase educational control was
completely abandoned; in the Occupation Statute there was no
reference to education at all. [42] There are six main features of
this phase: (1) There was, in September 1949, a real turning point.
The setting up of the Federal Republic changed the character of the
Occupation. There was henceforth a growing interpenetration of the
Zones not only by the Federal authorities but also by the Occupying
Powers. Educational activities were extended to the two other
Western Zones, though with care; in the French and American Zones,
activities were mainly left to the British Council and to the
Information Services Division, not to the Educational Adviser and his
educational staff, who acted only in the British Zone. (2) The
Germans were on the whole anxious to have in each Federal State a
British Cultural Relations Office and they took a big interest in
their continued activities. Sir Brian Robertson was much impressed
by this fact; he said: 'We have a unique opportunity due to the
extent to which our efforts are welcomed by the Germans'. [43] (3)
The whole of Western Germany was more and more open to
increased cultural activities by other Western Countries and by
UNESCO. German Authorities could more and more directly establish
normal international contacts. Organisations and individuals could
organise their projects (e.g. visits, exchange-programmes) on their
own, with a minimum of official help. The British-German
partnership which had already started in Phase Two and even to a
certain extent in Phase One, was henceforth rapidly assuming the
form of co-operation between equals. (4) The Cultural Relations
Groups maintained the activities of Education Branch in all fields:
Universities, Teacher Training, Schools, Adult Education, Youth,
Social Welfare. Emphasis was laid upon the Universities and Schools
where the mind of youth was formed. University Officers had a
particularly difficult task because of the rigid and authoritarian
academic structure and the academic pride of the professors.
Provided University Officers could win confidence as individuals,
they might have been able to turn the universities towards their
duties to society, perhaps on the lines of a German experts' Report
of 1948, the Blaues Gutachten, in which Lord Lindsay had
co-operated. (These difficult problems are dealt with in a publication
which David Phillips has prepared on the basis of the Oxford
Symposium held in July 1983.) [44] (5) The British Centres which
were established during Phase Two (then named British Information
Centres) were transferred to the direction of the Educational
Adviser on 1 January 1950. From now on, they formed the bases of
the Educational work. They were named in German 'Brücke' (Bridge).
The total number of Centres was at that time 50, but the number
was reduced within one year, for financial reasons, to 21 main
Centres and 14 subsidiary Centres which were attached to the main

Centres. Through these Centres, the direct contacts with German teachers and educational officials could be maintained. [45] These Centres employed the following methods: they compared British life and culture with German experience; they treated controversial questions with tolerance; they gave free access to news in a country long cut off from the outside world in this respect. These three methods were supposed to demonstrate the superiority of democracy and to make the Germans feel that their country had become an integral and equal part of Western culture.

During Phase Three, which ended in May 1955 with the full sovereignty of the Federal Republic, there was a gradual shift to complete German responsibility for the whole field of educational and cultural activities. The tendency was to leave British educational and cultural contributions in Germany to the British Council. In 1951 this agency took over the whole programme in art, music, and drama, and had a growing share of and finally complete responsibility for academic visits, lectures and exchanges. [46] Phase Three was a period of transition to the complete end of British occupation policy in Germany.

IV

Whether British and Allied Educational policy really worked, whether it did serve to integrate Germany into the Western Community and even into the Western mind, whether the differences between Nazi and post-Nazi Germany were not simply the result of defeat and collapse, are questions not at all easy to answer. In 1952 the Head of the German Education Department, de Saintonge, disagreed with the High Commissioner, Kirkpatrick, about the British achievement in Germany. de Saintonge visited the British Zone in April 1952. Kirkpatrick insisted on a revision of the ensuing report before it was presented to the Foreign Secretary. In his draft report de Saintonge was convinced of the political immaturity of the Germans, and concluded: 'It is unlikely democracy will develop in Germany in the near future.' In the revision this became- 'In spite of the fact that remarkable progress towards democratic Government has been made in Western Germany in the face of grave difficulties, it would be too much to expect from a people so immature and unstable a firmly established and responsible democracy in the near future.' The concern expressed in the draft, that 'the German people will turn to the East' was less dramatically expressed in the revision as 'the German people may turn to the East'. So far as de Saintonge was concerned, British 'help in the education of the people in the exercise of democratic responsibility' and in 'Western integration' was still required. [47]

Robert Birley, having left Germany in August 1949, was faced in Britain with the question as to whether German education (including political thinking and orientation) was being changed for the better. He was not prepared to answer the question. He thought that educational efforts are like seeds which need time to grow. He quoted his French colleague who was in charge of education in the French Sector of Berlin: 'You must wait for a generation and see.' [48] Looking, thirty-four years after the establishment of the Federal Republic, at Birley's criterion of 1945: 'the proof that Germany is being successfully re-educated will not be that she is submissive to the Allies, but that she is found capable of producing a stable and lasting democratic government' [49], it might be said that this has, over time, been met.

NOTES

1. The Times, 8 May 1945.
2. British Zone Review. A monthly Review of the Activities of the CCG (BE), Vol. 1, issue of 8 December 1945.
3. FO 371/70704 B.
4. FO 371/70713.
5. ibid. Memorandum of August 1948.
6. Georg Alexander, Essay (in German though under the English title 'Re-education'), in Denkendes Volk. Blätter für Selbstbesinnung. Organ der Volkshochschulbewegung, ed. by Adolf Grimme, March 1947, pp. 131-132.
7. Robert Birley's Memorandum of 20 December 1946. FO 371/64386.
8. Fritz Borinski, Ein Jahr Leben im neuen Geist. Heimvolkshochschule Jagdschloss Göhrde, in Denkendes Volk (see note 6), pp. 33-35.
9. On 3 December 1947, Robert Birley delivered The Burge Memorial Lecture 'The German Problem and the Responsibility of Britain'. Birley did not touch on the problem of 'Re-educating Germany'. See my article 'British Occupation Policy after 1945 and the Problem of "Re-educating Germany"', in History Vol. 68, Number 223, (1983) pp. 225-244.
10. Arthur Hearnden loc. cit. p. 46.
11. Hansard House of Lords 21 May 1942, cols. 1151-1152, 1163.
12. Ibid. col.1184.
13. FO 371/39093.
14. Four-Power in Germany and Austria 1945-1946: I. Germany by Michael Balfour, II. Austria by John Meir, Oxford University Press, London-New York, Toronto 1956, in the Series: Survey of International Affairs 1939-1946, ed. by Arnold Toynbee, pp. 80-92 (V) Potsdam.
15. See Hearnden op. cit. p. 46.
16. FO 371/85546, Letter of 27 January 1950.
17. Among the numerous publications, I wish to point out, (for its balanced views) Hans-Peter Schwartz, Die Ära Adenauer 1949-1957, in Geschichte der Bundesrepublik Deutschland, Vol. 2,

1981, Deutsche Verlagsanstalt/Brockhaus-Verlag, Stuttgart/ Wiesbaden; (for its outstanding documentation as to the negotiations between the Military Governors and the West-German Prime-Ministers) Der Parlamentarische Rat 1948-1949. Akten und Protokolle, Vol. 1 Vorgeschichte Editors: Der Deutsche Bundestag/Das Bundesarchiv, Harald Boldt Verlag, Boppard/Rhein 1975.

18. Birley's memo of 24 July 1948 to the Military Governor, FO 371/70716. I discuss Birley's view ('I do not consider that a democratic Order in Germany, in political life, social relations or education is any way assured.') in 'Zum Problem der "Political Re-education"', article in Umerziehung und Wiederaufbau. Die Bildungspolitik in Deutschland und Österreich, edited by Manfred Heinemann, Klett-Cotta, Stuttgart 1981, pp. 134-138.

19. Memo of 22 June 1950: 'The Future of Germany. General Robertson's Conclusions' FO 371/85381; Robertson to Younger 4 May 1950 ibid.

20. For the press Memo of 14 November 1951. Sir Ivone Kirkpatrick to Mr Eden on 'British Educational Work in Germany'. FO 371/93651.

21. See note 1.

22. See note 9.

23. See note 2 (Article: 'Can we re-educate Germany?').

24. FO 371/93650.

25. See note 19.

26. ibid.

27. Memorandum 'British policy towards Germany' (original version of May 1952, revised version of September 1952), FO 953/1285.

28. FO 371/84997-85010 (files under the heading: Political situation in Germany, activities of political parties).

29. FO 371/93456 (file concerning Dr Adenauer's visit to London in December 1951).

30. See note 19.

31. See German Universities after the Surrender: British Occupation Policy and the Control of Higher Education, edited by David Phillips, Oxford, Department of Educational Studies, 1983. See also the Transcript of the Symposium proceedings, Oxford Symposium, 8-11 July 1982 'British University Policy in Germany (1945-49)'; transcript compiled by Sarah Cox and David Phillips, University of Oxford Department of Educational Studies, 1982. The first mentioned publication is based upon the transcript of the Symposium proceedings. The transcript is confidential and intended for limited circulation only.

32. WO 220/214 (Military Government Handbook), and /228 (Military Government instructions, education and religion).

33. Transcript (see note 31), p. 24.

34. This Report is an Appendix to the memorandum 'A long-term policy for educational work in Germany', 29 April 1950. FO 371/85546.

35.   Robert Birley, Education in the British Zone of Germany, in Internal Affairs, Vol. XXVI, No. 1, January 1950 (Royal Institute of Internal Affairs), pp. 32-44 (quotation p. 33). This paper is an Address at Chatham House, 11 October 1949, a few months after Birley's return to Great Britain.

36.   I deal at length with Wilton Park in my contribution to Umerziehung und Wiederaufbau (see note 18), pp. 132-134.

37.   FO 371/70704 C.

38.   Memo on 'Prospects of a democratic order in Germany with special reference to Education', 24 July 1948 FO 371/70716.

39.   ibid. Letter to the Under Secretary of State, Sir William Strang, 6 August 1948.

40.   See note 19.

41.   See Note 39.

42.   Occupation Statute/Amtlicher Wortlaut des Besatzungsstatuts in Official Gazette of the Allied High Commission for Germany (Bonn-Petersberg), No. 1, pp. 13-15.

43.   General Sir Brian Robertson to Mr Younger, 4 May 1950, see note 19.

44.   See note 31. Special reference should be made to the Gutachten zur Hochschulreform (named after its blue cover 'Blaues Gutachten'), prepared by the Studienausschuss für Hochschul-Reform, Hamburg 1948. The members of the Committee of experts were seven Professors: Friedrich Drenckhahn (Kiel), Otto Gruber (Aachen), Lord Lindsay of Birker (Oxford), Katharina Petersen (Hamburg), Jean Rudolf von Salis (Zürich), Bruno Snell (Hamburg), Carl Friedrich von Weizsäcker (Göttingen); two clergymen: Lic. Joachim Beckmann (Düsseldorf), Robert Grosche (Prelate in Cologne); one trade-unionist: Franz Theunert (Cologne).

45.   Report on British Centres (1952), FO 953/1285.

46.   Sir Ivone Kirkpatrick to Mr Eden, 14 November 1951 (see note 25. The letter was printed for 'Confidential Foreign Office and Whitehall Distribution'. Sir Ivone Kirkpatrick described in this letter the perspectives of 'British Educational Work in Germany'.

47.   See note 27.

48.   See note 35.

49.   See note 1.

Chapter Four

THE EDUCATION BRANCH OF THE MILITARY GOVERNMENT OF GERMANY AND THE SCHOOLS

ARTHUR HEARNDEN

Could things have turned out differently? For a period of some twenty years after the war the German school system remained in a traditional form, largely impervious to the comprehensive transformation that was being experienced practically everywhere else in Europe. On the face of it the Federal Republic of Germany was educationally the most backward of the major countries, and the consultants paid by the various international organisations to analyse the development of national systems and draw general conclusions from comparisons were not slow in chiding the Germans for this backwardness. Indigenous educationalists were equally censorious, and the balance sheet was strikingly characterised by Saul Robinsohn and Caspar Kuhlmann in 1967 as 'two decades of non-reform'. [1] If, as is generally supposed, it is difficult to bring about reforms in the face of respected traditions and rooted vested interests, how could it have happened that in Germany of all countries, where a fresh start had to be made with the clean sheet of the Stunde Null, there was less disposition towards reform than anywhere else in Europe? Who was to blame? The occupying powers for setting the whole thing off on the wrong foot in the first place? Or the Germans themselves for thwarting any attempt that the occupying authorities made or might have made to introduce a more progressive system?

These are what might now be described as the conventional questions facing historians who, now that some at any rate of the contemporary documents are becoming accessible, are able to deploy their hindsight to try and find authenticated answers.

So far as the history of the Education Branch in the British Zone is concerned, much of the running has been made in the meantime by the members of the Branch themselves. The anthology of accounts of the work of the British education officers, entitled The British in Germany [2] was impressionistic and unsystematic, but to those who contributed to it, it was self-evidently a true record of what they had been doing at the time. To any of them looking back on those years the questions to which I have been referring would, I suspect, sound grossly out of keeping with the job they were given to do, alien and irrelevant to the nature of education as they understood it. At a time when they were straining every nerve to create some kind of order out of chaos, it would have been asking a lot to expect them to be luminaries of a comprehensive education movement which in the rest of Europe developed much later.

It is obvious that a balance has to be struck between the documentary evidence and the contemporary accounts, not only of how the British saw their work but also of what the Germans at the time thought was happening. About five years ago the Observer Magazine had a special issue containing a survey of what it described as 'Germany's new battleground'. The context was the murder of a prominent industrialist and the hijacking of a Lufthansa aeroplane by home-bred terrorists. Seeking to put the blame on what happened during the Occupation, the author quoted a German teacher who declared that 'the Allies' re-education programme directly after the war...had been a conqueror's programme, prepackaged and sloganised'. [3] Whatever the truth of this somewhat obscure accusation, it is interesting as a way of indicating that the view of their work taken by the British education officers was not necessarily shared by the German teachers in the schools. But while we do have a record on the British side which is representative of the experiences of Education Branch as a whole, it is much more of a problem to discover what was a representative view on the part of the Germans at the time.

There are two further points to bear in mind in trying to get the problem of educational reform in perspective. First, it is possible to look at what happened in the other Zones where some of the things the British have been accused of failing to do were tried by the Americans, the French or the Russians. Secondly, it is important to acknowledge that two decades of non-reform is a very loaded as well as a very catching slogan. It is quite true that for two decades the German education system remained stubbornly traditional, the odd man out among the European systems which by the 1960s were developing on comprehensive lines. It is also true that Germany was over the same period the most successful industrial country in Western Europe, a conjunction of phenomena somewhat embarrassing to analysts setting out to demonstrate that progressive educational development could be correlated with economic success. I suspect that one day it will be clear in retrospect that much of the talk about the economic benefits of educational expansion in the 1950s and 1960s was wishful thinking, if only because it was too soon to judge; that the driving force behind the introduction of comprehensive schooling was social; and that insofar as economic arguments were introduced, this was principally as a way of making it easier to convince the politicians that change was desirable.

I am not however going to explore the alluring hypothesis that the less a country embraces educational progress, as defined by progressive educationalists, the more it is likely to prosper economically. I merely want to establish that when we are talking about educational reform we are talking largely about a movement for social improvement. Otherwise it is questionable to use the word reform at all. What we are assuming is that if Germany had followed the path trodden by, say, Sweden, this would have brought about the greater good of a greater number of individual citizens. On this basis we must examine what this direction was, who was in a position to bring it about, and why they failed to do so.

The evidence for what it was is available readily enough. Under the aegis of the Reformpädagogik movement of the Weimar period various experiements with comprehensive schools were carried out. In 1919 there was the so-called Jena Plan for a comprehensive framework within which it would still be possible to promote the interests of the more able children. In the state of Thuringia there was actually a comprehensive school system of sorts in operation in the period from 1922 to 1924. So even though what was generally recognisable about education in Germany in the Weimar period was its selectivity, the prestige of the Gymnasium and the emphasis on vocational education for those not selected for it, there was also a radical alternative tradition. [4] But a word of caution may be in order. In analysing the origins of a movement that has transformed most modern school systems it is all too easy to ascribe a disproportionate role to the preliminary experiments in the context of their own time. This makes it all the more important to be aware of just how much of a minority tradition the comprehensive movement was in Germany, before trying to assess to what extent it could have been revived by those responsible for the planning of the occupation, or by the officers of Education Branch, or by the Germans themselves.

Throughout its twists and turns the discussion of re-education had very little to do with the structure of the school system. Not even the voluntary organisation of German émigrés, GER (German Educational Reconstruction) put forward any proposals of this kind. The atmosphere prior to the surrender was characterised by much more general propositions of the kind expressed by Conservative MP Wardlaw-Milne in a debate in the House of Commons in May 1944:

> There is no doubt whatever that in time to come Germany must have her place in a world which will want her great scientific attainments and her energy but, before that time comes, clearly she must be purged of the brutal doctrines which have caused her to plunge Europe into war over and over again in the last century and which.... have not altered in the German character for several hundred years past. That means a real re-education of the German people, and it probably means also a splitting up of Germany in some way or other. Above all things it means definitely the splitting of the Prussian influence from the rest of Germany. [5]

The fundamental idea of breaking up Prussia into smaller units was hardly conducive to the planning of a new national comprehensive system of education. When the whole emphasis of the re-education debate lay in the elimination of nationalism and militarism it was more natural to think in terms of what was actually going to be taught in the schools and by whom, rather than whether or not there was going to be a huge exercise of reorganisation, changing the age of transfer from one school to another for example, or eliminating selection.

Quite apart from the point that it is the substance of what is taught that constitutes education anyway, it would have been unrealistic to expect the planners to be thinking in terms of comprehensive education when R.A. Butler's 1944 Act, which was being hailed as a triumphant advance in Britain, was itself being interpreted in a selective way, with the division into grammar schools, technical schools and secondary modern schools on the basis of an examination at the age of eleven. It is difficult to believe that anyone was going to get worked up about the fact that selection for grammar schools in Germany took place a year earlier than in Britain. The kind of educational reform that was being envisaged by the British was, rather, a political re-education, restoring to Germany principles of democratic thought and practice, and few people at that time would have censured the selective system associated with the 1944 Act as undemocratic. It is hardly surprising therefore that the officers of Education Branch were not sent off to Germany full of ideas of how to introduce comprehensive schools.

How did the officers of the Branch go about what the Potsdam Agreement described as 'the elimination of Nazi and militarist doctrines and the successful development of democratic ideas?' One of the first tasks was to examine the centralised syllabuses for each school subject, to consult colleagues who were specialists in those subjects and to revise the syllabuses to ensure that all traces of National Socialist thinking were removed. Schools could not open until the education officers were satisfied on this score. [6] The process was obviously at its most critical in the case of the history syllabus. Let me quote from the first hand account:

> History was, without doubt, the most controversial subject of all. Prussia had, by order of the Allies, been deleted from the map of Europe whereas it had always loomed large in the history of Germany in the previous hundred years. The name had been synonymous with Germany as a whole in the eyes of the world. The word 'bolshevism' had also figured prominently in the syllabus of the Hitler Period. In the minds of German children it was synonymous with all things odious about Russia. This too was considered to be ein heisses Eisen and teachers were advised to keep off the subject. Colonial expansion, whether of Britain or any other country, was similarly taboo. The military achievements of Frederick the Great, much extolled under the late regime, were not to be over-emphasised. When the Lehrbuchprüfungsstelle was established in Braunschweig under the dedicated guidance of Professor Eckert, the difficulties encountered in trying to compile a history textbook unbiased as regards the traditional history teaching of any nation, proved well-nigh insuperable. In one of the meetings I attended

feelings ran high even regarding the nationality of Copernicus. Was he German or Polish? Neither, proclaimed the Italian representative, his spiritual home was Italy. [7]

This account makes the obvious point that hand in hand with the control of the syllabuses went control of the textbooks. It is not difficult to imagine the kind of racist propaganda that was incorporated in the existing ones - for example:

Of Race and Nation (Volk)...When the Ice-Age came to an end, the Nordic peoples poured westwards into the areas of what we now call Europe...the German Nation (Volk) is basically sixty per cent Nordic...Nordic blood - present in every German, even if his outward appearance does not reveal it! - determines the resolute character and the unity of German life. That is why National Socialism has a mission and an obligation to wage the fight against the Jewish people. (Werner May, German National Catechism for the Young German in School and at Work, Breslau, 1935). [8]

The Textbook Section of Education Branch had the problem of replacing textbooks which contained this kind of material and which were therefore unusable. When the preparatory work for this was done before the end of the war by T.J.Leonard, it was to history that he devoted nearly all his time. [9] But it was nearly two years after the end of the war before new books were available to replace those that had been banned. Again let me quote from the first hand account:

The most baffling problems were in history, in Heimatkunde (home regional studies), and in the Lesebuch, the German 'Reader'. History books had been completely banned in all four Zones. In the British Zone, two major efforts, very different in themselves, set the ball slowly rolling again. The first was the creation of a new comprehensive history for secondary schools, Geschichte unserer Welt (History of Our World), edited by Fritz Karsen at the head of a group of German academic émigrés living in the United States of America. They had begun work on it before the end of the War and Bermann-Fischer was to publish it. In the British Zone, there had been official insistence that new books, to be acceptable, must be written by teachers and authors living in Germany. But Textbook Section, to whom the first volumes were submitted in October 1945 and who studied the book critically as its parts appeared, urged its introduction, and the ban was waived by the summer of 1946. Herr Suhrkamp, who had the publishing right for Fischer in Berlin, appointed a team of German experts - historians and teachers - who made revisions and amendments, in consultation with Textbook Section. There were difficulties in interpretation, dramatic delays in production, but in early 1947, part I of Volume II (732-1660) appeared. Part II of Volume II (1660-1890) was ready for printing by July, when the edition of 50,000 of II/I was completed. The sheer size of the work - 480 pages of II/I, 360 pages of II/II - shows the scale and ambition of the project, and perhaps a certain lack of realism about conditions and shortages in a ruined country immediately after the War.

The second group of pioneers had no illusions and approached the problem from the opposite end. In Braunschweig, in December 1946, a History Working Party was set up by Herr Turn, a school inspector and member of the Central Textbook Committee, and Professor Eckert, Professor of History at the Kant Hochschule. This group produced the first curricula for the re-introduction of history in schools, taught on new lines. They held innumerable meetings and discussion groups with teachers at all levels, and they realised that the first necessity was to produce material for the teacher and teacher-in-training, based on 'actual sources of history' providing 'objective historical data'. At their own expense they set about publishing small booklets on specific subjects to form a series: Contributions to the teaching of History, Beiträge zum Geschichtsunterricht. The first, Dr Eckert's Der Bauernkrieg was printed on scrap paper discarded by the local newspaper, in an edition of 2,000. This remarkable enterprise, strongly supported by Textbooks Section, gained attention and influence throughout the Zone and beyond. By the end of 1948 the following titles had been published:

No.1: Georg Eckert, Der Bauernkrieg (The Peasants' Revolt)
No.2: George Eckert, Die Revolution von 1848/49
No.3: Karl Mielcke, Der Vormärz (Prelude to the March Revolution, 1848)
No.4: Georg Eckert, Arbeiterleben in der Frühzeit des Industriekapitalismus (Life of the Workers in the Early Period of Industrial Capitalism)
No.5: Georg Eckert, Freiherr vom Stein und die preussischen Reformen
No.6: Karl Mielcke, Städtewesen und Frühkapitalismus (Urban Life and Early Capitalism)
No.7: Karl Mielcke, Das Zeitalter der Entdeckungen (the Age of Discoveries)
No.8: Georg Eckert, Vom Bismarckreich zur Republik
No.9: Hermann Trimborn, Das Menschliche ist gleich im Urgrund aller Kulturen (Humanity is the Common Element in all Civilisations)
No.10: Fritz Wenzel, Der junge Luther

The Education Branch of the Military Government

No.11:   Karl Mielcke, Das deutsche Bürgertum im Zeitalter der Reichsgründung (The German Middle Classes and the Founding of the Empire)

No.12:   Georg Eckert, Das junge Deutschland und die Revolutionsdichtung des Vormärz ('Young Germany' and Revolutionary Poetry to 1848) [10]

The work of Professor Eckert and his colleagues serves as an illustration of the fact that what the British education officers remembered most clearly about the occupation was co-operation with their German colleagues rather than control of them.

This must, in part at least, account for the paradox of British education policy. For on the one hand it was possible to claim that the Potsdam Agreement, in going beyond the purely political and military aspects of victory, was concerned with fundamental reconstruction of German life, and that 'education would be the main vehicle of Allied influence not only because of the large number of people affected and the comparative ease with which they could be reached in their schools and colleges, but because most of them were in their most impressionable years'. [11] Yet once the decision was taken to build up in Germany a federation of potentially self-governing Länder, and it was essential that the new parliaments should acquire some genuine powers, education was among the first of the responsibilities to be handed over to these parliaments at the end of 1946.

It is important to keep in mind that the period of British direct control over education only lasted a year and a half, and that when the handover came it made remarkably little impact on the work of Education Branch in its relations with the schools. Whatever the feeling of re-education in the British attitude at the beginning of the occupation, by the end of the period of direct control the sense of co-operation was such that the formal act of withdrawing and handing over to the Germans did not in fact signify any great practical change in their work.

Perhaps it was in this co-operation that we can find the reason why the British Zone was not set on the road to a comprehensive education system. Was it simply that the British chose those Germans who would be faithful to reactionary policies? This would certainly fit in neatly with the theory of a conspiracy to restore capitalism and to suppress socialism in post-war Germany. According to this thesis, if Germany was to remain firmly within the Western sphere of influence, the most important aim was to avoid a left-wing political landslide. It was therefore expedient to maintain existing administrative structures in order to ensure co-operation in reaffirming capitalist principles, which had remained in evidence during the National Socialist period. In other words there was not really a Stunde Null at all because those Germans who really were disposed to make a fresh start were excluded from the emergency administrations immediately after the surrender. [12]

Whatever substance there may be to this theory in the more general assessment of post-war policy, in the particular sphere of education it is difficult to detect any strong political line in the appointments made to the education service. Among the early nominees there could scarcely have been two more politically divergent personalities than Josef Schnippenkötter - a Gymnasium headmaster of strongly traditional views - in North Rhine province, and Heinrich Landahl - a former headmaster of a progressive school - in Hamburg. This pluralist approach reflected the concern to reject centralisation and to build up education on a regional basis. When it came to elections it meant that it was perfectly possible to have strongly left-wing governments in Schleswig-Holstein and Hamburg which introduced legislation to establish comprehensive school systems in 1948 and 1949 respectively. The British authorities were disturbed, not by the fact that comprehensive schools were being introduced, but by the controversies that the legislation had aroused. Their attitude was shaped by the consensus on their own educational policy enshrined in the 1944 Education Act.

In practice the British found the idea of reform by consensus to be at odds with the realities of German regional politics. Schleswig-Holstein provides one illustration of the dilemma in which they found themselves. Its government had a clear Social Democrat majority and seized the opportunity to set about educational reform with speed and vigour. The Christian Democrat resistance was equally vigorous and the atmosphere was one of extreme bitterness. It was a measure of the precariousness of the legislation that opposition to it was a major factor in the electoral defeat of the Social Democratic Party two years later. At the time however the British were unable to persuade the Schleswig-Holstein government either to negotiate with the opposition and allow adequate public discussion of the new law, or to discuss its implications for the Zone as a whole with Ministers of Education in other Länder. This was an obvious source of disappointment to Robert Birley, the Educational Adviser to the Military Government.

The experience with Hamburg in the following year was similar. Hamburg was in a much better position to put its legislation into effect, being more prosperous and having a better supply of teachers. But as Birley subsequently recalled:

> ....the secrecy in which the law was prepared and the obvious disinclination of the Government to allow it to be discussed properly were, in my view, deplorable. I believe it is probably futile in any country to think that education can be kept quite apart from party politics. It is certainly futile to expect it in Germany; but it will be a sign of a genuine democratic tradition in Germany when it is felt that educational legislation is something which demands public discussion and that to hold negotiations on it with the Opposition, which would doubtless have to be informal, is not a sign of political weakness.[13]

The Education Branch of the Military Government

There is little doubt that the Schleswig-Holstein and Hamburg laws were ill-prepared and rushed. Perhaps if different nominees had been put in charge of the emergency administrations, the preparations could have been better. Perhaps the British attitude merely indicates paranoia at the emergence of strongly left-wing policies. This seems to me the obvious case study to test out the allegation of conspiracy.

It is however likely to be a formidable task to substantiate the allegation in relation to education. The charge of conspiracy to perpetuate capitalism is more commonly laid at the door of the Americans than of the British. Yet it was the Americans who in their Zone wanted to replace the existing school system with one which was organised along comprehensive lines. Whereas the British had from the outset or very soon afterwards been disposed to regard reconstruction as a matter for the Germans themselves, the Americans had shown something of a missionary zeal in their efforts to introduce changes. But the more energetically they went about it, the more fiercely the Germans resisted, so that in the end their plans for reshaping things made scarcely any impact, except in Bremen, which - like Hamburg in the British Zone - had a City Assembly favourable to radical reform. If this was the reception given to the progressive ideas of the Americans, is it likely that the same ideas would have been better received at the hands of the British?

To explore this kind of question means uncovering the political processes whereby those considered fitted for the task of getting the schools going again were actually chosen. The Russians in their Zone were careful to cultivate extreme left-wing groups, and to appoint to the most important posts administrators and teachers favourable to radical reorganisation. [14]

Already in 1946 they were in a position to introduce a new law which linked up with the comprehensive tradition. It did not matter that this was a minority tradition. To proceed in accordance with majority opinion was not considered relevant. In the eyes of the Soviet Union the Germans had forfeited the right to be consulted about the changes. They were to be told what was good for them and it will never be known what their verdict on the Russian initiative would have been, if they had been consulted.

Perhaps it is true that the Western powers were equally partisan in their appointments, in excluding those with strong left-wing affiliations from the most important posts. But it would have been inconceivable for them not to put what was done to the test of public opinion in free elections. Whether a different initial policy, at the instigation of Germans of a more radical disposition, would have survived this test seems to me to be what the questions with which I began this paper were about. Turning over the stones of the political processes of the first year of occupation is by this token a more fruitful area of research than the relations of Education Branch with the schools.

NOTES

1. Saul B. Robinsohn and J. Caspar Kuhlmann, Two Decades of Non-Reform in West German Education, Comparative Education Review, Vol. XI No.3 Oct. 1967 pp. 311-330.

2. Arthur Hearnden (ed.), The British in Germany (London, 1979).

3. Werner Burmeister, 'Were the British too neutral?' in Adult Education, July 1978. pp. 98-100.

4. For a full account see Helmut Sienknecht, Der Einheitsschulgedanke (Weinheim, 1968).

5. Quoted in Günter Pakschies, Umerziehung in der Britischen Zone 1945-1949 (Weinheim, 1979) p. 40.

6. Edith Davies, 'Der britische Beitrag zum Wiederaufbau des deutschen Schulwesens von 1945 bis 1950' in Manfred Heinemann (ed.) Umerziehung und Wiederaufbau (Stuttgart, 1981) p. 143.

7. Edith Davies, 'British Policy and the Schools' in Hearnden op. cit. p. 101.

8. Kathleen Southwell Davis, 'The Problem of Textbooks' in Hearnden op. cit. p. 118.

9. Kathleen Southwell Davis, 'Das Schulbuchwesen als Spiegel der Bildungspolitik von 1945 bis 1950' in Heinemann op. cit. p. 159.

10. Hearnden op. cit. p. 123. But see also, Maria Halbritter, Schulreformpolitik in der Britischen Zone von 1945 bis 1949 (Weinheim, 1979) pp. 156-234.

11. George Murray, 'The British Contribution' in Hearnden op. cit. p. 70.

12. Christian Kubina, 'Anmerkungen zur Verwendung des Begriffs Restauration' in Benno Schmoldt (ed.) Zeilkonflikte um das Berliner Schulwesen zwischen 1948 und 1962 (Werkstattbericht Berlin, 1983).

13. Robert Birley 'Education in the British Zone of Germany' in International Affairs Vol. XXVI No. 1, January 1950 p. 36.

14. Marion Klewitz 'Allied Policy in Berlin' in Hearnden op. cit. pp. 199-200. For a full account see Klewitz, Berliner Einheitsschule 1945-51, Colloquium, Berlin 1971.

Chapter Five

THE PRESS IN THE BRITISH ZONE OF GERMANY

KURT KOSZYK

I. Planning

The term 're-education' only came to be generally used in connection with the mass media after the war had ended and the Allied military government of Germany began to function in practice. During the period of planning which started in earnest in the late summer of 1943, and even more so before it, 're-education' was mainly understood either in the context of influencing German schools and universities after the war, or more immediately, in the context of influencing the outlook of the some 500,000 German Prisoners of War (POW) held in Britain and in the Middle East and North Africa. On the 18th September 1944 the Political Warfare Executive (PWE) under its Director of Plans, Ritchie Calder, was formally given the task of 're-educating' German prisoners of war. Even in the POW context there was still 'extremely little theory or experience to aid the re-educators' working first under Wing Commander E.H. Hitch and his Chief Executive Officer Cyrus Brooks (a writer of detective stories and translator of Erich Kästner and Alfred Neumann) and later under Lieutenant-Colonel Henry Faulks when he was seconded to the Political Intelligence Department of the Foreign Office and its POW Branch a few months before the end of the war. [1]

Although the word had been used by R.A. Butler in a more general sense in the House of Commons on 27 May 1943 when he said '...the best way to start re-education is by means of an overwhelming military defeat', a view reflecting what Anthony Eden had already told the Foreign Press Association on 29 July 1941 without using the word 're-education', there had certainly been no systematic approach to re-education in the making, in the sense of integrating the control of the mass media into an overall concept. One reason for the lack of a broadly based integrated approach to 're-education' was the initial reluctance to consult those who had sufficiently intimate knowledge of Germany necessary for it: not even the most eminent or best known German refugees then living in Britain had much chance of being consulted by Whitehall. On the political level ignorance about the internal realities of Germany persisted close to the end of the war. Winston Churchill, for example, believed that the explanation for the plot against Hitler of 20 July 1944 was that the top people in the German Reich once again started murdering each other as they did in 1934 when Hitler eliminated the leadership of the SA and a number of former political enemies. It was as late as November 1944 that Churchill began to feel it necessary to learn more about Germany, when he asked his Personal Assistant Major Sir Desmond Morton to call at the Foreign Office and find out 'what there was for him to read about Germany'. [2]

Thinking about re-education was developing however somewhat faster at the level of officials, but until the summer of 1943 're-education' and the methods to be employed for it remained minor matters left mainly for the consideration of the relatively low level personnel working in the Political Warfare Executive. The potential role of the mass media was perhaps first seriously considered by the German Sub-Committee of the Joint PWE/MOI/ BBC Re-Occupation Committee (constituted by agreement with the Foreign Office and the War Office) which held its first meeting on 11 August 1943. [3] In the chair was Con O'Neill who had been in the Diplomatic Service in Berlin until Munich and who subsequently became a key figure in the development of these plans together with John M. Troutbeck. [4] O'Neill had prepared a secret paper of 6 July 1943 'Lines for Emergency Plan, Propaganda to Germany after her Defeat'; the main points and presumptions were:

(a) The long-term aim is presumably to integrate Germany into a peaceful and prosperous European order.
(b) Although the means of propaganda (press, radio, film etc.) will play an important part, the most important propaganda for or against Britain will be carried out by the occupying armies and officials.
(c) The tone should be maintained which has been adopted in BBC broadcasts - the tone of the strong but just enemy.
(d) If Britain could convince the Germans that the aim is to establish the rule of law, they will probably be automatically attracted into the British or Western sphere of influence.
(e) Under the heading of entertainment and instruction no attempt should be made, as had been the German way, to ram the victor's culture down the vanquished's throat.

The Committee had many other long-term problems to consider amongst which re-education still came last, after Territorial Problems, Security against further German aggression, Economic Problems and Germany's place in a future World or European organisation. It had been agreed that all planning should allow for the strong negative feelings toward the German people which had developed in Britain by autumn 1943. [5] From the beginning, the German Sub-Committee devoted much time to discussing the personnel (staffing) problems which would eventually turn out to be most aggravating. [6] In October 1943 O'Neill became Secretary of the Sub-Committee of the Post-Hostilities Planning Committee, which was chaired by John M. Troutbeck, until then Principal Assistant Secretary at the Ministry of Economic Warfare, which was originally in charge of all subversive operations including 'black' propaganda'. On 17 November 1943 O'Neill presented to the Sub-Committee a survey on action to be taken concerning the re-education of Germany. He repeated the statement already made in the paper submitted to the War Cabinet on 8 August after the initial meeting of the German Sub-Committee: 'Germans alone can re-educate their fellow countrymen, and Germans will make the attempt only if they are themselves convinced that the future of their country lies in co-operation with her neighbours.' [7] In O'Neill's opinion 'the real re-education of Germany, in the sense of a permanent "change of heart" and conversion to tolerable European behaviour' could be brought about, if at all, 'only by the general development of events in Germany and the world at large'. re-education by propaganda or means within the sphere of education could play only a comparatively subordinate, though still important, role. 'If it cannot influence events, it may at least influence the manner in which Germans judge events', O'Neill stated. He proposed to work through German educational agencies. He thought censorship to be better than propaganda in the sense that it would be better to insist that certain things should not be done instead of ordering that other things should be. A forecast of the same sort came from PWE at the end of 1943, in the form of a proposal contained in a draft Foreign Office Declaration that Britain should not 'intend to impose a constitution on Germany, or ourselves to undertake the re-education of the German people'. [8]

From the beginning of 1944 the preparation of detailed plans proceeded by informal contact between PWE and the Publicity and Propaganda Section of Headquarters, Chief of Staff, Supreme Allied Commander (COSSAC) established in London as an integrated US and UK staff in March 1943 after the Casablanca Conference and which became the Supreme Headquarters Allied Expeditionary Force (SHAEF) under Eisenhower in January 1944.[9] Director of Publicity and Propaganda was the American Brigadier-General Robert McClure. The German Sub-Committee remained responsible for all British plans for long-term control of the German press with special regard to the question of the financial basis of the German newspaper industry and to that of paper supply. [10] It proposed to define the degree of control as the 'minimum degree consistent with the attainment of our objectives'. Incorporating this policy-ideal, PWE had drafted a paper, [11] early in December 1943 which was to be submitted to the European Advisory Commission (EAC) and which intended to serve as a guidance in future planning for Germany.

While the highest priority was given to the preparation of German textbooks for use in German schools the lack of activities in the field of the press (and film) was due to the fact that no experts were in the employ of any of the Departments concerned - except PWE. When Troutbeck asked the PWE on 14 January 1944 to prepare a short draft for a Political Section under the High Commission for

Germany he thought it better 'not to discuss the content of propaganda or the policy of re-education...any more detailed proposals for radio, press, films, books etc. being added as annexes to it'. And he thought the Section 'of course' to be a tripartite body, including the Russians. [12] The reason was that the EAC which did not much care for propaganda policy remaining the sole prerogative of each of the Allies, had not so far reached any agreement. On the other hand, as O'Neill complained to Duncan Wilson on 20 January 1944, the PWE drafts did not succeed in 'avoiding the appearance of total control of German intellectual life, and leaving as much scope to German initiative...as possible'. [13] O'Neill, in any case, thought it improbable that education in Germany should be controlled by those responsible for the issuing of propaganda. If the Germans drew the wrong conclusions from the events of the last 30 years, 'we may find ourselves obliged to take forcible action. But it seems to me that the likelihood of our having to do so will be much increased if we incur their resentment and discredit our own ideals and the sincerity of our liberal principles by trying to exercise a total supervision of German intellectual activities'. O'Neill doubted that it would be easy 'to reconcile Russian objectives in this field with British ones'. It would be more prudent to avoid a possible clash 'by agreeing to leave the field free for the exercise of German initiative'.

The PWE Draft Directive of 17 February 1944 on use, control and censorship of the Press, Publications, Broadcasting, etc., was based on the powers which were contained in Article 15 (c) of the Draft German Armistice. The United Nations should have the right 'to make such use of the press and publications generally, of broadcasting and of publications of all kinds, and to establish such control and censorship of these and of all forms of publicity and intercommunication...as the United Nations may see fit'. [14] The PWE draft did not contain the word re-education. The main aim of the Allied Forces was to give orders and instructions to the German population and control, or close down, certain newspapers and periodicals of a purely National Socialist, or otherwise particularly undesirable character. Before a revised draft was sent to the War Office on 2 March 1944, German Planning Committee of SHAEF under R.H.S. Crossman had taken up its work. It included as its members Brig.-General McClure and on the British side Ritchie Calder, Duncan Wilson and Hugh Greene.

The main problem was to decide whether or not an attempt should be made to establish a completely tripartite Anglo-American-Russian control and direction of all information and propaganda services in Germany. Quite separate and unco-ordinated information and propaganda zones were regarded as undesirable, since propaganda by its very nature could not be contained within geographical boundaries. [15] Differences could have the disastrous effect of strengthening in the German mind the conviction that fundamental conflicts of opinion existed between the three major powers, a conviction which it had long been German policy to drive home. Such a propaganda war might well result in quite disproportionate deterioration in Anglo-American-Russian relations generally. The need for endeavouring to secure agreement with Russia to these proposals was thought to be a matter of extreme urgency. In April 1944 O'Neill in an urgent letter to Captain Harrington of the War Office asked: 'Do we want to institute censorship between the Anglo-American and the Soviet Zones?' [16] Internal censorship would be against the idea of governing Germany as a whole. There were reservations concerning tripartite organisation on the part of the military planners. They, unlike the Foreign Office, regarded Anglo-American arrangements as not necessarily anti-Soviet. [17] On the other hand it was thought wrong to assume, when making strategical appreciations, that the Soviet Union would be 'our permanent friend'. Also, the Psychological Warfare Division (PWD) of SHAEF under McClure agreed with the Service Departments to impose censorship from the start, mainly to prevent a leakage of information through Russia to Japan, as there was still a Japanese embassy in Moscow.

Matters became urgent after the invasion had started. Ten days after the Allied landings in France, McClure asked Sir Robert Bruce Lockhart, Director-General of PWE, for a provisional list of key personnel suitable for work in Germany. [18] This time proposals for implementing tripartite control over the media in Germany were still being considered. [19] O'Neill criticised the version of 30 June 1944 because of the 50:50 division of functions, as being contrary to the principle of equality between the three powers. He modified the idea of tripartite control on 18 July 1944 by interpreting the application as being the responsibility of the authorities in each zone.

Two memoranda completed the planning process before August 1944. The Armistice and Post War Committee of the War Cabinet under Clement Attlee passed the Memorandum on Control and Censorship of Public Information and Means of Intercommunications on 10 August 1944. The aim was to minimise resistance and to promote co-operation in the implementation of the terms of surrender, and to eradicate Nazism and militarism and encourage democratic initiative and ideas within the framework of Allied policy. [20] The second memorandum - Operation TALISMAN, Psychological Warfare Requirements and Plan - of 19 August 1944 contained the basic aims of P.W.D / SHAEF It was thought to be of prime importance that the Allies (including the Russians) should speak to the defeated Germans with one voice. [21] On 5 September 1944 the British Deputy Commissioner Kirkpatrick and his opposite military number Kirby saw McClure and agreed to the TALISMAN Plan. It called for the location of Headquarters and regional Press Control Units in some 21 German cities.

The Basic US Directive to Eisenhower regarding the Military Government of Germany in the immediate post defeat period on 26 September 1944 coincided with the publication and circulation to the EAC of the Handbook of British policy directives. [22] The US directive ordered the suspension of all German newspapers and other publications. The formal agreement was to be disturbed a month later when the French asked for participation. Lockhart feared that the presence of French officers would serve as an excuse for independent action by PWD, two members of which, namely Crossman and Newsome, appeared to him 'individualistic by temperament'. [23] The British Handbook separated re-education (Directive No. 8) from Control and Censorship of Public Information (Directive No. 27). The reason for this is not clear, but it may be found in Hitler's Mein Kampf, where the press was called the main adult education instrument of the government. Directive No. 27 more or less repeated the PWE version.

The Talisman Memorandum No. 15 of 17 November 1944 followed the American line that, in the initial phase of the occupation operation of German information services should be prohibited. This was also the aim of Military Government Law No. 191 added as Annex 'A'. [24] Both were the basis of the SHAEF Handbook governing policy and procedure for the Military Occupation of Germany published in December 1944. [25] The Americans turned out to be far ahead of the British in the application of the regulations, in spite of some rivalry between McClure and the press team of Hans Habe. [26] By March 1945, on the British side, only the plan of having an Informational Blackout got through. [27] This was the austerity line decided upon by McClure and the PWD in January 1945 and extended in March. According to this, until June, there should be no broadcasting, news services etc. in or to Germany and Austria other than (a) a brief and objective news broadcast programme (b) simple Allied news-sheets of world news and occupation instruction (c) informational activities for foreign workers, deportees and prisoners.

This should, in the opinion of PWE, create a total break between Nazi indoctrination and Allied re-education and finally the emergence of acceptable German informational activities. It should give an opportunity to diagnose the problems within Germany, in contrast to schemes based on prior judgements, or plans improvised in the confusing first few weeks. It should also give time for a serious attempt at concerting post-blackout plans with the Russians, Americans and French. It was thought that this approach would prevent the 'moral hypocrisy' of re-educational work, preaching the virtues of democracy etc. at the time when the Germans were experiencing for the first time the realities of defeat and occupation, such as deportation, starvation, disease and imprisonment. After the first drastic purge of the Nazis and the re-distribution of Allied troops and occupation authorities into their separate zones, post-blackout activities could start in relatively stable conditions.

II The SHAEF Period

The German situation was found to be more difficult than had been forecast in most of the plans. [28] The decision at Potsdam turned out to be very general. The Allied powers were unable to settle the main question of how to deal with Germany as a whole on a common basis. In Britain, the general elections caused an administrative vacuum for some time. In the British Zone all sorts of problems came up. There were no personnel at hand able to deal with the problems of the media. There were not enough experts with knowledge of the German language to scrutinize the Germans; there was the non-fraternization order; and last but not least, the sense of rivalry between Montgomery and Eisenhower on the one hand and the antagonistic feelings of the Corps Commanders towards the Americans. These were only some of the factors which have to be kept in mind in discussing the story of the re-education of the Germans in 1945. Some problems could have been solved more easily, if there had not been a feeling of animosity towards the employment of German speaking emigrants, especially Jews, on a larger scale. Some of them had been useful in the planning phase, but now the British were afraid of reintroducing the old Weimar problems by repatriating them. It was commonly accepted among British experts that those who had emigrated after 1933 were also somehow responsible for Hitler's seizure of power. Another motive often mentioned in British official documents was the anxiety not to impair the German collaboration with the occupation authorities. Thus, the re-educators saw no reason to urge re-education. When, at last, the work actually started it already faced that conflict between the Western Powers and the Russians that had first become obvious in the minutes of the Control Council meetings. It then became the main interest of the British not to lose control of the German media, which might publish unpleasant information of what was going on among the Allies and what German journalists might have heard or seen from foreign sources. It was not until fairly late, perhaps too late, that re-education actually took shape in Germany. The problem was that, by always postponing decisions, the British lost the chance to co-ordinate the task of publishing model newspapers under British control and thus gradually transferring licensed German newspapers to scrutinised, experienced and approved Germans.

The Americans hastened to leave all responsibility to the Germans in their Zone only seven months after the end of the war. When the British became more familiar with German problems, which until the spring of 1946 had taken second place to those of India and the Near East, it was obvious that the licensing of newspapers as an important means of counteracting Russian propaganda sweeping to the West had been postponed for almost too long. Ernest Bevin suddenly took notice of the documents dealing with the Social Democrats fighting against Communist pressure in Berlin and the Soviet Zone. But in their dislike of Schumacher, the SPD leader in the British Zone, most Labour politicians felt hesitant to support an early integration of the German Socialists in the Socialist International. The Clacton Conference of the Labour Party in May 1946 had to debate the problem presented by the French, Belgian and Danish initiative, aimed at giving the SPD more support by extra rations of newsprint to newspapers supporting the SPD and by other similar measures which led led to a re-organisation of the paper supplies for the Berlin Telegraf. [29]

*

Let us however return to the actual events of 1945-46. At the end of March and the beginning of April 1945 some personnel decisions were being taken. The most important result was that in July 1945 Major-General Alec Bishop, formerly Deputy Director-General of PWE became chief of Information Services and Public Relations (later PR/ISC) of the Control Commission. Duncan Wilson and Cedric Belfrage were released by PID to be employed at PWD [30]

It took months of discussion in London before the idea of an overt British Prototype Newspaper could be realised after the retirement of Sefton Delmer who had proved to be most successful in organising a new German News Service in Hamburg. Accurate news presentation was the formula on which all re-educational endeavours in the media concentrated. This was contained in the programme formulated by PID on 21 May 1945, and emphasised that the technique of presentation in all British-sponsored media would have an even greater impact on policy than it had during the war. It would play a primary part in re-educating the taste of the German public to those journalistic ideals and standards 'for which Great Britain stands'. [31] Of course, those who wrote policy-papers like this aimed at an ideal which was not universally to be found in Britain herself: the idea of a newspaper represented, and indeed developed, by The Times and the Manchester Guardian. The planners concentrated only on the journalistic make-up, not on the economic implications of the press, of which most of the planners seem to have understood nothing, even though there had already been published by then at least one book which gave a more realistic picture of the problems; and they were being widely discussed in Britain in other books and before the Royal Commission on the Press. [32] William Harris found that no problem in (British) journalism was more acute than that arising from the relationship between the proprietors of a paper and the editor, especially because of 'the irresponsibility with which proprietors are ready to sell a paper outright regardless of what its new owners intend to make of it'. Robert Sinclair saw that the main dangers might come from two general directions: (a) that the world of newspapers might become dominated by a few powerful proprietors and (b) that the proprietors must necessarily develop, as their sincere personal philosophy, the traditional outlook shown by industrial magnates. [33] It was not long before the same happened with the licensed German press which enjoyed a profitable monopoly until 1949. The years afterwards were filled with a kind of battle between the licensees and the old publishers returning to the market.

Another problem arose from the complicated and bureaucratic structure created for implementing the plans concerning the press. The military Commanders in the American and the British Zones had to observe the 'Manual for the Control of German Information Services' of 16 April 1945. It had to be read in conjunction with the 'Handbook of Military Government in Germany' and the 'Handbook Governing Policy and Procedure' for the Military Occupation of Germany. The 'Manual' prescribed the following three phrases: Blackout (according to Law No. 191), overt Allied Information Services and the reconstruction of German services, and finally the gradual transition to German information services under Allied supervision. [34] A United States Information Control Unit augmented by British personnel worked in areas of the British Zone occupied initially by US Forces, while at Bremen a British Information Control Unit was stationed until the end of SHAEF in the middle of July 1945. One major administrative problem concerned the acquisition of property for the use of Information Control. Confiscation without payment applied to all Nazi and German State property. In all other cases, the use was subject to requisition; the owner was entitled to reimbursement at a future date. A German licensee was (theoretically) not allowed to make 'a windfall gain from the operation of confiscated or requisitioned properties'. He had to pay 'a fair rental value' for the use of both non-consumable and consumable property. Payments were to be deposited in a special account. The publisher was permitted to keep the net profits of his business. At the end of the licensing period he owned - subject to the applicable provisions of the German law - the intangible assets he had acquired such as the name of the paper, customers' list etc. Where necessary, local banks were directed by the Military Government to make advances to keep a newspaper running.

Since 24 January 1945, the four page weekly Aachener Nachrichten was published by German personnel under Allied control. The newspaper was taken over by the British in July of the same year. The poor impression this newspaper had made produced all sorts of problems and had made McClure prohibit the publication of all information concerning what was happening in Aachen. [35] After this experiment, only overt Military Government newspapers were published, 15 altogether, during the SHAEF period. The papers received selected news from the Allied Press Service in London. it was beamed daily to the continent by radio. Daily contact with objective and truthful world news was expected to help the Germans to draw their own conclusions on Nazi propaganda.

McClure in a press release of 25 May 1945 did not expect a sudden change. [36] Three days later, Directive No. 2 authorised a certain relaxation of the austerity programme laid down in Directive No. 1 and corresponding to the Joint Chiefs of Staff Directive 1067, forwarded to Eisenhower in the middle of May. It now was possible to start selecting the Germans for executive positions in Phase Three. For McClure, this implied the difference between the simplicity of a paper policy and the actual hard-rock problem of making it work. Obviously, after 12 years of Nazism, there were not many people of high calibre available with an active devotion to democratic ideals. Directive No. 3 of 22 June 1945 laid down policy for the immediate future. [37] Sufficient evidence was available that desirable groups of potential licensees were emerging in various parts of Germany. SHAEF still followed the model of non-partisan group papers, since single individuals would inevitably be resented by equally reputable leaders and sections of the community having differing political or religious beliefs. Each group should be representative, within the limits of those experienced newspaper men available locally, of the main anti-Nazi groups. Shortage of newsprint made it impossible to license more than one newspaper in each city.

The Foreign Office paper on 'Policy British Information Services for Germany' of 29 May 1945 defined again the methods of presentation to be used in all British-sponsored media which were to play a primary part in re-educating the taste of the German public 'so that they may unconsciously become more accessible to the ideas and standards for which Britain stands'. [38] Among these standards, the rule of law, the sanctity of contract and impartial reporting were mentioned.

While the Americans, shortly after the end of SHAEF, licensed their first newspaper run by Germans, the Frankfurter Rundschau on 1 August 1945, the British were in danger of rushing into licensing prematurely, merely in order to have newspapers to carry the instructions of the Military Government. Delmer warned that before licensing German journalists and the German public should be educated to Western standards of newspaper production. The military commanders attached priority to Hamburg and the Ruhr, and to regional trade unions. In spite of an interdepartmental meeting, which transferred the functions of information policy-planning from PID to the Control Commission, there was continued inaction. The Foreign Office attributed it largely to the difficulty in establishing the Control Council, until after the Potsdam Conference. But it was found that the German people were allegedly tired of hearing about their crimes. More pleasant news seemed to come from Russian controlled radio stations. The Russian non-fraternization order was much less strictly interpreted than that of General Eisenhower in the West. The Russians had started to license German parties, trade unions and newspapers. In this context, Con O'Neill stated on 23 June 1945: 'Unless the Control Commission is more successful than most people seem to suppose it will be in conducting the control of Germany on a genuine Allied basis, then the danger is very great that we and the Americans on the one hand, and the Russians on the other, will before long find ourselves engaged in a struggle for the soul of the German people'. [39] The main handicaps the British had to overcome in competing with the Russians were (apart from non-fraternisation) the intemperance of British public opinion towards Germany and in consequence of that, the restraining effects of Parliamentary Questions. Nevertheless, O'Neill wanted PWE to be a little more encouraging and forthcoming in their propaganda to Germany.

A memorandum by the C.C.G of 14 July 1945 proclaimed a five-stage plan which still postponed the licensing of the German media, because it was thought that the opportunity of teaching the

116

Germans western standards would only be available during the period of Allied control. The Germans should learn to abstain from 'the dangerous mix-up of information and tendentious comment, which has passed as news-writing in German newspapers for the last sixty years'.[40] Editorial comment and explanation, letters to the editor and other opinion material should be confined to one page. The news stories on the other pages should be written, selected and presented in such a way as to make the German reader feel 'he is getting an accurate, objective, interesting and readable service of world and German news'. In this way the German readers should feel 'that items have been included or left out, purely from considerations of news value, not because of policy considerations'. The planners rather contradicted themselves when they unveiled their real aim: 'If we succeed in giving the German reader this impression it will be all the easier for us to introduce those items which are intended to influence him into identifying his interests with those of this country without his resenting them as propaganda.' A central newspaper should serve as a model of what was wanted.

Instead of implementing these ideas, the search for the causes of the problems went on. Bruce Lockhart asked for 'very energetic action' to overcome the communication and transport difficulties and to bring home the importance of the information services forcibly to the Corps Commanders who, like Montgomery, had more or less boycotted the PWD and SHAEF orders. [41] The Americans withdrew their own trained personnel in PWD into their zone which gave them a strength of approximately 1,700, while the British had less than 80 without training or facilities, and PID had no formal status recognised by the War Office. [42] Thus by 2 August 1945, there were ten four-page overt newspapers appearing twice a week in the British Zone providing about one copy for every five of the German population. In the district of Schleswig-Holstein, daily news-sheets were being provided, because of the large number of undisbanded German army units and displaced persons. [43]

At this point Montgomery caused considerable irritation by an unauthorised personal message to the German people. [44] The Foreign Office considered his promises as 'running far ahead of the possibilities of efficient performance'. The policy of gradually handing over the responsibility for newspaper production to carefully selected and trained Germans seemed to be endangered, as there were 'very few of these, and no-one seriously expects to see a good, free German press under a couple of years'. Montgomery had promised free papers with leading articles.

No systematic effort to find suitable Germans had been operating in the British Zone. Ritchie Calder thought the methods of Corps Commanders, to license group newspapers similar to the American principle, 'by pre-war standards, ill-defined'.[45] There were no qualified personnel in the ISC to do the selecting of qualified licensees' groups willing to work together and hold the balance between views. In another paper of 21 August 1945, Calder wrote that he believed the British had failed to achieve the moral acceptance of defeat by the Germans, or a sense of individual guilt.

The Germans even tended to put blame for the Nazi crimes on the victors arguing that they had tolerated Hitler. In the British Zone, according to Calder, the constructive plans had rapidly deteriorated into short-term improvisations.[46] Tactics had replaced strategy, and the 'object of the exercise' was to humour the Commander-in-Chief. The more outstanding the combat Generals were, the less fitted they seemed to be to Calder for the complex task of administering Germany. One can only guess that Calder acted in close agreement with the Labour Cabinet. Demilitarising the administration of the British Zone soon began, and it led to the creation of a Control Office for Germany and Austria in October 1945, a solution which, according to Balfour, developed 'certain defects'.

On 18 August 1945, the PR/ISC Group, originally part of the Political Division of the CCG, became a separate group; it was organised under Major-General Bishop in two branches, Public Relations and Informations Services Control. Following a meeting in London at the same time, PID personnel in Germany were transferred to the ISC, among them Michael Balfour. [47] It was also decided at the ISC meeting in London on 25 September 1945, that aliens, especially emigrants, could be transferred to Germany for one or three years service at ISC The Guide to the Functions and Organisation of the Allied Control Authority and the Control Commission for Germany (British Element) was published in October 1945. Paragraphs 30-33 dealt with PR/ISC, but contained nothing new. It was made clear that the policy and directions as laid down by the ISC Branch, were to be executed in the field by Information Control Units in Berlin, Hamburg, Kiel and Düsseldorf.

III Licensing and Slow Progress

By the end of November when in the American Zone there were already 18 licensed newspapers, the second largest group after those in the Russian Zone, there were none in the British Zone, which was being served still only by the 18 overt Military Government newspapers. [48] At this time Major N.B.J. Huijsman became Controller of Press and Publications Branch in PR/ISC (as successor to Duncan Wilson and Arthur Galsworthy.) His first duty was 'to streamline the organisation' and to carry through the policy of replacing the overt Military Government German-language press by a licensed press. [49] In Huijsman's opinion, the decision to license German newspapers with political viewpoints had been taken at Cabinet level, but the nature of any political link between licensees and political parties they supported was not stated. German political leaders, such as Schumacher and Adenauer, maintained to Huijsman that they had the impression that it was the political parties who nominated and controlled the licensees. As there were no instructions from the CCG, Huijsman followed his 'common sense'. In each Land there were published in the major centres of population a number of newspapers of the kind described, supporting the political views of the main parties as far as possible, but they were not party papers in the strict sense. The biggest problem remained the shortage of newsprint and the availability of printing presses. [50] Newsprint was rationed on the basis of one copy to five persons. To ensure that each newspaper had a print-run that made it financially viable, it was also generally necessary to publish only one newspaper in each rural area.

Huijsman toured all Land Information Control Units and instructed them to put forward licensing proposals. The first licence was granted to Braunschweiger Zeitung on 8 January 1946. The decision to grant licences had been published and candidates were left free to come forward and of course the political parties were fully involved. An applicant for a licence had be employing at least one senior qualified journalist with a clean political background. In Braunschweig it was Fritz Sänger, who had been working for the Frankfurter Zeitung until 1943 and, in this instance, both the capital and the journalistic expertise were provided by Eckensberger, who thus became sole licensee and had bought the presses from their previous owner. A week later Lüneburger Landeszeitung followed. Here four local businessmen provided the capital and entered into a partnership with a Social Democrat journalist.

Whenever the printing presses belonged to either the Nazi press or a family with close Nazi connections, licensees could enter into arrangements with the official custodians for a lease of the machinery, the rent being paid into a blocked account pending a final decision on the disposal of the property concerned. ISC took no rigid line: in Oldenburg for example, where the Nordwest-Zeitung started on 26 April 1946, the custodian of a family newspaper, who had paid a nominal subscription to SS charities to keep the paper from being acquired by the Nazi press was permitted to become the licensee. In other cases, such as Lensing in Dortmund, ISC refused a licence. Obviously, the decision greatly depended upon the opinion of the regional licensing officers.

The situation in North Rhine-Westphalia was most difficult, as, after the withdrawal of the American 12th Army Group, virtually no newsprint remained - some even seemed by a mysterious process to have found its way into neighbouring countries. In Essen, it took six months to get the large presses in working order. Oelde, where the Neue Westfälische Zeitung an overt paper had been published, had a press in excellent condition, but was deemed an unimportant location - contrary to the opinion of some press officers. Most applicants coming forward in NRW had either only weak financial standing or were journalistically inexperienced. Some licensees complained about constant pressures from their local party organisations. In the end, only in Hamburg was it found possible to license newspapers of differing political complexions.

Licensees' proposals had to be accompanied by a mock-up of the proposed newspaper and submitted to the Land Information Control Unit, which was responsible for its approval, before submitting recommended proposals to PR/ISC Bünde, where, in most cases, the final decision was made by Huijsman and the head of the

ISC, Brigadier W.L. Gibson. Initially, there was pre-publication censorship, but after a short time (sometimes only a few issues) only post-publication scrutiny was exercised. Complaints were very rare, and only two or three cases had to be dealt with at the (Bünde) Zonal Executive Office.

In February 1946, a conference of both the already licensed and the aspirant publishers was held with representatives of the editorial staffs of overt Military Government papers. This led to the foundation of the Nordwestdeutscher Zeitungsverlegerverein. The newsprint situation remained very tight until the currency reform in June 1948. At this time the Military Government licensed three non-party newspapers, Springer's Hamburger Abendblatt (14 October 1948), Brost's Westdeutsche Allgemeine Zeitung (3 April 1948), starting in Bochum (later Essen, today the largest provincial in Germany) and the Norddeutsche Zeitung (Hanover, 30 April 1948); the reason was to impart more balance to the new system. [51] The original idea of publishing a British model 'quality' newspaper never worked properly. When Die Welt, at last, came out on 2 April 1946 a dozen British licensed papers already existed. There was constant trouble with the character of Die Welt, which was judged by the Germans to be more or less the voice of the British Occupation Authority. Circulation dropped from 1 million copies in February 1949, until it was sold to Springer in September 1953.

When the licensing process under its new civilian chiefs [52] eventually started, it worked at first in a very pragmatic way, with a liberal interpretation of the directives to be observed. Thus the unfavourable comparisons drawn by Christopher Steel, Political Adviser at this time, between British and American actions in respect of the Press have to be viewed with some reserve. Steel had noted the praise for the 'orderly administration and systematic progress' certain American officials in Berlin had for the work in the British Zone. [53] In Steel's opinion the Americans were attempting to complete in a few months a task that the British had expected would take years to achieve. In doing so, the Americans had omitted 'vital stages in re-education of the German people according to democratic principles'. Steel thought the Americans had produced a semi-authoritarian regime by handing over responsibility in their zone to the German authorities on 1 January 1946. Whereas in the British Zone, the Military Government was attempting 'stage by stage, with considerable patience and no mean success, to re-educate the Germans to a well-tried system of democratic government', the Americans, Steel thought, would produce 'disastrous results', unless their supervision were stricter than it appeared to be. On the one hand the Americans had shown themselves remarkably efficient in re-establishing an outward appearance of normality, 'but in matters political and in an understanding of German psychology and history, they have shown themselves to be inexperienced and inept'.

In some way the British authorities considered the licensed newspaper as a means of giving the political parties 'something to do and help them to sort out and formulate their ideas' before they could assume definite governmental responsibilities. To allocate newspapers on a party basis was thought to contribute to this end. The new policy was based on all available information on the strength and the distribution of political parties and religious groups as well as on political licensees. At a later date, when free elections had demonstrated the proportionate strengths of the various parties, the fixed circulation figures in relation to the newsprint at hand were readjusted. [54] Since the first licensing applications had been approved by the middle of December 1945, the process had worked, and in the middle of February more than one third of the 40 planned party newspapers had been licensed.

The SPD was slightly favoured in the arrangements. According to the ISC memorandum of 27 February the intended allocations were as follows:

15	Social Democrat	(circulation	2,050,000)
10	Christian Democrat	(circulation	1,100,000)
7	Communist	(circulation	760,000)
2	Liberal groups	(circulation	450,000)
5	non-party groups	(circulation	600,000)
1	Free Democrat	(circulation	80,000)

Of this total, 17 newspapers should have been in production by March 1946, the rest by the middle of the year, but actually, only 11 were being published by March, the bulk, namely another 12 and Die Welt, as the zonal newspaper, started in April 1946. The number of 40 was not reached until April 1947. The reason obviously was that, in some cases, complicated legal and financial adjustments had to be made before the licensees could take possession of the printing plants. The licensed newspapers were four-page and appeared twice a week only. By this time 278 branches of political parties had been licensed - 109 of the SPD, 87 of the KPD, 54 of the CDU and 28 others.

The issue of the different policies pursued by the Information Services Control Branch towards the licensing of German newspapers in the British and the American Zones respectively, no doubt also needs to be seen against the background of political developments in the Russian Zone. Here the occupying power speeded up the merger of the two workers' parties, the Social Democratic SPD and the Communist KPD. The Foreign Office itself was aware of the importance of developments in the Russian Zone in the winter of 1945-46 and was trying to collect information about them. [55] The problems raised by these developments in the Russian Zone were compounded by the fact that there were also quite a few members (albeit conservative) of the House of Commons who favoured the fusing of the workers' parties in Germany. The Minister in charge, John Hynd, tried to make it clear that while the government favoured 'understanding' between the parties, this did not mean 'merger'. The debate about this issue helped to emphasise the relative importance of the mass media in the overall policy of 're-education'. So we find the first document, 18 April 1946, which deals simultaneously with schools, universities, youth welfare organisations and the information services. Submitted to the Foreign Office by the newly established Central Office of Information which had taken over much of the functions of the wartime Ministry of Information as well as some of its personnel, it described the information services as 'the most obvious vehicle for re-education'.[56]

The anti-Soviet feelings in the CCG escalated in May 1946. Sir William Strang wrote to Bevin on the Berlin press situation.[57] He even accused the Soviet licensed press of imitating the style and the lay-out of the Nazi press, and the claims that the Berlin public were indifferent to 'what the Communists tell them'. As German public opinion remained suspicious and unstable, the British endeavoured to ensure 'that any propaganda we try to put across is strictly objective and also that it is not overdone'. Only a year after the end of the war, Major-General Bishop emphasised that the main task had been to find the right Germans, who were sound in mind and thought, and then 'leave them as free as possible to work out Germany's spiritual salvation'.[58] When Bishop wrote this on 27 June 1946, the search for his successor had started, who, in his opinion and own emphatic words should be 'a student of human nature with a very broad and humane outlook, and a keen interest in education', to lead the team of individualists (ISC) with 'artistic temperament'. After much searching, in Robert Birley the British eventually found the best man available for the job of re-education on the lines that Con O'Neill had had in mind since 1943. These views were shared at the political level too. John Hynd in a letter to the Foreign Office of 2 July 1946 wrote 'it always has been and still is our firm policy not to impose political ideas from above but to let them develop spontaneously from the lowest levels, thus ensuring that the growth of political institutions shall be truly democratic in character'. [59]

*

In the end the British were lucky enough however to find the right way - 'per ardua ad astra'. As far as the position of the information services in general and the Press in particular was concerned by the autumn of 1946 this was outlined in a letter to George Houghton at the Control Office by Michael Balfour writing from the Zonal Executive Office of Information Services Control, which deserves extended quotation:

> I wonder whether you realise how restricted are our opportunities for presenting the British - which is to say, the government's - point of view. We have no Ministers to make speeches, no Parliament in which to ask and answer questions or reply to opposition criticisms, no pro-Government newspaper (except 'Die Welt'), a radio which, by deliberate policy, leaves most to the initiative of the Germans, no press advertisement, no poster campaigns and no documentary films. We are dependent

upon press hand-outs, occasional press conferences by anonymous 'high military Government officials' (which, at the zonal level, are not attended by many German journalists, and at the regional level, have to be very cautious in discussing matters of more than zonal interest), reports of Parliamentary Debates and speeches in Britain, and the information which is given in such programmes as 'Military Government Question Hour' in N.W.D.R. Consequently, the British case is often in danger of going by default and that too at a time when feeling against us is increasing and some of our competitors are very vocal in their accusations.

The German parties, who fear accusations of subservience if they are too cooperative, have no particular anxiety to print facts favourable to us because these might reduce the effect of their leaders' criticisms. We can issue background material, and some of it will be used as a basis for feature articles, editorials etc. But this is a method in which points tend to get missed and arguments blunted.

I am as anxious as anyone to build up a Democratic press in Germany. But democracy to me means largely Government by discussion, and you are not really achieving that objective if the arguments of one of the most important groups in the country, namely the Government, are not introduced into the discussion because the public is unfamiliar with them. It would be undemocratic to interfere unduly with the liberty of the Press to criticise us and our measures. But I cannot see that it is undemocratic to insist upon them explaining the reasons behind our measures.

Of course, such open intervention does provoke some resistance and should for that reason be sparingly used. But I would be most reluctant to accept the view that it cannot be used at all.

Balfour's comments accurately described the problems faced by the British in 'the fight for the soul of the German people'.

In 1946, 44 newspapers including two weeklies and Die Welt were licensed in the British Zone, as were some 80 miscellaneous publications which needed 3,000 tons of newsprint per month.[60] Each week, 15 million copies were printed for 22 million people; 38 newspapers appeared twice a week, whereas a large proportion of the 80 papers in the Soviet Zone were dailies. It was estimated that the American Zone (population 17 million) received about 20 million copies and the Soviet Zone (population 19 million) about 45 million copies. Such comparisons have to be read in conjunction with the propaganda which had started early in 1946. All sorts of criticisms were being levelled by licensed newspapers against the measures of the occupation powers of the opposite site. At the end of January

1947, the Foreign Office were 'very much impressed by the growing volume of hostile and inaccurate criticisms against the British Authorities which appeared in certain German newspapers' and by the 'apparent unwillingness of the authorities concerned to suppress such criticisms'. This was directed at the Russians. [61] The Control Council Directive No. 40 did not improve the situation by authorising the suppression of Communist newspapers.

IV The End of a Monopoly

A further relaxation of British control took place when ISC was turned into I.S.D. - Information Services Department. Since the late spring of 1946, the establishment of Zonal and Land Press Advisory Committees was discussed and was at last introduced by Ordinance No. 108. This was a decisive step in handing over the licensing producedure to the German Land Ministers of Education and Culture. [62] These Press Advisory Committees had at least 12 and not more than 20 members one third of whom would each represent the associations of licensees, the general public and the associations of journalists and printers. Within half a year, in North Rhine-Westphalia the number of licensees among the 19 members of the Press Advisory Committee had grown from 7 to 11. The Regional Commissioner Major-General Bishop complained to the Minister President, Karl Arnold, who disbanded the Committee on 24 December 1948. The American Zonal newspaper Die Neue Zeitung on 19 January 1949 charged that the establishment of the Press Advisory Committees in the British Zone was an 'authoritarian solution of press freedom'. Emil Gross, licensee of the Bielefeld Freie Presse (SPD) and Chairman of the Zonal Press Advisory Committee, defended their work by mentioning the licensing of 256 newspapers and periodicals within seven months compared to only 247 licences of the British Military Government between 1945 and May 1948.

A month after the currency reform of 20 June 1948, the circulation of newspapers and periodicals was set free from control. [63] When the Occupation Statute was discussed, the consequences were again carefully considered by CCG at a conference of the Regional Commissioners on 28 January 1949.[64] It seemed to be generally agreed that certain powers should be retained to maintain the prestige and security of the Occupation in relation to the Press, but it was found to be unnecessary to define these powers in an Ordinance, as they were already contained in the Statute.

Robert Birley found it necessary to distinguish between freedom of the press in the British sense, and the economic freedom which, in Germany, might enable malignant influences, such as syndication, to destroy that freedom. Perhaps the best method of approaching the problem would be to draw the attention of the Germans to the potential dangers inherent in the situation, and use the British influence to secure suitable legislation. This referred to the problem of printing plants which the proprietors, after the fall of the licensing system, would certainly use in their own interest. It

124

was thought advisable that Ministers President should by legislation compel German printers to prolong their contracts for periods up to five years. [65] British Ordinance No. 185 came into force on 29 April 1949 and enabled Laender legislatures, in spite of Military Government Ordinance No. 57, to enact the required protective legislation. The Press Advisory Committees prepared the drafts of this legislation.

The former publishers under the Nazi regime had powerful organisations, and owned most of the printing plants of the 53 British licensed newspapers. Early in 1948 they had formed the 'Arbeitsgemeinschaft für Pressefragen' which became the Gesamtverband der Deutschen Zeitungsverlegen in 1949. They had announced their intention of publishing their former newspapers, some with their original titles, from 1 September 1949. If the Military Government would not permit this they threatened to print their newspapers in the US enclave of Bremen, and distribute them in the British Zone.

Matters were brought to a head by two telegrams from I.S.D. to the F.O. German Section on 29 August 1949; they contained alarming news from the US Zone, where the General License No. 3 had gradually permitted free publication of newspapers and other printed matter after the passing of press laws in the Laender of the Zone. [66] The Occupation Statute similarly changed the situation in the British Zone from 7 September 1949. High Commissioner Sir Ivone Kirkpatrick, still in London and about to move to Bonn, sent a secret telegram to Military Governor Robertson on 31 August saying:

> The news that a large number of German newspapers are likely to appear shortly attacking Allied policy and propagating Nazi doctrines is having a lamentable effect on public opinion here towards Germany. Behaviour of this sort coming on top of the election campaign is certain to make any liberal policy towards Germany completely unacceptable here and even more in France. This development will also undermine the whole of the work which we have done in Germany since the occupation in improving the standards of the press.

Kirkpatrick thought the best method of nipping undesirable developments in the bud was to strike quickly and firmly. He proposed to stiffen the draft Press ordinance by adding the power to confiscate printing presses, and ban offenders from carrying on the profession of journalism. [67]

The excitement over this development died down when W.L.Gibson informed the Political Adviser, Steel, of his talk with Emil Gross on 1 September at Bielefeld, where Gross chaired the meeting of the three western Zonal Newspaper Publishers' Associations which were about to merge. Gibson found Gross' position contradictory: on the one hand he followed the line of the Associations which wanted to establish a 'qualified friendship

125

towards the "Heimatpresse" sponsors and their colleagues, the printers', as it would enable the licensees to maintain their present circulation and political influence; on the other hand he asked not only for an assurance that law 191 and the old Information Regulations 2 and 3 of 1945 remain operative until the promulgation of the Occupation Statute, but that the British should not allow 'would-be publishers to beat the pistol'. After Gibson had given this assurance Gross pointed out, according to Gibson's report, 'what a good and salutary step' it would be if the British authorities would 'immediately close down any unlicensed paper after only one edition: because the venturer would be heavily hit in his pocket'. Gibson recorded with interest the discrepancy between these proposals and Gross's simultaneous assurance that he was not worried by fears of competition. I.S.D. chief's opinion was that the new papers, especially those which revived old titles, would win quite a number of present subscribers from licensed papers, a few of them would get the final push over the precipice from the new competition, but the majority would survive the ordeal - in some cases with considerably reduced circulation.

Gibson was not in favour of firm action, since it would be difficult for the High Commission to decide 'when to suppress a newspaper because its cleverly-expressed ideas' were harming the minds of its readers 'so that they, at some unspecified future date, may disturb the 'prestige and security' of the Occupying Powers', as the Occupation Statute put it. [68] There were questions in the House of Commons. On 12 October 1949 the High Commission outlined what became part of the Foreign Office's reply. [69] It was stated that the Allied High Commission Law on Press, Radio, Information and Entertainment of 21 September had not been introduced because newspapers were appearing under their former titles and with former Nazi editors; however it became effective at the same time that the Allied High Commission Occupation Statute and the Basic Law of the Federal Republic of Germany were passed. It repealed that part of the legislation passed by the former British Military Government regarding the Press which was inconsistent with these two measures and, at the same time, placed safeguards into the hands of the Allied High Commission, to be used if any undemocratic Press tendencies developed in the future. In pursuance of the principle of the Freedom of the Press, as enacted by the Basic Law, anyone who had been cleared by the German denazification panels since December 1947 could produce a newspaper without obtaining prior permission. In the meantime Kirkpatrick had stated that it was for the German authorities in the first place to prevent the emergence of undesirable trends in the German Press. The Federal Government had announced that it would give priority to the problem. The Law (No. 5) on Press, Radio etc., was agreed on a tripartite basis and any action to be taken under its provisions also had to be agreed on a tripartite basis.

The main difficulty from which the licensed press was suffering at this time was however not so much political but financial. The licensed newspapers were unable to amass sufficient capital to purchase their own printing presses. The currency reform had greatly reduced their income and in some cases as much as 80% of the profits of licensed newspapers were taken by the outside printers on whose goodwill the licensed press depended. The monthly subscription rate thus could not be reduced much below 3.20 DM as long as they were being charged about 2.50 DM by the printers for actually printing the paper.

There were also still some political fears at the end of the period of monopoly and close allied supervision. Early in 1948 the pre-1945 newspaper publishers formed the Arbeitsgemeinschaft für Pressefragen, which in 1949 became the Gesamtverband der Deutschen Zeitungsverlegen. At the same time it was feared that the German News Agency, which had been established under Allied aegis as the common news-gathering and distributing agency for the German press might get a competitor under the name 'Telepress' with financial backing coming 'from pronounced Right Wing industrial circles'. Altogether, amongst High Commission officials there was little doubt that 'the new press will support or even initiate, a resurgence of German Nationalism as enthusiastically as it had done in the past'. [70] This prophesy however was not to be proved by reality.

V Conclusion

Anxieties concerning the possible ruin of the system of licensed papers made the British and the American authorities take precautions against possible undesirable consequences of what has been called the end of the monopoly or the opening of the free market. Developments up to 1954 fostered the illusion that the liberation of the market really was possible. Actually, only the proprietors of printing plants returned to the newspaper business. At the end of 1949 there were 87 licensed papers in the British Zone including weeklies and official periodicals. Within three months 197 newspapers of the old publishers, some under their old titles, had reappeared. In the other two Western Zones the disproportion seemed even greater, with 59 licensed and 240 old newspapers in the US Zone, and 19 licensed against 150 old newspapers in the French Zone. But, in spite of this, the larger share in circulation remained with the licensed press. It soon became obvious that the newly published newspapers were competing mainly with the regional or local editions of licensed papers, 400 of which were in the British Zone, 120 in the US-Zone and 174 in the French Zone. A significant reduction in the number of licensed papers, from 29 to 19, had occurred only in the French Zone. The situation in Berlin remained stable until the sixties.

There was one notable difference after 1949 which prevented a mere return to the situation of 1932. In 1932 only 1.4% of the German newspapers had a circulation of over 50,000 copies. In 1949 there were only 1.4% with a circulation under 20,000 copies, but over 80% with more than 50,000. By 1952 the return of the old publishers resulted in over 60% of all German newspapers having less than 20,000 copies, but more than 10% with over 50,000 copies: seven times more than in 1932.

Today, the majority of the 120 newspapers have a circulation of well over 50,000 copies and, among the largest the majority were licensed before 1949. Since 1952 the non-subscription popular newspapers with a circulation of up to 5 million daily gained a growing share in the entire German newspaper circulation, said to be about 21 million copies in West Germany and West Berlin.

Circulation figures, of course, have little relation to the standards which the British tried to implement, which amounted to the well-known formula of separating news from comment. This did not survive for long even amongst the British themselves. In November 1947, a member of the Foreign Service, J.O. Reichenheim, of German Jewish origin, in a document arguing against Sefton Delmer's emphasis on 'news value' as defined in British journalism, referred favourably to 'the valuable traditions and trends in the German press and publicity'. [71] Reichenheim recalled 'the still existing remnants of qualified (German) journalism' thinking of the Frankfurter Zeitung, Berliner Tageblatt and Kölnische Zeitung, all of which had continued to be published well into the Nazi era, and were either turned into Nazi organs or, at least, had been forced to follow suit. In some way, nevertheless, the journalistic standards they had represented until 1933 have been absorbed into the new German press, and presentation of world news is practised in the regional German press on a much larger scale than in Britain and the U.S.A.

When the organisations of the licensed and the old publishers merged in 1953, the professional journalistic market became open to change. The German newspapers of today are as much a result of the principles that the British and the Americans tried to introduce as of the good traditions for which names like Theodor Wolff, Georg Bernhard, Bernhard Guttmann and others stand. The newspapers referred to by Reichenheim had led the field - and were of course as atypical of the press as whole in Germany as were The Times, The Guardian or the Observer in Britain, or the New York Times and the Washington Post in the U.S.A. The bulk of the present-day 120 German newspapers, with their 400-odd local editions are as regionally-oriented as ever, following the typical German custom. They represent regional shades that make it difficult to speak of the Germans.

Like their readers, newspapers are only receptive to changes if they accord with long-term developments in - public opinion as a whole. Newspapers are anxious to keep in touch with their public through personal contact and to live in complete harmony with public opinion. New, alternative, political groupings to the generally established trends come therefore to be noted by the media only when they become likely to lead to some representation in parliament. Thus the ecologists and the peace movement are less ridiculed in the German media since they entered the Bundestag, and they even get a disproportionately high coverage of their activities.

All newspapers observe the liberal economic opinions of those who run them or pay for the advertisements - except a very small number of 'alternative' newspapers. In fact, the average German newspaper of today is as 'normal' as one perhaps would call British newspapers. In its best examples the German press achieves the qualities for which the British - partly at least - stood in 1945, but the dogma of separating news and comment, which the Americans favoured even more than the British, is still a questioned principle among German journalists.

One of the differences today between German and British journalism may also be a result of the problem of self-regulation in Germany. The German Press Council has been practically dead since 1982. It became obvious that the Council had become more or less an arena for political antagonism between representatives of the publishers' organisations and the journalists' organisations. The conflict escalated because of the publishers' unwillingness to accept criticism of doubtful journalistic methods employed in some of their papers, and of the journalists' defence of other doubtful practices relating to investigative journalism. Once again it was revealed that Germans are rather inclined to solve problems by using political power, rather than by persuasion and discussion.

On a more pragmatic level we may well accept that Sir Con O'Neill told the author in February 1978:

> The development of affairs in Germany in the first five, six or seven years after the war was extraordinarily fortunate, uncommonly successful. It could, quite easily, have gone very much worse, in a large variety of different ways. It didn't, it went well... I don't have the feeling there is anything fundamentally wrong with the society of the Federal Republic.

If so, could there be much wrong with its media?

NOTES

1. Henry Faulk Group Captives, (London 1977); Matthew Barry Sullivan Thresholds of Peace, (London 1979), p.90, thinks the word 're-education' to have been used first 'in letters to the press in 1941 by writers of Vansittart's persuasion, suggesting that a body of Englishmen take up residence in Germany after the war and dedicate themselves to this self-sacrificing task'. Sullivan's book has been translated into German. See also Michael Balfour Four-Power-Control in Germany, (London 1956), p.28, referring to Sir Alan Herbert's poem from Punch Sept. 1939 'No Quarrel'. For the British authorities see Ulrich Reusch 'Die Londoner Institutionen der Britischen Deutschlandpolitik 1943-1948', in Historisches Jahrbuch,

100, Freiburg 1980, pp.320-331. Also M. Balfour Reforming the German Press 1945-1949, in Journal of European Studies 1973, 3, pp.268-269.

2. FO 371/39226/C 16074. Churchill even tried to bring into 10 Downing Street a young man to act as his adviser on Germany. Morton managed to stop this, pointing out that his adviser on Germany was the Secretary of State. Con O'Neill, who prepared a paper for Churchill, expressed relief on hearing this.

3. FO 898/370. The weekly meetings took place in Duncan. Wilson's room on the 6th floor of Bush House (BBC). With O'Neill there were Hugh Greene, Dr John Hawgood (later Professor of Modern History and Government at Birmingham), Patrick Gordon Walker and Marius Goring participating. In October 1943 O'Neill became Secretary of the Sub-Committee of the Post Hostilities Planning Committee the chairman of which was John M. Troutbeck. FO 371/34460.

4. Con 'O'Neill, born in 1912, Eton, Balliol, entered FO in 1936, became Head of the News Dept. O'Neill left the FO on 8 April 1946 and became leader writer for The Times until June 1947, when he returned to the FO and was seconded to the Political Division of the Control Commission Germany in March 1948. Troutbeck, born in 1894, Westminster, Christ Church, entered the FO in 1920,and was transferred to the Ministry of Economic Warfare in 1940 becoming Prinicipal Assistant Secretary. From November 1943 Heinz Koeppler functioned as Secretary of the German Sub-Committee. WO 193/290 and FO 371/34460 and 34461.

5. M. Balfour Four-Power-Control, p.29, also M. Balfour Propaganda in War, (London 1979), pp.74 and 312-313. See also Richard Crossman's Considerations Concerning SHAEF Policy Towards the German Civil Population (FO 371/46729/C 319 Annex A, pp.136-142) in 1944 and how in his view the Morgenthau plan had a profound and saving effect on German fighting morale.

6. FO 371/34461. The Personnel Paper of 6 Nov. 1943 mentioned a number of 26 Press Control Officers (10 Advanced Party, 16 Second Stage) to undertake immediately the central control of the German press by controlling the news agencies and organising for the future the positive direction of the German press. At the end of 1943 just a control of still existing German newspapers seems to have been planned, not a blackout yet.

7. FO 371/34462. O'Neill, in 1943, thought re-education 'a complicated and important issue of foreign policy'. In an interview in his London home on 28 Feb. 1978 he stated 'I don't think, I had personally much to do with it... It was a very vague notion and, I think, rather a foolish notion...re-education was a kind of ambitious semi-propaganda concept which fizzled out as it deserved to do.' O'Neill submitted a draft on re-education on 26 Nov. 1943 to PWE, Ministry of Information and War Office. On the same day N.B. Ronald (FO) expressed concern to Cyrus Brooks (PID) about the

progress of plans for the control of the press in Germany after the war. See also John Wheeler-Bennett's memoranda of 31 May 1943 and 5 April 1944 (FO 371/34459/C 6883 and FO 371/46868).

8. FO 371/39076/C 124.

9. Norfolk House, St. James's Square. FO 898/408, 28 Dec. 1943. See F.S.V. Donnison Civil Affairs and Military Government North-West Europe 1944-1946, (London 1961), pp.4-8.

10. On McClure see Hans Habe Im Jahre Null, (München 1979), p.31. Responsibilities remained conflicting especially with the Civil Affairs Directorate at the War Office.

11. FO 898/408. The authors were Dr Hawgood and Major Jenkins.

12. FO 371/39054.

13. FO 371/39054. O'Neill stated this as the official view of his Dept. Duncan Wilson, born in 1911, Winchester, Balliol, brother in law of Michael Balfour, came to the FO in 1941, belonged to the CCG 1945/46, back in London until Nov. 1947, then in Berlin until 1949, Ambassador to Yugoslavia 1964-68, Peking 1957-59 and Moscow 1968-71. Master of Corpus Christi College, Cambridge.Died in 1984.

14. FO 371/39054/C 2609. See H.-G. Kowalski Die European Advisory Commission, in Vierteljahrshefte für Zeitgeschichte, 1971, p.270.

15. FO 898/193 and 370. In FO 371/39054 a letter of McClure to Chief of Staff of 24 April 1944 using the same arguments. The Committee proposed on 2 April 1944 a Tripartite Propaganda Policy Control Committee which never came to life.

16. FO 945/848. O'Neill pointed out that if German central administrative services continued to work from Berlin vital instructions might be delayed for a long time, if censorship intervened.

17. WO 193/290, statement of Lieutenant-Colonel C.S. Cole of 22 May 1944.

18. The Combined Chiefs of Staff Directive 551 of 17 April 1944 prohibited the employment of political personalities or leaders in exile in the political or military administration.

19. FO 371/39054 and FO 898/400.

20. FO 371/39054/C 10354.

21. FO 371/39078 and 39054.

22. WO 220/222. The Russians never responded to British proposals (see also FO 371/46868, 2 July 1945). The Americans considered the British directives as being much more detailed than they would be prepared to issue to an American C-in-C. An Anglo-American working party agreed on the compromise that the short general US directive would rely for detailed guidance on the British handbook.

23. FO 371/39078. In the end French liaison officers became attached to, but not embodied in PWD In January 1943 Lockhart had

called a memorandum by Crossman on the possibilities of influencing Hitler's decisions 'ingenious' (FO 371/34444/C 608).

24. FO 898/400. The US Delegation to the EAC tabled some 40 directives similar to the British ones on 23 Nov. 1944 (FO 949/880, also FO 371/39055/C 16516). The British Directive No. 26 dealt with Broadcasting. The American sequence started with Censorship (No. 1); No. 3 dealt with Public Information and No. 4 with Information and Archives.

25. FO 371/46730, and WO 220/221.

26. Hans Habe op. cit., pp.31-43. Harald Hurwitz Die Stunde Null der Deutschen Presse, Köln 1972, pp.45-68.

27. See the memorandum of Lockhart's Deputy, Walter Adams, FO 898/404. For the situation in Germany see M. Balfour Four-Power-Control, pp.76-78.

28. The Times stated on 7 July 1945 that the Allies had not yet got far in working out policies for Germany. Among the reasons the FO (371/46733/C 3816) mentioned (a) The unco-operative Russian attitude in the EAC, (b) the lasting Russian refusal to agree to the Control Council meeting, (c) the need to await the natural death of a lot of half baked ideas like the Morgenthau plan, (d) the situation in Germany herself. See also FO 898/401.

29. See FO 371/46910/C 7492 (21 Oct. 1945) and FO 371/46910/C 8825 (17 Nov. 1945) for the British estimation of Schumacher, who is constantly spelled 'Schuhmacher'. M. Balfour Four-Power-Control, p.61. See also the letter of the Political Adviser of 5 May 1947 to Bevin on the occasion of the first birthday of Telegraf (FO 371/64342/C 6819). To support the Telegraf in May 1946 the proportion of newsprint for the Berlin papers was raised from 20 to 28% of the newsprint available in the British Zone (FO 945/536). Similar measures were taken to launch Der Bund (DGB) by cutting the newsprint supply of the licensed press by 10% (FO 946/54). Bevin asked the FO to send the relevant minutes of the Clacton Conference to Hynd (FO 371/55366/C 5922).

30. FO 898/404. Belfrage, being a Communist, later worked for OMGUS Hesse.

31. FO 898/401. Control Office decided on 21 Oct. 1946 that from 1 July 1947 commercial news agencies should be granted permission to operate in the British Zone (FO 945/534/C 772).

32. William Harris The Daily Press, (London 1943), 1946; Robert Sinclair The British Press, (London 1949). Harris was a Fleet Street journalist for about 25 years and Sinclair was editor of The Spectator. It lasted until Nov. 1947 when after a critical article by Ernst Friedländer in Die Zeit J.O. Reichenheim blamed Delmer's thesis 'which completely ignores those traditions and trends in the German press and publicity which are valuable and which we should try to revive' (FO 371/64317/C 13156).

33. Harris, pp.113 and 117; Sinclair, pp.256-257. The Report of The Royal Commission on The Press (London 1949) p.149, pointed out

approvingly that mass-circulation newspapers were skilful in gauging the public taste and meeting a wide public demand: 'Great affairs of national and international importance may not always get the space of the dispassionate treatment that is their due, but they are not neglected...'. Stronger criticism of the British press may be found in the books by James Margach The Abuse of Power, (London 1978), and James Curran (ed.) The British Press: a Manifesto, (London 1978).

34. WO 219/974.

35. M. Balfour to the author on 11 Nov. 1979. See also Hurwitz op.cit. pp.58-63. The Aachen publisher Heinrich Hollands received his formal SHAEF license only on 27 June 1945. This made the British accept the situation at last. It was one example of the many irregularities embarrassing London. A detailed history has to be postponed until the Military Government files become open in the PRO in 1984

36. WO 219/974. McClure defended the Aachen experiment as he thought that 'between an experienced publisher who is suspect and a man whose technical knowledge may be faulty but whose political philosophy is right, the latter is our best bet'.

37. WO 219/947.

38. FO 898/401. At this time Sefton Delmer visited Germany and wrote a detailed report on the media situation 'By contrast to the American, the arrangements in the British zone were still woefully incomplete.' See also the Minutes of a FO/WO/PID meeting at the Treasury on 30 May 1945 (FO 945/905) which mainly contemplated the future of news agencies in Germany.

39. FO 371/46867/C 3225. Duncan Wilson, on 21 May 1945, proposed a similarly 'elastic' attitude towards the different groups of Germans. Otherwise one would 'run the risk of stultifying our own schemes of the re-education of prisoners of war outside Germany' and losing support of a small but potentially influential element in German society. ibid.

40. FO 945/848.

41. FO 898/401, message to Oliver Harvey, 10 July 1945. Even the French had more than 160 officers in the information services. By March 1947 the British employed 360 of all grades in the ISC (FO 371/64578).

42. Permission to grant licenses had already been asked for on 4 June 1945. Lockhart after reading a report by Sir William Strang recommended on 20 July 1945 not to relax suddenly the current information policy and to examine carefully the situation in Germany.

43. FO 945/905. Major-General Bishop regarded the overt newspapers as inadequate because they had no German home news service. Due to their monopoly they made considerable profits anyway.

44. FO 371/46735 C 5132, a statement by Commander McLachlan (PID). Bevin on 25 Aug. 1945 signed a FO draft letter to Montgomery trying to explain to him the danger of such messages which should come from all four Cs-in-C: '...it might indirectly have some educative effect in weaning them from their custom of looking to a single Fuhrer for guidance...'.

45. Ritchie Calder's harsh comments of 23 Aug. 1945 on the Corps Commanders 'Observations on Information Services in Germany' (FO 898/401). See also Calder's remarks of 31 Aug. 1945 on the 'benevolent autarchy' of the Military Government. (FO 37/46973, marginal correction 'autocraty').

46. FO 898/401 and 371/46973. See Falk Pingel 'Die Russen am Rhein?', in Vierteljahrshafte für Zeitgeschichte, 30/1982, No. 1, p.104, pointing at the problem of the military commanders which did not arise only in Dec. 1945. It was the problem of the political administration of the British Zone. Obviously the officers did not feel like reading all the directives, instructions and orders, if these seemed to be purely political. Similar experiences in the American Zone where the Military Government did not care much about Washington. See also M. Balfour Four-Power-Control, p.99, on the Control Office. There were discussions in March 1947 already to merge the COGA with the FO (FO371/64578/C 4846).

47. FO 898/401, 371/46735, 371/55576/C 128 and 944/432. See also M. Balfour's Notes on Some Aspects of German Affairs of 10 Aug. 1945 (FO 898/193), defending the Military Government situation by pointing out the problems.

48. FO 371/46702/C 10124, report of PID German and Austrian Intelligence of 19 Dec. 1945. Even the French had licensed six newspapers by that time.

49. We follow Huijsman's own words in an interview on 3 Feb. 1978 in London. Huijsman had been a member of the Union of South Africa's Foreign Service. He remained in the position in Germany until July 1948. He was stationed in Berlin, but divided his time between Bünde, Hamburg and Berlin aiming at three days travelling in the zone. His report is in general supported by the FO files 946/8 and 936/148 and by a letter of M. Balfour on 1 Jan. 1979. After a year in Germany Huijsman had to go on leave to avoid a breakdown (FO 946/54, a letter of Balfour, 3 Sept. 1946). See also K. Koszyk Kontinuität oder Neubeginn? (Siegen 1981). Duncan Wilson returned to the FO German Dept. He re-visited Germany in Sept. 1946. FO 945/534/B 659.

50. When the British founded the overt newspaper Der Berliner on 2 Aug. 1945 they employed 36 Germans after screening and had to send forward three linotypes from Bielefeld. See Calder's report of 23 August 1945, FO 898/401. M. Balfour learned from Christopher Steel in Oct. 1945 that licensing proceeded on another basis than in the US Zone.

51. See for the Norddeutsche Zeitung FO 953/535/PC 1522, 3 May 1949 and FO 953/534, 4 Apr. 1949, for the zonal paper. On 2 July 1945 already Brig. Neville of 21st Army Group thought that the time for the use of a model newspaper had gone by. FO 945/905. See also Die ersten Jahre, Hamburg 1962. Heinz-Dietrich Fischer Reeducations-und Pressepolitik unter Britischen Besatzungsstatus, (Düsseldorf 1978), relies on printed material only. Die Welt had to compete with the suprazonal weeklies Die Zeit (Hamburg since 21 Feb. 1946) and Handelsblatt (Düsseldorf since 16 May 1946).

52. On 24 Aug. 1945 Germans were notified that they could apply for press licenses. Bishop's successor as Chief PR/ISC Group was C. Sprigge, Director of Information Services Control since Sept. 1945 Michael Balfour. FO 946/35. See also Balfour's letter to the author of 1 Jan. 1979. In April 1948 G.R. Gauntlett became Chief of Information Services Division (ISD) as a result of the changes in ISC (FO936/242).

53. FO 945/30. See also adverse remarks by a Military Government officer on 8 Feb. 1946 'that the CCG is badly managed, overstaffed and lacking in sufficient understanding of its task'. The officer 'knew little of what directives go out', but doubted 'if we have a fixed aim and policy and, what is worse - the thing that really matters, i.e. whether communism may ultimately come to Germany, is a question that has the least attention paid to it'. FO 936/236. A similarly adverse American voice was Waldemar Gurian 'Re-educating Germany'. in The Commonweal, 27 August 1948, pp.466-469.

54. M. Balfour '...the impulse (of having political party newspapers) might quite well have come from Mr. Hynd or other Ministers in London, who again might well have been influenced by representations from the SPD. But if it had been so, I do not see why Steel should not have mentioned it and I have absolutely no memory of his doing so.' See also FO 946/8. Huijsman, in May 1947, had a great deal of sympathy with the newspapermens' point of view that relating circulations to election results excluded journalistic quality and perpetuated the danger of domination of the press by the political parties.FO 946/54.

55. Pingel, pp.104-107, comes to similar conclusions, although the criticism of what the Russians were about to do was very general even before 3 April 1946 when the decisive meeting took place in the FO. There were secret talks with Grotewohl who openly admitted to be under Soviet pressure FO 946/2. The Observer told the public on 17 February 1946 that it was through the disunity of the SPD and KPD that Hitler had come to power.

56. FO 946/54. pp.23-33.

57. FO 945/536, enclosing a memorandum of 7 May 1946 by Peter de Mendelssohn, the Berlin Press Controller, on the 'Progress and Prospects of Telegraf'. Strang asked Bevin for more newsprint: 'We shall, in fact, not effectively exert our due influence in

Germany, or make satisfactory progress with the re-education of the German people, until we can do something more to spread our ideas among them.' See also FO 371/55366/C 5922.

58. FO 936/290. After considering to bring Francis Williams, Clement Attlee's Press Secretary, to the British Zone (James Margach The Abuse of Power, pp.90-91), in the end Robert Birley became Educational Adviser of the CCG. In summer 1947 it was even proposed to merge the PR/ISC Group with the Education Branch, FO 371/64578. See R. Birley, Worauf es ankommt, in Die Welt, No. 144, 4 Dec. 1947.

59. FO 945/27. The situation in the four zones is described in a Control Office telegram of 10 July 1946. FO 946/58.

60. FO 946/54.

61. FO 946/58. The numbers from the Soviet Zone seem to be exaggerated, since there were only 21 newspapers with 80 sub-editions.

62. FO 371/64342/C 2060 and FO 371/64411/C 5307 3 April 1947. On 5 Feb. 1947 the Russian representative in the Control Council, General Kurochkin, answered British complaints by pointing out that since November 1946 there was no censorship in the Soviet Zone, FO 371/64409/C 2276. On 17 April 1947 Christopher Steel noticed a growing party influence on the British licensed press, but the British did not dare to extend the circulation of the few independent papers as this might cause an 'explosion' in the 'present difficult situation' as there was a danger of the main political parties withdrawing from responsibility. FO 371/64271/C 5658 and 6086. Military Government started suppressing Communist newspapers under Directive No. 40 for a shorter period in June 1947 (Koszyk, op. cit., pp.18-19). The Americans followed in July 1947. See also FO 371/70482/C 1970, 70481/C 1586 and 64540/C 15643 and C 16536. Several withdrawals of licences happened in 1948 in connection with the Berlin Crisis which speeded up the foundation of the Federal Republic of Germany. Already in Feb. 1948 the CCG forwarded an SPD memorandum which considered it necessary and possible to make it clear to the German people, that if a partition of Germany takes place, it will be the fault of the USSR Undated memorandum FO 371/70481/C 1606. In June 1948 the French complained about an anti-French campaign of Die Zeit. FO 371/70647/C 4971 and 6200. In Oct. 1948 Der Spiegel was on the list because of an article on the Netherlands Royal House. FO 371/70647/C 8146.

63. FO 371/64834. Draft Ordinance of 27 May 1947. See Koszyk, pp.22 and 27-29. The Advisory Committees were a kind of manifestation of the Zonal Advisory Council for the press, founded on 15 Feb. 1946 to constitute German administrative functions on a zonal basis (see Konrad Adenauer Erinnerungen 1945-1953, pp.64-81). The Military Government never used its right of veto.

64. The US Military Government announced on 30 September 1948 a termination of the licensing system progressively by Länder as acceptable legislation became effective. Daily publication of newspapers was possible since 1 April 1949, but involved the danger of collapse for some licensed papers because of a 15% increase in printers' wages. Die Welt started daily publication on 1 July 1949, all German newspapers on 1 September 1949. FO 953/535/PC 1522. For the Conference of Regional Commissioners see FO 953/534. It was decided not to discuss the problems with the Zonal Press Advisory Committee, but with some form of ad hoc representative body.

65. This approach was different from the American which tried to enforce prolongation of contracts. FO 953/535/ PC 1452 and 1818, also FO 953/536, 29 August 1949. See also FO 953/538/PC 3407, 17 November 1949. In NRW printers promised not to stop existing newspapers and no legislation was passed. In Lower Saxony the law had passed by August 1949. At this time 106 new newspapers were expected to be published in Bavaria against 27 licensed papers.

66. FO 953/536/PC 2600. The Press Laws became valid in Wuerttemberg-Baden on 1 June, in Hesse on 22 July, in Bavaria on 22 August and in Bremen on 8 September 1949.

67. The Office being in Wahnerheide. The new Chief of ISD was Brig. W.L. Gibson who had been in charge of press control in 1945. Lance Pope was Head of the Press Section. Labour was returned to power in the General Election in February 1950.

68. Gibson promised to make a special study of new publications and to endeavour to watch their trends. See FO 953/536/PC 2672, Gibson's letter of 5 September 1949 to the FO German (soon Education and) Information Dept. R.A.A. Chaput de Saintonge '...I admit that our appreciation of their efforts over the past four years, to ensure a building up of a reasonable objective German press, also binds us to give them all support we possibly can.' ibid. See also Gibson's explanatory letter to the Regional ISD Branches of 3 Sept. 1949.

69. FO 953/537, by J.H. Moore. He stated that most of the newly appeared newspapers were small and none was the official organ of the Nazi Party, 'though it is undoubtedly true that all of them "went with the tide" '. In 6 cases it had been found that former editors were back with the newspapers. Only in Lower Saxony after 1 Sept. a few announcement sheets were stopped for a short time on the request of the Land Press Advisory Committee. Up to 7 October 32 and by mid-November 150 newspapers under their former titles had reappeared, 99% of which were Kreiss and Heimatblaetter. See also FO 953/538/PC 3277. Chaput de Saintonge expected on 3 November 1949 'a continual stream of questions and enquiries during the next few months'. See also FO 953/538/PC

3407, in which Moore expected 600 new newspapers by the spring of 1950.

70. FO 953/538/PC 3407. As the licensed publishers were reticent it became increasingly difficult for the High Commission to obtain information. British authorities thought the situation in the American Zone less difficult as an order issued in 1947 made it possible for OMGUS to enforce suitable contracts on printers for five years.

71. FO 371/64317/C 13156.

Chapter Six

IN RETROSPECT: BRITAIN'S POLICY OF 'RE-EDUCATION'

MICHAEL BALFOUR

*

The talk on which this chapter is based was not intended to be a
survey of 're-education', something which it would in any case have
been difficult to give, even in outline, in 45 minutes. I assumed,
rightly or wrongly, that those coming to the Conference would
already know something about its subject. I thought it might be
helpful if, at the outset, I tried to call attention to a few of the
background constraints under which we were operating. My original
intention was to speak for only ten minutes and confine myself to
explaining why, in my view, something like 're-education' was
inevitable if a purely punitive treatment of the Germans was to be
avoided. I then decided that a few explanatory words about
organisation might be useful and that the audience might be
interested to know that somebody who had had charge of an
important part of re-education efforts thought about them in
retrospect.

*

In mid-September 1939 A.P. Herbert published in <u>Punch</u> a poem
which can be taken as the plain man's reaction to Chamberlain's
statement that 'we have no quarrel with the German people':

> We have no quarrel with the German nation,
> They're fond of music, poetry and beer:
> But all the same, with tiresome iteration,
> They choose a fool to govern them - and cheer.

After touching on the possibility that

> It might be better if they did not breed

he came to the conclusion that

> some major operation

(On heart and head) may be the only way.

I understand that the term 're-education' was first used by Vansittart or one of his votaries in 1941. By November 1942 it was cropping up in British official documents. On 27 May 1943 the egregious MP for Marylebone, Cunningham-Reid, attacked it in an adjournment debate:

> What a fantastic idea it is to attempt to educate a whole race to be peaceful, a race that for centuries has had an instinct for war deep down in its nature. I believe it would be much easier to educate 80 million baboons.

What solution the gallant Captain himself offered for Germany was not altogether clear. After saying that 'unless at the end of hostilities we intend to fight the Russians, we may have to take their advice about Polish frontiers', he got involved in a slanging-match with Lord Hinchinbrooke which exhausted the time available for debate. But he appeared to want to wipe Germany off the map altogether.

Henry Faulk, an outstanding practitioner of re-education, was later to say that its real inventor was the British people. According to him the British public was immensely afraid of future wars and was convinced that Nazism was a political form of nationalism and aggressive nationalism a peculiar German disease. It therefore looked for a way of preventing another war and the suggestions varied from the violence of a Vansittart to the popular demand for re-education.

On five occasions between May 1942 and April 1945, Mass Observation asked a cross-section of the public what kind of settlement should be imposed on Germany. The commonest answer was 'preventive' but 'revengeful' always came close behind and once was in front. Those who wanted something 'constructive' formed a much smaller fraction and in April 1945, just after the Belsen camp had been uncovered, fell to 7%. A fortnight before the end of the war, the Sunday Express wrote that 'the Germans are moral lepers and should be treated as such until we are sure that the race has been purged and redeemed'. Churchill was struck in January 1945 by the depth of the feeling which would be aroused by a policy of 'putting poor Germany on her feet again'. Noel Coward's 'Don't let's be beastly to the Germans' had a distinctly ambivalent undertone. And this is to look at Britain alone. I will not take time recording the opposition of some Americans to anything which looked like leniency and in particular of Roosevelt who was in a position to impose his will throughout the Anglo-American policy-making hierarchy.

Some may be inclined to criticise the use of the term re-education because it was ambiguous. To some it meant (quoting Faulk again) that Germans were capable of being better than Nazi doctrine allowed them to be. To others, it was Hochnäsigkeit, arrogance and, as such, likely to prove counter-productive. I suggest its ambiguity was a considerable advantage. It was acceptable to the

British hawks even if not to the lunatic fringe. Nobody knew precisely what it meant or how it was to be carried out. I cannot think of any other phrase which so aptly described what the public wanted and which would not have brought down on itself the anathema pronounced by Mr Morgenthau on the draft British Civil Affairs Handbook. In the meantime it provided cover behind which those who recognised its shortcomings could get ahead with operational planning. As early as May 1943 R.A. Butler, as President of the Board of Education, in answering the Cunningham-Reid motion, said 'we would be wise to realise that the re-education of a people comes better from inside that people themselves... We may hope to start such a leaven within the country that a real self-education and re-education arises'. Responsible people on the British side were from early on aware of the problems involved in the idea of re-education. But for them to have been too open in questioning its practicability would have played straight into the hands of those who were out simply to punish. It would be a mistake to spend time deploring the use of the word re-education or trying to define what it was originally intended to do. Public attitudes in Britain made the use of some such phrase indispensable: public attitudes in Germany meant that its use was bound to give offence.

There is however another angle to be remembered. I have just quoted R.A. Butler as saying that the re-education of a people comes better from inside that people themselves. There were others who reminded us that you cannot force ideas down people's throats. But a fact much in mind during the war and immediately after it was that in 1918 we had pretty well left it to the Germans to decide for themselves how their society should be changed at a time when, in Rilke's later words, much of Germany preferred to persist rather than to change. There was general agreement that they had made a pretty inadequate job of it. Mr Attlee, as Deputy Prime-Minister and Chairman of the Cabinet Armistice and Post-War Committee, twice represented to it the need to deprive the Prussian landowning class and the industrialists of the social power which they had so far managed to retain. The surrender of Ebert and Noske to Gröner and Seeckt in 1918-20 was a fairly familiar story. Brigadier-General Morgan, a lawyer in uniform, was assiduous in reminding us how the Versailles disarmament provisions had been evaded. The German disregard of the provisions about war crimes led to the conclusion that next time responsibility must be taken out of their hands. That was one reason why as early as January 1944 Britain proposed, despite the misgivings of some of the Cabinet, that this time the occupation should be total and disarmament complete. I do not think it would be fair to say that we underestimated what a much greater effect a second and indisputably complete defeat would have on German thinking. That was a main reason for insisting on unconditional surrender. But we were - and I suggest wisely - sceptical as to how far the treatment would be effective. There was wide support for the view - exaggerated but not altogether unfounded - that the roots of National Socialism lay deep in German culture.

Accordingly many Britons were unable to accept without qualification the view that all the Germans had to do was to go back to their traditions. What they had to do was to go back to the Liberal tradition which had by common consent existed in Germany and to which some Germans had all along remained faithful. But one then had to ask why that tradition had not prevailed in the past and what must be done to see that it prevailed in the future.

*

I must now say something about the various organisations involved in re-education. Let me start with the one to whose Intelligence Division I belonged – the Political Warfare Executive, set up in 1941 to reconcile the conflicting claims in the field of enemy propaganda between Eden, as Foreign Secretary, Bracken as Minister of Information and, for a few months, Dalton as Minister of Subversive Operations. Its Director-General, Robert Bruce Lockhart, said its function was to act as a buffer (I would prefer 'insulating blanket') between the enthusiasm of the temporaries and the cold cynical experience of the permanent officials. Its staff were almost all temporaries, from a variety of backgrounds, though a number of them were in uniform. It settled the lines of output policy with the Foreign Office and either carried them out itself or transmitted them to the BBC European Service, whose Controller, be it remembered, was himself an FO official, Ivone Kirkpatrick. Within broad lines laid down by the FO, responsibility for settling media policy in Germany after the surrender rested with PWE as the only body combining the necessary political with the necessary technical knowledge. It was they who formulated the well-known 3-stage policy towards the German press: closure of existing Nazi papers; a temporary filling of the gap by papers with contents openly decided by Military Government; the issue to suitable Germans of licences to publish papers. On the American side neither OSS nor OWI were really an equivalent of PWE in this respect.

PWE was for intelligible reasons a secret department. As cover it used the name of the Political Intelligence Department of the Foreign Office. From 1939 to 1943 this body really existed as a small group of eminent if ageing gentlemen, one for each area, established at Woburn. Their principal product was a green weekly printed Survey of Foreign Political Information widely circulated in the Foreign Service; a selection from the series has just been reprinted. In 1943 they were embodied in the new FO Research Department (where 'Research' was not the euphemism for subversive propaganda it has since become). But PWE still used the title PID as cover. After VJ-Day, when it became a little absurd to have a Political Warfare organisation without a war, but where the work which PWE had been doing latterly still had to be done, PWE came out into the open calling itself PID. As far as we are concerned, PID can be forgotten and PWE used instead. Wherever one comes across the acronym PID one has to ask 'was this the real PID or was it PWE in disguise?'

PWD, however, Psychological Warfare Division, must be carefully distinguished from the Political Warfare Executive. PWD was a Division of Eisenhower's Supreme Headquarters, SHAEF, with a combined Anglo-American staff, in which Americans and officers predominated, though a few civilians of both nationalities including myself masqueraded rather uncomfortably in uniform without rank. It was formed in England early in 1944, on the basis of experience in the Mediterranean, moved to Paris in September 1944, on to Bad Homburg in June 1945 and was dissolved with the rest of SHAEF in July 1945. Its chief was a regular American soldier, Brigadier-General Bob McClure, whose principal original qualification for the job, besides integrity and common-sense, was the confidence of Eisenhower.

PWD's primary task was propaganda to the forces opposing the Allies in Western Europe. But PWD got involved in general propaganda in three ways. Firstly some of its output, and notably its transmissions from Radio Luxembourg, inevitably reached civilians in battle areas. Secondly, until the end of hostilities (and in practice for some time longer), responsibility for government behind the Allied lines, particularly in Germany, rested with Civilian Affairs, another Division of SHAEF, and as Civilian Affairs had no Information Branch of its own, PWD acted for it. Thirdly PWD was made responsible for what would happen mediawise in Germany between surrender and the establishment of the quadripartite Control Commission. Moreover in practice, for lack of any other qualified body, it did the media planning for what would happen in the American Zone after the Commission was set up. Generally speaking the views of PWE and PWD were not far out of line; in particular, PWD took over PWE's three-stage press plan. But PWE was putting forward through the FO and European Advisory Commission proposals for quadripartite media policy and wanted to keep as free a hand for the Control Commission as possible; it was apt to get restive when PWD started planning for what would happen in the inevitable gap between surrender and the establishment of the Commission for fear lest that should present the Commission with a number of faits accomplis. What might have been a clash, however, was averted by the failure of the EAC and everybody else to frame a quadripartite media policy.

PWD had subordinate teams for psychological warfare with its three Army Groups, 6, 12, and 21. It had some difficulty in maintaining policy control over the 12 AG team, partly owing to the personality of General Patton but even more to that of the versatile Hungarian, Hans Habe, whom it had put in control. But its difficulties with 12 AG were as nothing compared to those with the Anglo-Canadian team at 21 AG who, in keeping with the spirit of independence which Monty had brought with him from the desert, went their own way without regard for any superior, American or British. 21 AG paid equally little attention to the planning for the post-surrender situation which was going on in PWD SHAEF and to that going on in PWE in London. A certain number of officers were collected in England in the autumn and kept kicking their heels as shadow Information Control Units. PWE gave a certain amount of help in their rather rudimentary training. But while it was easy to foresee that Bob McClure would move into Germany as the Chief of US Information Control, with a trained team behind him, there was no obvious figure to take charge on the British side. Lockhart was too ill, his deputy Major-General Brooks had gone back to the Marines and Neville, Monty's Brigadier for Psychological Warfare, was ploughing his own furrow. This weakness was, in my view, intensified by the fact that the two people responsible for planning the information side of the Control Commission, Kirkpatrick as Political Chief and Brigadier Gibson, the shadow head of the Information Control branch, both belonged to that valuable class of administrator who is inclined to doubt the value of doing anything and therefore inclined to underestimate the size of the job to be done. The net result in my view was a failure to bring to bear on the media problems in the British Zone anything like enough of the expertise in official management of information services which had been accumulated by painful trial and error in Britain since 1939. It is true that in the late summer of 1945 the Deputy Director-General of PWE, Major-General Alec Bishop, did come to Germany as head of Public Relations and Information Services Control. But Bishop was a regular soldier who had only been in PWE for three months.

The Allied Control Council for Germany was set up by quadripartite proclamation in Berlin on 5 June 1945. It first met on 30 July and only announced its existence to the Germans on 30 August. During the next few months it gradually got established and built up a staff in Berlin. But of course the Allied troops had been governing increasingly large parts of Germany ever since the Americans crossed the frontier near Aachen on 11 September 1944, while Military Government went on at all levels below the top until May 1946. Military Government had naturally been built up to correspond with military formations. With the change to civilian control, the Generals commanding the I, VIII and XXX Corps handed over to civilian Land Commissioners for Schleswig-Holstein, Hamburg, Lower Saxony and North Rhine-Westphalia. This did not make as much difference as might be thought because both Monty and his Corps Commanders had for long had Deputies for Military Government alongside their seconds-in-command for military matters while each Military Government unit had naturally dealt with such German government units as had been established in its area. But the change of personnel from generals to civilians was accompanied by the gradual departure of the Military Government officers on demobilisation and their replacement by civilians freshly recruited in Britain, or by themselves re-employed as civilians. The War Office also handed over its responsibilities for German administration to the Control Office, anomalously headed by the Chancellor of the Duchy of Lancaster, John Hynd, because the Foreign Office resolutely refused to get immersed in the detail. But it was not a help that over the next few months the Foreign Secretary had nominally no responsibility for Germany, a country he found distasteful anyhow. Bevin carried weight in Cabinet, Hynd did not.

The European Advisory Commission's plan for the Central Council envisaged that, under the Council and the Co-ordinating Committee immediately subordinate to it there would be Directorates to supervise the work of each of the main Departments which had existed in Weimar Germany. Thus there was a Political Directorate, a Legal Directorate, a Finance Directorate and so on. Each national element in the Commission was similarly divided. But under Weimar there had been no single Department responsible for the media and to resurrect the Propaganda Ministry was unthinkable. Consequently there was no Directorate responsible for it, the theory being that the Political Directorate would do whatever might be necessary. Equally no formal provision had been made in the British organisation for an Information Division. The Americans, as I said, simply rechristened their Psychological Warfare Division the Information Control Division. In the autumn of 1945 the British put Public Relations (the handling of non-German press and radio correspondents) along with Information Services Control into what was known till 1948 as the 'PR/ISC Group': it was this of which General Bishop became Chief. But the other part of the Commission primarily concerned with re-education was of course Education Branch, which was part of the Internal Affairs Division. Between the Information Control Branch of PR/ISC and Education Branch there was no organisational link below the Co-ordinating Committee nor did Political Division have any responsibility for education. The Deputy Military Governor held weekly meetings of his Divisional Directors but at these Education Branch was normally only represented by the General directing all home affairs (until Birley arrived as Educational Adviser early in 1947).

There were a number of other reasons why Education Branch and ISC saw little of one another. Schools are by their nature widely scattered, whereas printing-presses and radio stations tend to be confined to the larger towns. Thus while Education Officers were fairly widely scattered, living among the grass roots and coming to know a lot of Germans personally, ISC staff congregated in their detachments at Düsseldorf, Hanover, Hamburg, Kiel and Berlin (as well as at their Zone headquaarters at Bünde). I got the impression – and this is not a criticism – that Education Officers shunned things like headquarters, committees and policy discussions. I would not be surprised if they also suspected us as people who were trying to sell a line, to force things down German throats, whereas they regarded their role much more as that of guide, philosopher and friend. Initially all their energies were absorbed by the material job of getting the schools and universities going again, of providing not only text-books but pencils and paper and window-glass (and it must be remembered that the procurement of these usually had to be done in competition with other units of MG and thus could not be left entirely to Germans). They had to try to see that the right Germans got appointed to the key posts and decide with them how many of the compromised teachers could safely be allowed to teach again.

They did not have to worry about how far things being said in schools might affect Allied security whereas in Information this was something which we were never allowed to forget. And while control over the media was maintained (admittedly with progressive laxity) till 1949, Education Branch's direct responsibility stopped at the end of 1946. For in line with our policy of decentralising Germany, we then handed over to the new Land Governments all the jobs which did not have to be kept as Federal responsibilities - and Germany's central Ministry of Education which had only existed from 1934 to 1945 was another institution everyone was determined not to revive.

As a result, more was done to remould the German media (and particularly the press) than was done to remould German education where the deliberate refusal to give orders meant that the Germans put things back pretty much where they had been before 1933. The opportunity to make a break with the past was not taken. Some Germans have criticised this refusal to enforce a policy, saying that it in fact amounted to a policy and that Education Branch, by insisting on more attention being paid to their advice, could have saved German education from some of the troubles that overtook it twenty years later. But thorough-going reforms would have had to be carried through in the teeth of German academic opinion and would probably have been reversed immediately responsibility had been put back into German hands. This is only one aspect of a wider question. If the British had pushed through nationalisation of the German coal and steel industries; if, in conjunction with the Americans, they had convened the Parliamentary Council in 1946 instead of 1948, German society would have assumed a distinctly socialist character and education as well as everything else would have been affected. Schumacher Germany would have been very different from Adenauer Germany but this is not the place to start asking whether the world would have benefited.

The changes we made in the media were of course designed to ensure free discussion and the free flow of information but had relatively few party political implications. It may be that, by requiring any would-be publisher to get a licence from us, and only licensing people we thought financially as well as politically respectable, we discouraged experiments. Not having been a journalist myself, I accepted as the pure milk of the C.P.Scott gospel the principle of separating news from comment but I must say I did sometimes wonder how far papers like the Daily Express and Daily Mirror were doing it at home. And recently I read with interest a 1944 comment by a German journalist - 'there is one way the British, despite the narrowness of their political thinking, are ahead of us - they know that news can be a weapon and are experts in its strategy'. All the same, we refused to make Selton Delmer Editor of the paper we kept under our own control to be an example to the Germans and we did so because of disbelief in his capacity to handle news with real objectivity. As he was easily the ablest journalist at our disposal, and we never solved the problem of finding an alternative, I think our restraint deserves credit. But I shudder to think what the reaction would have been if it had come out, as it must have done, that our chief agent in teaching the Germans the virtues of objective news was the man who had shown such a brilliant ability to pervert it in his black transmissions during the war.

Of the media, the press and radio were by a long way the most important. After that, I would put books and information centres (Die Brücke), of which we had at one time 62. I'm afraid that I attached - and still attach - little importance to films. New German features were in the nature of things slow to emerge. A selection of old German features was admitted on sufferance because of the need to reduce German boredom by having something to show in the cinemas. Rank, under pressure from Monty, made a number of British features available but it was hard to find ones which showed the kind of Britain we would like the Germans to imitate. So dislocated was transport that the master copy of the newsreel made in the U.S. Zone as often as not got lost on the journey to the British Zone with the result that the time-lag before it got into cinemas was even more than the pre-war Nazi gap of 8 weeks. The most valuable work to my mind was done by Buckland-Smith of Education Branch in making documentary films for teaching. I persuaded the Ministry of Information to lend me Arthur Elton for over a year in the hope that he could implant something of the Grierson inspiration in Germany. He was a stimulating person to have around but I've no clear idea of what he achieved.

Our intention had been that, after newspapers had been licensed, they would be kept under fairly close control and pulled up whenever they began to make trouble for the authorities. But in practice this was not done. Pre-publication censorship was given up almost at once and post-publication censorship proved too big a job to be done with the necessary amount of speed. Representations were of course made on occasion by Press Officers. Three 'itinerant preachers' were sent round in the summer of 1946 to visit editors and persuade them to widen their views. Anything more than that, such as suspending a paper for one or more issues, would have had to go up to Chief PR/ISC at the lowest and by the time all the documentation had been got together, a lot of water would have flowed down the Rhine. Goebbels had been able to take accusations of high-handedness in his stride. We had to be seen to be acting fairly.

The real difficulty with the press - and radio - was one of balance. In the circumstances of the time, almost anything done by the Allies, if looked at in isolation, could be made the object of what looked like legitimate criticism. Take the question of coal supplies. If more coal had been left in Germany, a lot of useful things could have been done with it (besides keeping the Germans warmer) and Europe as a whole would probably have benefited. But some of Germany's neighbours, particularly France, having had their coal industries wrecked by German action during the war, insisted that they had a prior claim on German coal and no doubt some of the ways in which they were going to use it also benefited Europe as a whole. Most of the coal was produced in the British Zone and the British authorities had the thankless task of sharing it out. Those left unsatisfied had what appeared to be a perfectly good case for attacking the decisions. Not unnaturally the German press repeated those criticisms when the verdict seemed to have gone at Germany's expense. To get a clear and defensible statement of the opposite case was not easy and to get publicity for it in Germany even less easy.

In retrospect it is possible to see that one of the problems was the lack of parliamentary government. If there had been Ministers having to answer questions and make speeches defending their policies to a House of Commons or on platforms round the country, a lot more information would have come out and some of it at any rate would have got to German eyes or ears. But we only had officials, often soldiers, and they are trained not to usurp the function of politicians. I myself felt that we ought to be making more use of the right the licences gave us to require the printing of articles setting out the factual background of controversial subjects. But those articles would have done more harm than good if they had made mistakes of fact or unfounded claims, and what I really needed but did not have was a first-class journalist to write them. Much of the news and factual information which was needed to put the picture straight had to come from outside Germany.

I still wish we had been more active but by now I doubt whether it would have done much good. The frame of mind of Germans in the closing months of the war is a fascinating subject calling for a book on its own. But 30% of them retained their faith in Hitler till near the very end. The proportion of those professing to think Nazism 'a good thing badly carried out' never dropped below 42% between November 1945 and January 1948. There is good evidence that 10% of the adult male population remained convinced Nazis - 4 million people. Yet the incontrovertible evidence of total defeat was hard to overlook or excuse away by stories of treachery or corruption. We did not stress 'collective guilt', preferring to talk about responsibility. Yet it was a concept most Germans must have been aware of, even if only to repudiate. That is what distinguishes Germany from any other defeated country. Goebbels had left behind a deep scepticism about anything officials said. The Germans may have had a little more faith in us, because, after all, our wartime forecasts had come true. But they were not trusting anyone much. For the time being German patriotism must have seemed to consist in conceding as little as possible. Coming to terms with the past was going to be a very slow process.

That is why the most important part of re-education remains to be described. It had little to do with the media. I remember Heinz Koeppler saying about 1946 that what re-education really involved was rebuilding the cultural links between Germany and the Western world which the Nazis had been so concerned to destroy. To some extent we rebuilt those links by bringing in material from outside - news, books, plays, the accumulated backlog of the years when democratic literature had been discouraged in Germany. But what did most to rebuild those links was personal contact. I am not so starry-eyed as to suggest that every contact between British and Germans was beneficial. In many cases no doubt existing prejudices were strengthened and fresh misconceptions born. But my guess would be that the harmful ones were fewer than the beneficial ones, especially as time went on. First of all there were the British already in Germany, especially those who saw themselves as being there to do a job, not simply because they had been part of an invasion. Then there were the considerable number of British brought on visits to talk to Germans - particularly their opposite numbers. More valuable still were the Germans taken on visits to Britain. In 1949 a Professsor at Münster told Birley that a quarter of the students had already been abroad since the end of the war, whereas after 1918 it took 8 years for the first party of German students to visit England. Such contacts, being face-to-face, were more likely to establish personal trust than the written or broadcast word. Secondly they gave Germans chances to see for themselves things in the outside world of which they had hitherto only heard by report. Let us hope that that strengthened the credibility of the reports.

Finally I would be guilty of a grave dereliction of duty if I did not say something about the Prisoner of War programme. At the end of the war we had 2.7 million prisoners on our hands outside Germany. For a variety of reasons the last of them were not to get home for over three years. But on 18 September 1944 the Cabinet decided they should be re-educated and gave PWE the job. The staff available for doing it consisted at that moment of a Wing-commander who spoke no German and a former literary agent. Some 200 more were soon brought in, many part-time, many from the teaching profession. In the end some 400,000 prisoners were handled. What was going on had largely to be concealed from the British public or it would have been interfered with. Perhaps the most remarkable testimony to what was achieved was that, when the Germans got around to writing their official history of their POWs, in 18 volumes, they gave the writing of the one on re-education to a British officer, Henry Faulk.

The first step was to screen each prisoner and segregate the incorrigibles. Remember that up to May 1945 Nazi discipline was maintained in the camps and there was a case of an anti-Nazi being executed as a traitor as late as December 1944: the British thereupon held a trial and executed five Germans who had formed the Roll-Kommando. About 10% proved to be already convinced anti-Nazis; they were either kept to act as leaven or given accelerated release so that their capacities could be put to use at home. The primary object with the remainder was to make them think and provide them with materials for doing so. Every prisoner was required to sit through an American film on the liberation of Belsen. Special camps were run for theological students and for youths under 26. An obstacle was the ban on fraternisation with the local population, maintained until the end of 1946, largely to protect prisoners from vindictive treatment by the public. But even before it was lifted, and much more so afterwards, human-kindness kept breaking through.

The show-piece of course was Heinz Koeppler's Wilton Park, opened in January 1946 as a residential college at which 300 prisoners could take a six-week course and discuss in a civilised atmosphere burning problems of the recent past and immediate future, with many distinguished visitors, both British and German, coming to join in. Those who had attended went back to their original camps and helped to spread what they had absorbed. From January 1947 civilians brought from Germany began to take part in the courses. Altogether 2400 people went through the mill in the first two years. By the time Wilton Park held its Jubilee conference in 1971 in the presence of the Prime Minister, the number had risen to 12,000 from all over the Western world.

In the dingy days of the Stunde Null, nobody would have foreseen the Wirtschaftswunder. But anyone would have been accused of equally wishful thinking if he had supposed that within a few decades two-thirds of the German people could attain the level of political judgement which in my view they have displayed during recent years. The overwhelming credit for both achievements must of course go to the· Germans themselves. Of course the economic success contributed a great deal to the psychological one. The Russians also contributed in their own way.

In 1947 a Dutch lady said to Robert Birley 'the last war was not the kind of war that could be won by winning it. That had to come after it was over'. On the evening of 28 September 1969, when the polls showed he had won the election, Willy Brandt is said to have remarked 'To-night, finally and for ever, Hitler lost the war'.

This paper is based primarily on personal knowledge and memories. Some of the material used has already been published in M. Balfour Four-Power-Control in Germany 1945-6 (Oxford 1956) and Propaganda in War 1939-45 (London 1979). Sir Robert Birley's talk in A. Hearnden (ed.) The British in Germany, and M.B. Sullivan Thresholds of Peace, have also been drawn upon.

Chapter Seven

WELT IM FILM: ANGLO-AMERICAN NEWSREEL POLICY

ROGER SMITHER

Welt im Film was a newsreel produced jointly by the British and American occupying powers for compulsory screening in the cinemas licensed to operate in their respective zones and sectors of Germany and Berlin; a variant of the newsreel was produced for distribution on a similar basis in Austria and Vienna. [1] The first issue of Welt im Film for Germany was released on 18 May 1945, just ten days after VE Day, and over 200 weekly issues followed before the ending of its compulsory (and monopoly) status at the creation of the Bundesrepublik in September 1949. The newsreel continued in production and distribution on a normal commercial basis under joint Anglo-American auspices until 1 June 1950, when the British withdrew, and under the Americans alone until 27 June 1952, when production ceased altogether with issue 369.

Planning for Welt im Film began in London well before the end of the war. A progress report to the Foreign Office, German Section on 15 February 1945 refers to the screening of 'a new set of dummy reels' and the test-recording of potential commentators. [2] The first few issues were compiled, again in London, by an OWI team working for the Psychological Warfare Division of SHAEF; formal participation by the Political Intelligence Department of the Foreign Office was agreed in June 1945. In August, arrangements were implemented for the making of release prints of the joint newsreel in Germany, and in the autumn of the same year the whole of the production function was transferred to the requisitioned Bavaria Filmkunst studios at Munich-Geiselgasteig in the American Zone. [3] Munich remained thereafter the base for production with, as joint editors, an American, Sam Winston, and a Briton, George Salmony, usually described as respectively managing editor and supervising editor. Meanwhile, supervision was transferred to the Information Services Control sections of the Office of Military Government and the control Commission as these bodies took shape.

Before the move to Munich, the newsreel echoed the harshest interpretations of occupation policy directives which 'enjoin a tone of great austerity in presenting material to Germans... They specify objectives of inculcating a sense of war and atrocity guilt into the German people'. [4] The attitudes of non-fraternisation and collective guilt dominated: the commentary, which was obviously the translation of an English text rather than an idiomatic German composition, lectured rather than informed and most certainly did not entertain, while the images stressed German defeat and allied power and, most controversially, actually showed the execution of 'spies and saboteurs'. [5] German stories for the newsreel were derived from the work of cameramen of the British Army Film and Photographic Unit and the American Army Pictorial Service. International stories were obtained from the British Newsreel Association and its American equivalent, apparently in rather grudging response to appeals to their patriotism, and in the early issues such stories were impressive neither for their topicality nor their pictorial quality. [6]

From these severe beginnings, Welt im Film could only improve. The first element corrected was the attitude to German guilt. Scenes of executions were dropped (the last was in issue 10) in response to the predictably negative audience reaction. 'It had a terrible effect on the spectators. They did not see the crime the spies committed. They only saw Germans shot.' This was the reported reaction of one German civilian, while 'execution scenes would not have been portrayed even in Nazi Germany' was a reaction from prisoner of war camps in Britain. [7] The emphasis of the coverage of this topic in the newsreels was switched to the victims of war crimes and the due process of proceedings against perpetrators. The same analysis of prisoner of war reactions also reported on the good effect of stories honestly reporting the difficulties of the war in the Pacific: two camps were said to have been impressed by coverage of American landings in Okinawa 'because accidents to aircraft of the US Fleet Air Arm [sic] were not concealed as would have been the case in a German film'. The fact that the people responsible for information control needed to learn empirically that a German audience like any other could be more favourably moved by appeals to its reason than by outright intimidation demonstrates the unflattering opinion the re-educators initially had of those to be re-educated.

The appearance of the newsreel also improved after the move to Munich. It was acknowledged that camera crews from service film units (which were in any case being run down) were not the ideal sources for news stories aimed at the citizens of an occupied country, and moves were initiated to recruit local staff. [8] In time, Welt im Film was to have news desks, in addition to those at the headquarter sites of Munich, Hamburg and Berlin, based in Cologne, Dusseldorf, Essen, Frankfurt, Nuremburg and Stuttgart and (for Austrian stories) in Linz, Salzburg and Vienna. [9] Foreign stories were acquired more rapidly and reproduced in better quality. With attention also paid to the improvement of the commentary, titles, music and so on, Welt im Film acquired the framework of a recognisable newsreel. The contents also became closer to the standard product with the gradual inclusion of stories that were not wholly related to the major themes of defeat, retribution and postwar planning – first on the international scene (an aeroplane crash into the Empire State Building and an athletics meeting in London, both carried in issue 16, released 31 August 1945) and then inside Germany (football from Hamburg in issue 22, released 12 October 1945).

Financial responsibility for Welt im Film was established as an equal division of costs, and of any resulting profits, between the two participating allies. Expenditure involved the payment of staff, the purchase of equipment and the acquisition of rawstock. [10] This last was the chief problem, as the major German source was in the Russian zone and sources outside Germany were not very forthcoming. Even the British Board of Trade, approached for rawstock for use in the British zone, was to say 'that they prefer the limited quantity available for export to be sent to markets where they expect a long term goodwill'. [11] These difficulties affected both the length of the newsreel produced and the number of copies of each issue that could be printed.

The impression so far offered of a steady development or evolution of Welt im Film is more than a little misleading. There were several uncertainties about the nature of allied news film in the nine months following VE Day, beginning with the question of the length, frequency and number of news film releases to be made for the Germans. In April 1945, the US Office of War Information was giving consideration to the preparation of a weekly four reel (or even one hour) compilation of news, documentary and propaganda, although Welt im Film actually appeared from May as two reel (twenty minute) weekly issues. In July an expansion to three reels 'to provide more scope for handling allied information policies in this medium' was discussed, and in August mention was still being made of news compilations 'aside from the newsreel coverage'. [12] These proposals represented an idealist approach to news film usage: there were reflections of a harsher reality as well. In September-October it was variously suggested that the newsreel be reduced either to fortnightly issues or to a single reel [13], the motivation this time being strictly practical considerations such as the availability of rawstock and the frequency with which cinema operators were managing to change their programmes. Inevitably the realists won. From February 1946, the newsreel was reduced to single reel (ten minute) issues, though continuing as a weekly release.

More fundamental than the topics of size and frequency was the question of whether Welt im Film had a secure future at all. Although routine operating procedures had been pragmatically evolved as described in the first nine months, it was still possible to note as late as February 1946 that 'it has developed that there is no written agreement between the British and the Americans regarding the joint newsreel'. [14] Beyond the standard difficulties in agreeing anything involving commitment to future expenditure in two different bureaucratic environments, especially when responsibilities were moving between individuals and offices, the chief reason for the delay in formalising arrangements for Welt im Film was the official hope that the Anglo-American newsreel was a temporary expedient. Two possible alternatives were considered. It was either to be replaced (once a suitable agreement could be worked out) by a quadripartite newsreel covering the whole of Germany, or, in keeping with the official allied policy, which was particularly strongly endorsed by the Americans, it was to give way to a licensed German operation. In either case, agreement on an Anglo-American Welt im Film was scarcely a priority, and indeed the formal establishment of the Anglo-American official newsreel might threaten the long-term goal. [15]

The two alternatives were both involved in a dispute within the US Military Government in late 1945. General Clay (Deputy Military Governor, and firmly committed to the rapid ending of 'overt' American activity in favour of licensed German operations) took the opportunity offered by the winding-down of OWI to order the immediate dissolution of the joint Anglo-American newsreel. This order was opposed by the staff of Brigadier General McClure (Chief of the Information Control Division). In arguing against Clay's order (and against even letting the British get to hear of it), McClure's staff concentrated on the issues of inter-allied relations. They claimed that premature dissolution of Welt im Film might alienate the British to the point where they would not co-operate in quadripartite negotiations, which, they claimed, were currently proceeding with encouraging signs of imminent success; they also joined this comparatively idealistic argument to the more materialistic one of the economy of scale in producing a joint newsreel for two zones rather than separate newsreels in each and to the fact that Welt im Film was a successfully established enterprise. These arguments carried the day, although where the British were concerned McClure's staff were being unnecessarily cautious: whether or not they heard of Clay's specific order, the British were aware of a question-mark over the future of Welt im Film and had already been taking precautionary steps. [16] Official hopes for a four-power newsreel may account for the prominence, and the wording, with which the US Information Control Division reported that 'during December [1945] "Welt im Film" included shots taken by British, Russian and French, as well as by American newsreel photographers'. [17] Such hopes cannot, however, realistically have survived the replacement of the stop-gap Russian zone newsreel Neues vom Tage by Der Augenzeuge in February 1946.

As for the second alternative to continuing Welt im Film, there would have been many difficulties in determining who should take over the task of newsreel production if Military Government let it go. American and British film companies had their eyes on the Central European market, but official occupation policy wished to prevent foreign domination of German markets and favoured the licensing of 'clean' Germans for the establishment of post-war information media in Germany. [18] Official policy was in addition set against the possible re-emergence of anything like the Third Reich's propaganda ministry: newspapers and radio stations were licensed for local rather than national operation. There was no easy application of this policy for newsreel activities. Nazi control of the film industry had been such that 'clean' Germans were thought to be in short supply: 'The screening of film people was a long and difficult task, since the industry had been completely dominated by the Third Reich...Military Government policy was more concerned with laying a sound basis for a democratic film industry than with rushing production.' [19] Besides the issue of political cleanliness, the economics of newsreel operation were giving even the two allies problems. All in all, the preservation of Welt im Film presented the easiest solution. Neither its closure nor the removal of its obligatory status and the licensing of competitors was considered seriously during the following three years.

A Basic Agreement on Welt im Film was finally concluded by the British and the Americans in the first half of 1946: although even the version dated 4 March 1947 [20] was referred to as a draft and continued to pay lip-service to the goal of a quadripartite newsreel, Welt im Film was firmly established on a two-power basis. A Joint Newsreel Control Board was established to oversee the work of the joint editorial staff in Munich, and a conference was held in Munich on 21/22 June 1946, in the words of a report from the (British) Information Services Directorate, 'in order to tighten up the make-up of the newsreel...The conference was most satisfactory and a complete set of directives, based on the original contract, were formulated.' [21] These directives were relayed to newsreel staff in the shape of the following instructions from Munich:

Directives to Outpost Assignment Desks
1.   The object of the Joint US-British Newsreel operation, 'Welt im Film', is '...to contribute to the enlightenment of Germans and Austrians by presenting news in pictures from throughout the world, including the four zones of occupation in Germany, and from Austria.'
2.   The following excerpts from the basic agreement will indicate the channels into which we are to direct our efforts:
3.   'In pictures from occupied countries the aim should be to assist the Control authorities and to show reconstruction and restoration, particularly through the efforts of the local population.'
4.   'The object of the newsreel is to keep the German people informed of those current events which are likely to have a bearing on their lives. To stimulate interest, the reel must also have entertainment value, but this is definitely secondary in importance.'
5.   'Humour and documentary items, which cannot be classed strictly as news, may be included when they contribute directly to the object of establishing a peaceful, tolerant and democratic Germany.'
6.   'Deprivation suffered....in consequence of the war should be emphasized.'
7.   'Items illustrating military pomp and display, or celebrating the Allied victory over the Germans, shall be

included only when they are of first-class news value, and emphasis on them should be avoided.'
8.   'A section of the newsreel shall....be devoted to sports items....' ....
11.   If at any time a question of policy arises in connection with the shooting of a news story, please get in touch with the Managing Editor. [22]

These instructions are quoted at length partly because of the degree to which they show the sophistication, or at least normalisation, of Welt im Film compared with its early issues, but principally because they represent virtually the total extent of intervention by higher authority in the preparation of the newsreel by its production team. The files available for study contain practically no evidence of significant intervention from the Joint Newsreel Control Board or from other agencies in what went on in Munich except in connection with treatment of the developing Cold War - a topic considered below. Apart from occasional complaints about the balance of British and American stories, commonly from the British, and some post-release critiques of individual newsreel stories which, like the complaints, cease about mid-1946, the most significant instances of intervention are some requests to the newsreel to cover the world food shortage, with one British official rather testily remarking 'there is no harm in letting the Germans see that we have to queue too'. [23]
As well as being spared significant interference from allied authority, the production team was also shielded from direct intervention by Germans. As late as January 1948, the Joint Newsreel Control Board discussed an approach on this subject from the British Zonal Advisory Council and agreed that 'it would be impossible to take advice on the actual compilation of the reel', offering only to allow 'any representative group of Germans' to comment on the newsreel, make general observations on policy, and recommend stories for coverage. [24] The other significant decision taken by the JNCB at about this time was the addition of a third form of distribution to the extant pattern of weekly issues for Germany and Austria. In October 1947, 'it was agreed to issue a junior version of the newsreel...for schools and other non-theatrical showing'; two specimen issues were seen and approved by the January meeting, and it was agreed to continue monthly with the option of up to three supplementaries per year'. [25]
More important developments than the addition of a new form of distribution came up for discussion in 1947. For its first two years, the newsreel had handled cautiously or ignored stories that did not fit in with the positive world-picture it was directed to present, using to the full the channel of escape offered by the directive on 'humour and documentary items' to replace contentious topics. Chief among the subjects to which reference was not made was, of course, any hint of a rift between the victorious allies. The classic encapsulation of Welt im Film's approach to such issues was the coverage given in issue 44 to Winston Churchill's 'Iron Curtain'

speech at Fulton, Missouri. The occasion was reported, but the commentary described the speech only in the words 'Churchill acknowledges bestowal of the degree in his own humorous manner and then addresses the assembly of 3,000 in a half-hour speech'. Because the Basic Agreement on Welt im Film reflected its status as an allied operation, this policy of silence was not formally stated in the newsreel directives, as it was, for example, in the instructions to German licensees in the information services (the American wording expressly prohibited 'Dissemination of any type of news, information or editorial which constitutes a malicious attack upon policies or personnel of Military Government, aims to disrupt unity among the Allies, or seeks to evoke the distrust and hostility of the German people against any Occupying Power'). For Welt im Film operatives, this constraint was contained only by implication in section 3 of the Agreement, which stated 'In pictures from Allied countries the aim should be to show the Allied purpose, standards and ways of life'. [26] During this first period there was no question but that the impression of allied unity was to be maintained. By mid-1947, however, the interpretation was beginning to change.

The first cautious gloss on section 3 was made at the Joint Newsreel Control Board's meeting with its editors on 23 July 1947 when 'It was agreed that the newsreel editors should hereafter deal frankly with political and other provocative issues provided that due care would be taken to present the respective viewpoints objectively and fairly... In general the JNCB undertook to serve as a shield for the editors so long as they would continue to treat every subject as news and thus to prevent the newsreel from becoming an obvious instrument of propaganda, as were the newsreels in Nazi days'. [27] This directive was followed within a month by the first criticism of the USSR voiced on Welt im Film, when a story in issue 117 (released 22 August 1947) on prisoners of war returning from Russia made much of their poor physical condition. In October, the stakes were raised by an American announcement. 'Because of the harsh and baseless attacks against the United States, its policies, and its principles made by Soviet-sponsored and licensed information media in Germany, US Military Government on 28 October began an educational and informational program to explain to the German people the basic concepts of democracy as opposed to the communistic system'. [28] The British were initially reluctant to follow this American lead, and George Salmony was privately informed of 'instructions from the highest quarter that the line of British controlled sources of information in Germany was not to be changed in this regard, that is, we are not to engage in anti-communistic warfare...the status quo prevails'. [29] This reservation was honoured in Welt im Film, which covered most of the build-up to the Berlin crisis in a spirit close to the July 1947 decision. Once the airlift had started, however, the newsreel became firmly a mouthpiece of the western side.

Reports on the blockade were compiled within Berlin itself by the documentary film unit established by the American Military Government in July 1947. [30] These complete compilations were flown out of Berlin and most of them were incorporated more or less unchanged into the general issues of Welt im Film. There was thus a degree of back-door entry of American attitudes into the joint newsreel, but there was in any case no question of British reluctance to countenance direct anti-Soviet statements after the east-west rift became overt. Once taken, the decision to use the newsreel on the side of the 'democratic' German ex-enemy against the Russian ex-ally and 'his' Germans was not rescinded, and Welt im Film lost the appearance of political innocence or ignorance that had replaced the strict lecturing tone of the early issues. Political discretion was not lost completely - coverage of Soviet actions was not matched by equal coverage of the Saar question which involved the French, whose alliance of course continued, or of the details of some of the politicial divisions, other than those echoing Cold War developments, within the emergent Federal Republic of Germany. These last elements of control, however, were not especially conspicuous, and with the presence of at least some relevant political coverage the last obvious distinction between Welt im Film and a normal newsreel faded.

With this change of complexion, and with the way smoothed by generous reductions in rental charges in June 1949 [31], it is no surprise that Welt im Film weathered the transition to non-compulsory, non-monopoly commercial operations in September 1949. It continued to receive subsidies from the allied governments: as late as 1951, an enthusiastic American account was still having to predict rather than report the newsreel's self-sufficiency. (It was presumably largely for this reason that the British withdrew from the joint newsreel in 1950.) The subsidies no doubt helped, but Welt im Film retained a very creditable market share well into its 'commercial' life: the same American account noted that 'despite competition from the Fox Newsreel and the German production "Die Neue Deutsche Wochenschau"... "Welt im Film" is still very popular and is being purchased by 63 percent of the theaters in Germany'. [32]

Is it possible to evaluate the effectiveness of Welt im Film over the four years of its existence as an organ of information policy for the Anglo-American occupation government? The question breaks down into two parts: what were the expectations of the British and American occupying powers in creating and maintaining this obligatory component in the cinema programmes of the occupied, and how did the German audience react to its presence?

The staff of the American Information Control Division and the British Public Relations and Information Services Control Group do not appear to have attached much importance to film in general or to Welt im Film specifically. There are occasional expressions of belief in the film medium, such as the American announcement in the Military Governor's report for July 1947 'Because of their value in the reorientation and the reeducation of the German people, Military Government has established in Berlin a new documentary Film Unit as a special producing agency for the purpose of expediting and increasing the efficiency of documentary film production' [33], but a more realistic indication of the importance attached by the Americans to film may be read into the normal ordering of the section of such reports covering information services, typically placing Motion Pictures at the end of the section, after General, Press, Publications, Radio, and Information Centres and Exhibitions. In the words of an official historian, 'higher priority was given to other fields such as the press and education'. [34] The British shared this view. A policy paper on Information Control in the British Zone of Germany drafted in June 1945 says ' Of first importance among the media of information is the Press... Next in importance is the Radio', and the head of the PR/ISC Group wrote in February 1946 'It is considered that the written word has more influence on the German mind than any other medium'. [35]

Compared with these media, where subtle arguments could be developed at length or rapid response made to sudden developments, the newsreel could only react rather belatedly and in a circumscribed and cumbersome framework to stories which its staff would frequently themselves have picked up only through those other media. [36] Film production and distribution in the western zones of post-war Germany were moreover beset with logistical problems. Perhaps some of the preference for press and radio could even be traced to a feeling that if the media glories of the allies in the war just over had been the BBC and a free press, the newsreel had been the Nazis' equivalent. Whatever the reason, film is repeatedly ignored, or given only the most cursory of mentions, in both contemporary reports on Information Services activities [37] and retrospective memoirs and histories of the period. [38] The conclusion is unavoidable that if the files reveal little evidence of high-level policy direction to Welt im Film it is primarily because Welt im Film was not considered a very important policy mouthpiece. The provision of a newsreel for the occupied Germans was treated as an obligation, not as a challenge or an opportunity.

Whatever its rating by those responsible for it - and if they did not treat it as the flagship of the information fleet, neither did they scuttle it - Welt im Film was the newsreel voice of the British and Americans throughout this period, and was seen as such by the occupied Germans. Initially, it must be assumed, the audience would have been small, at least in the American Zone. US occupation policy called for the immediate closure of all cinemas, and only began to permit their re-opening in July 1945. Even then, the number of cinemas open increased slowly: 'ICD's reluctance to sponsor entertainment for the Germans persisted longer with regard to films than to any other medium. ICD slowed the opening of movie houses through the summer of 1945...The gradual approach would probably have persisted longer than it did if the advent of winter had not intensified the need to take the Germans' minds off the hardships of cold weather and to keep the young people off the street.' [39] By mid-February 1946, the US Zone was reported to have 351 cinemas open while the British Zone had had 767 as early as November 1945. [40] By Welt im Film's second anniversary in May 1947, however, 2000 cinemas were open in the British and American Zones combined. By the time of issue 200 of the newsreel, in April 1949, it was estimated that the weekly audience was ten to fifteen million. [41] The existence of a cinema was of course necessary to screen a newsreel, but the newsreel would not in itself guarantee an audience. Attractive features were the main draw, and they were not always easy to come by, again especially in the US Zone. In the Military Governor's report for October 1945, Information Control observed that 'many motion picture theatres had little to offer during their first few weeks except out-dated newsreels and shorts' and as late as October 1947, the Americans had only passed for release sixty pre-occupation German films, although these were what the audience most wanted. [42] This tardiness is only explicable in terms of priorities, not perception - in fact in the very first Monthly Report of the US Military Governor covering July 1945, Information Control clearly described the appetite of the Germans for appropriate cultural or media nourishment:

> The Germans...display an avid desire to resume their cultural activities...and to obtain newspapers and books to fill the gap of factual knowledge which existed during the Nazi regime. These desires are evident from the reaction to the resumption of musical concerts and cinemas and to the sale of newspapers. In every case the output is completely absorbed. Care must be exercised, however, to refrain from obvious propaganda....The Germans have been filled to overflowing with propaganda, and will reject in disgust any output which tastes even faintly of an attempt to propagandize....To accomplish the objectives of re-education by reconciling this interest with the ability to recognize propaganda presents a problem of greatest delicacy. [43]

As to how audiences would react to the newsreel, reports and opinions differed. Conceivably, Welt im Film would drive the audience out, invoking the ability to recognise and the disgust felt at propaganda mentioned in the paragraph just quoted. Thus in May 1946 there were reports

> From all parts of the British and US zones...of demonstrations by cinema audiences against such scenes as the pictorial report of the Nuremberg trials, the removal of Nazi emblems from German buildings or German generals in captivity. There are reports from a number of towns in both these zones that people are wont to leave the cinema after the main feature film when the newsreel is shown at the end of the programme. The French newsreel is also reported to have been the subject for similar demonstrations. [44]

(The newsreels were not alone in generating this hostility, however, as war scenes in feature films were also said to be 'thoroughly disliked'. Neither was the hostility confined to the audience: Hanus Burger recalls an incident suggesting that at least one newsreel story was sabotaged by Welt im Film's German personnel on the grounds that 'the thing to do was to forget the [concentration] camps as quickly as possible'. [45]) If not driven out, the audience might be simply baffled by the newsreel, like the one described by Gladwin Hill. [46] A 'forbearing, bewildered silence' was of course open to another interpretation, as in the remark by the US Chief of Film Production William Patterson that 'I have been impressed by the almost rapt attention given to newsreels in the various theaters I have attended'. [47] Finally, a more positive reaction does seem to have been possible, especially once the crassness of the early issues was left behind: one thing a Goebbels newsreel had not provided was a view of the outside world, and some observers do suggest that the newsreels were indeed a major incentive for German cinemagoers. [48]

Another factor affecting the likely response of the audience was the topicality of the newsreel seen. Occasional mention has been made in this paper of the logistical problems attendant on the production of Welt im Film, and a report quoted from as early as October 1945 referring to 'out-dated newsreels'. To understand what these problems could entail at their worst, it is necessary only to read a cable sent to the Chief of the Film Section OMGUS ICD from the office of the Military Governor of Bavaria on 24 March 1948:

> This is to call attention to the fact that for servicing 549 cinemas in Bavaria the week of 19th March 1948 there are only 33 prints of the newsreel Welt im Film available. This means that many prints of Welt im Film are playing 18 weeks....Please note that Welt im Film has lost its timely value and that according to many cinema operators the public does not come into the cinema until after Welt im Film has played because the stories shown are so much outdated.

A letter from one of the cinema operators referred to also survives to make the same point in more picturesque fashion: 'Unser Publikum...schlaegt einen weiten Bogen vor einer so unaktuellen Wochenschau. Wenn fuer unser Theater die Wochenschau vor dem Hauptfilm trifft, kommen die Leute 20 Minuten zu spaet, um nicht ihren Bart rauschen zu hoeren; wenn wir die Wochenschau nach dem Hauptfilm spielen, verlaesst alles fluchtartig unser Theater. Wir koennen es ihnen nicht verdenken: wer hat am Aschermittwoch noch Appetit auf Weihnachtsstimmung?' [Our public gives a wide berth to so un-topical a newsreel. If the newsreel plays before the feature in our cinema, people arrive twenty minutes late, so that they do not have to listen to their beards rustling; if we run the newsreel after the feature, they all leave our cinema in a rush. We cannot blame them: on Ash Wednesday, who still has a taste for Christmas fare?] [49] It is against this background that a plan to reduce play-off time to a maximum of nine weeks was an achievement worth reporting.

161

[50] Logistics could mean a more specific problem in the city of Berlin where the blockade left the western sectors very short of electric power, necessitating strict quotas and many blackouts. 'Military Government', reported the American Governor, 'has warned a number of motion picture house operators against their practice of projecting the feature picture and "Welt im Film" at twice normal speed in an effort to show an entire programme.' [51]

The only known efforts by the Allied Military Government to evaluate the penetration of the German audience by Welt im Film are found in the OMGUS opinion surveys. [52] In the first directly relevant survey, conducted between November 1945 and February 1946, 3687 Germans in the American zone were questioned on their motion picture attendance and attitudes; the replies of the 985 questioned in February are analysed in most detail. 23% of that sample had been to the movies since the beginning of the occupation; 26% had not been because there were no movies in their town, while 33% had not been because they had no time or no interest. (That some at least of them might have found that time or interest given different programmes is suggested by the finding that 55% of the non-moviegoers stated they would like to see an old German film again.) 18% of the sample (i.e. three quarters of the moviegoers) had seen Welt im Film; 11% (two thirds of those who had seen it) said they thought it good, most of them because it brought in news from the outside.

Despite the increase in the number of cinemas opened during the following two years, the picture is not very much altered in a second survey, carried out in February 1948, when 3700 adults in the parts of Germany administered by the USA were questioned. On this occasion, 28% of the sample went to the movies at least once a month. This overall figure includes the much higher figures of 40% for Bremen and 54% for Berlin, suggesting that the rural attendance was much lower. (A survey in Vienna in January 1947 found a comparably high urban ratio, 57% of a sample of 1499 saying they went to the movies.) Social analysis of the German sample provided interesting food for thought for those inclined to share the opinion of a US official historian that film is 'the information medium which has the greatest impact on the less well educated and more impressionable elements of the German population'. [53] Looking at the audience breakdown suggested by the survey, the same historian (though in a different publication) noted

> The regular German movie audience of commercial theaters is drawn largely from people of the higher socio-economic levels rather than those of lower status; well-educated people in contrast to the poorly educated; unmarried people rather than married, and childless married people rather than those who have children. Among the occupational groups, white collar workers are most likely to go to the movies while farmers are the least likely to go. The fact that the attendance of farmers

162

is much lower than urban dwellers is probably due to the lack of opportunity. [54]

The survey also described the audience as being largely young (56%). Most of the moviegoers - 88% - had seen Welt im Film. Of these, 65% were satisfied, 25% dissatisfied. The criticism of the latter group 'centred around the view that the newsreel tended to be superficial or frivolous, ignoring the serious aspects of life in Germany at that time'.

In considering these findings, it should not be forgotten who was asking the questions; on the other hand, it should also not be forgotten that Welt im Film would not have been the only newsreel in the 1940's or at any time open to charges of being 'superficial and frivolous'. In addition, some of the other OMGUS surveys suggest widespread apathy or cynicism about the news media generally at the time of the second survey. In January 1948, for example, only half the American zone population claimed to be regular newspaper readers (three quarters in Berlin), while over 40% claimed to be consistent non-listeners to radio. 49% of those questioned had no opinion on whether they were getting more accurate news coverage than during the war. Interestingly, however, a survey in November 1948 found that 59% of those questioned in the American zone felt that movies could strongly influence people's opinions. [55] Perhaps the Allied discrediting of propagandist uses of the media had had successes in unanticipated directions.

The body of evidence available on the reception of Welt im Film thus suggests that its potential use to allied information policy may have been underestimated by the makers of that policy. On the negative side, it is true that the logistical problems of film production in post-war Germany meant that the rural audience was not well served by the newsreel; either independent of that fact, or because of it, the statistics suggest a low penetration of the audience outside the major towns by Welt im Film. Within the towns, however, the audience was far from negligible and, moreover, although there were appreciable minorities hostile to the tone of the early issues and resentful of the superficiality (or out-of-date appearance) of the later ones, there is evidence to suggest widespread acceptance and occasional enthusiasm for the newsreel. This acceptance or enthusiasm was usually attributed to the extent to which Welt im Film lived up to the promise implied in its title and offered the cinema audience glimpses of the wider world, and this fact in turn suggests a possible opportunity for an interested information policy to explore, had the motivation been there. Since it does not seem to have been present, Welt im Film remained on the periphery of allied re-education policy. The reels that survive in the world's archives may be seen by today's students as competently made reflections of that policy rather than as valued instruments of its implementation.

NOTES

This paper draws on three principal sources of information, and to prevent unnecessary repetition they are hereafter referred to in these notes in abbreviated form. They are:

(A) papers from the Foreign Office series in the British Public Record Office, hereafter referred to as FO;

(B) papers from two files in US National Archives Record Group 260, OMGUS ISD MPB, 'Newsreel General' and 'Film - newsreels OWI & PID' which were microfilmed for the Imperial War Museum by the National Archives during 1982 and studied by me in this form: they are hereafter referred to as NA RG 260/1 and NA RG 260/2 respectively;

(C) information in either the Monthly Reports of the Military Governor for the US Zone or in the supplementary Information Control reports also published by OMGUS in conjunction with the main reports: they are hereafter referred to as 'US Monthly Report' and 'Information Control/US Monthly Report' respectively. The month given is the month covered by the report; publication was always during the month following.

All other sources are fully cited.

*

1. The starting point for this paper was my work in the early 1970s on the cataloguing of the Imperial War Museum's holding of Welt im Film material, published by the Museum in 1981 as Microfiche Film Catalogue No. 1: Welt im Film. I should like to acknowledge the help given to me by the Museum and by Kay Gladstone and my other colleagues both in that original work and in its continuation.

2. FO939/352, 1944-45 POWs: films. 'Progress report, situation as at 15 February 1945.'

3. NA RG 260/2. Taylor to McClure 'German Newsreel' 2 June 1945; Taylor to Executive Office 'Priority for Courier of Newsreels' 27 July 1945; Patterson to McLachlan 19 September 1945.

4. Information Control/US Monthly Report No. 1 (July 1945), p.2.

5. As presented at the Conference, a considerably abridged version of this paper was accompanied by screenings of two pieces of Welt im Film material. The first was an issue of the newsreel (No. 7, released 29 June 1945) selected to illustrate the description in this paragraph. An idea of the complexion of the issue screened may be obtained from the translation of the commentary included in the appendix.

6. FO 936/148, Information Services Directorate: organisation. Memorandum from Deputy Director, Information Services 2 August 1948.

The minutes of the meetings of the Council of the Newsreel Association of Great Britain and Ireland make no direct reference to the creation of Welt im Film but retrospectively confirm the existence of an arrangement - and of the Association's misgivings - both in 1948 (Minute 2474 etc.) when the Association discussed the supply of Welt im Film stories by the Central Office of Information to BBC television news and in 1949 (Minute 2950 etc.) when the Association considered competing with the commercial Welt im Film. The newsreel for Germany was presumably covered by earlier agreements on the supply of newsreels for liberated territories and of newsreel material for Government films. Typical of the Association's discussions of such arrangements is the description given by Sir Gordon Craig of British Movietone News of the dual motivation of the newsreel companies: 'firstly, the overwhelming desire of all the companies to pull their weight in the national interest and, secondly, to secure their business against outside parties' (Meeting of the Council of the Association 14 September 1943).

NA RG 260/1 contains correspondence on the supply of American newsreel material as well as approaches from Welt im Film proposing exchanges of material with newsreels in European countries.

7. Julian Bach, Jr America's Germany (New York, 1946), pp. 232-233; FO 939/234 Films: general policy. Seeds to Hitch 'P/W reactions to summer film programme' 27 October 1945.

8. NA RG 260/2. Montague to Taylor 7 August 1945.

9. Information Control/US Monthly Report No. 23 (April–May 1947), p. 19.

10. FO 936/152, PID: German and Austrian Division: Part I. Earle 'Future of the German/Austrian Division' 31 January 1946. An illustration of the pragmatic workings of this arrangement is given (from the American side) in suggestions made about finance in a letter from Lefebre to Goodman 28 December 1945 (NA RG 260/2).d

11. FO 943/549, 1945-48 Film (Rawstock). Selwyn to Ripman (Doc 8A).

12. NA RG 260/2. Montague to Patterson 'Regarding the German news operation' 7 April 1945; Patterson to Paley and Patterson to Taylor 13 July 1945; Lefebre to Taylor 23 July 1945; Montague to Taylor 7 August 1945.

13. NA RG 260/2. Murphy to McClure 4 September 1945 (and manuscript annotations); Schwartz to Roemheld 'Suggestion of Producing a One-Reel Newsreel' 3 October 1945; Patterson to Roemheld 'One-Reel Neewsreel' 20 October 1945.

14. NA RG 260/1. 'Report of a meeting regarding joint newsreel financial accounting held on 7 February 1946.'

15. NA RG 260/2. Patterson to McLachlan 'German Newsreel Operation' 1 August 1945. This draft agreement reflects both the American commitment to licensed newsreels and their quadripartite aspirations; the former disappears from the correspondence in about February 1946.

16. NA RG 260/2. Patterson to Murphy 'Lt. Gen. Clay's order to dissolve the joint Anglo-American newsreel immediately' 6

November 1945; FO 936/124, Information Services Control Branch (PR/ISC Group). 'Information Services in Germany, Meeting at the Treasury on 25 September 1945'. These minutes indicate that the British were aware of the possibility of difficulties following the closure of OWI at the end of the year and were making contingency plans for a newsreel for their zone only.

17. Information Control/US Monthly Report No. 6 (December 1945), p. 1.

18. FO 939/391, Manual for control of German information services. See also Albert Norman Our German policy: propaganda and culture (New York 1951) for a personal evaluation by an ex-member of ICD USF(ET) (later OMG (US)).

19. Henry P. Pilgert Press, Radio and Film in West Germany 1945-1953 (Historical Division... Office of the US High Commissioner for Germany, 1953), p. 32.

20. FO 946/73, 1947-48 Joint Newsreel Control Board. 'Basic Agreement between WDSCA and Control Office ' 4 March 1947.

21. FO 946/22, British Information Services in Germany. 'Information Services monthly report' June 1946.

22. NA RG 260/1. 'Operating Instructions WELT IM FILM assignment desks' (Summer 1946).

23. FO 946/73. Crawford to Brown 23 June 1947.
See NA RG 260/1, (cable) Keating to ICD Newsreel 20 May 1947. The American files also contain representative story criticisms, such as the question of whether a Norwegian army march past should have been omitted on the grounds that the Norwegian parade step resembled the goosestep.

24. FO 946/73. Minutes of JNCB meeting 22/23 January 1948.

25. Monthly Report of the Control Commission for Germany (British Element) Vol. 2 No. 10 (HQ CCG(BE), October 1947), p. 50; FO 946/73. (loc. cit.) reports the specimen issues and the continuation agreement.

26. FO 946/73. 'Basic Agreement...'. The US Instruction quoted is 'Responsibility of German Licensees: Policy Instruction No. 3 to All Licensees in German Information Services' Section 2(c) (September 30 1946), reproduced in Germany 1947-1949: the story in documents (US Department of State, 1950), pp. 596-598.

27. FO 946/73. Minutes of JNCB meeting 21/22 July 1947.

28. US Monthly Report No. 28 (October 1947), p. 28.

29. FO 946/73. Elton to Salmony 10 November 1947.

30. NA RG 260/1. 'Informal Newsreel meeting' 23 July 1948. One of the Berlin compilations provided the second piece of Welt im Film material screened at the Conference. The commentary is transcribed in the appendix.

31. US Monthly Report No. 48 (June 1949), p. 46.

32. Henry P. Pilgert The History of the Development of Information Services through Information Centers and Documentary Films (Historical Division... Office of the US High Commissioner for Germany, 1951), p. 70.

33. US Monthly Report No. 25 (July 1947), p. 31.

34. Pilgert 1953 (op. cit.), p. 32.

35. FO 945/905, 1945 Information Services Control: Germany and Austria. This quotation is from paragraphs 6 and 7 of the paper; film is reached in paragraph 11.
FO 946/8, Overall policy: Films, Theatres, Books. Bishop to P.M. Balfour 20 February 1946.
36. The operating instructions to Welt im Film assignment desks (see note 22) list as news sources in the following order '1. German, American and English newspapers; 2. DANA [the news agency]; 3. Public Relations Offices; 4. Contact - reporters; 5. Radio check: local and BBC; 6. Military Government Reports'.
37. For example FO 371/55514/C 9008, Overhaul of our information services in Germany (1946) or FO 936/195, Organisation of German Information Department (1948).
38. As noted in chapter 9 (following fn 41) 'one looks in vain... for any reference, even in passing, to Todesmühlen or Welt im Film in Lucius Clay's Decision in Germany, or the thorough surveys of American occupation policy by Peterson, Gimbel and Tent'.
39. Earl F. Ziemke The US Army in the occupation of Germany 1944-1946 (Washington DC, 1975), p. 376.
40. FO 939/234, Films, general policy, 'The film situation in all the zones of Germany' May 1946.
41. Information Control/US Monthly Report No. 23 (April-May 1947), p. 16; Monthly Report of the Control Commission for Germany (British Element) Vol.4 No. 4 (HQ CCG(BE), April 1949), p. 35.
42. Information Control/US Monthly Report No. 4 (October 1945), p. 1; US Monthly Report No. 28 (October 1947), p. 29.
43. Information Control/US Monthly Report No. 1 (July 1945), p.2.
44. FO 939/234, (loc. cit.)
45. Hanus Burger to Imperial War Museum 29 July 1983. Burger, then in Munich for the final editing of Todesmühlen (as described in his autobiography Der Frühling war es wert: Erinnerungen (Munich 1977), had arranged the filming in October 1945 of a story for Welt im Film about concentration camp orphans in the care of monks at a monastery in Indersdorf. The German cameraman voiced the opinion quoted during the drive to the monastery. The exposed film was subsequently damaged and rendered unusable by sand in the developing machinery.
46. See chapter 9 fn. 37.
47. NA RG 260/2. Patterson to Roemheld 'One-Reel Newsreel' 20 October 1945.
48. For example, Norman (op.cit.), p. 66 - 'audiences not infrequently going to the movies just to see news' - or Harold Zink The United States in Germany 1944-55 (Princeton NJ, 1957), p. 243 - Welt im Film 'enjoyed considerable popularity among the German moviegoers because of its good technical and interest-holding qualities'. A more sceptical note is struck in Helmut Regel 'Der Film als Instrument allierter Besatzungspolitik in Westdeutschland' in Deutschland in Trümmern: Filmdokumente der Jahre 1945-1949 (Oberhausen, 1976) pp. 44-47 and 49-50.

49. NA RG 260/1. Cable as described; Witter to Allgemeiner Filmverleih 19 February 1948.

50. Monthly Report of the Control Commission for Germany (British Element) Vol. 3 No. 7 (HQ CCG (BE), July 1948), p. 19.

51. US Monthly Report No. 38 (August 1948), p. 31.

52. Anna J. Merritt and Richard L. Merritt Public opinion in occupied Germany: the OMGUS surveys 1945-1949 (Chicago 1970), Report No. 20 (pp. 100-101), Report No. 39 (pp. 128-129) and Report No. 116 (pp. 232-233).

53. Pilgert 1953 (op. cit.), p. 86.

54. Pilgert 1951 (op. cit.), p. 73.

55. Merritt and Merritt (op. cit.) Report No. 100 (p. 211) and Report No. 188 (p. 311).

Appendix

Two WELT IM FILM commentaries

1. Welt im Film Issue No. 7, 29 June 1945
(Translation of German commentary by Roger B.N. Smither and Kay G.T. Gladstone)

UPRISING IN PRAGUE
In the last days of the war, Prague, after six years of slavery, rose against its oppressor. This was not the revolt of a faction – it was the uprising of the embittered citizens of a nation. The struggle began in a city still under the control of SS troops. The Czechs captured the radio station, from where, calling repeatedly for assistance on the nations of the free world, they fought in the streets their desperate fight against the overwhelming adversary. The Czechs knew that the SS took no prisoners. They fought with the courage of desperation. They did not yet know that help was already on the way, that the Americans from the west and the Red Army from the east were approaching. The 9th of May dawned. The whole free world was celebrating Germany's surrender – Prague still lay in darkness. German soldiers were flushed out of cellars. As the battle began to turn in the Czechs' favour, some of the SS pulled back from the city and left others to their fate. They were taken prisoner. So were the traitors. On the 10th May, the first Russian armoured spearheads entered the city. The struggle of the freedom fighters was over. Prague was free. Six days later, an enormous crowd gathered at the station. They were greeting their President, Eduard Benes, who was returning home after seven years' exile. Czechoslovakia, which had been among the first nations to lose its freedom, was the last to win it back. Now she will take her place among the nations of Europe, and join, in freedom and peace, in the collective work upon which the world's hope rests – the building of a happier Europe.

STOLEN ARTWORKS DISCOVERED

In a mountain cave near Berchtesgaden, American troops discovered a collection of art treasures. This was where Goering stored his loot, sculptures and paintings stolen from European museums and private collections. Now, these treasures will be carefully packed, and will be returned under the direction of the allies to their rightful owners. This officer is an American art expert, entrusted with the checking of the collection. Here too, in Neuschwanstein, in Ludwig II's castle, Goering had secreted a matchless collection of art treasures. A coffer of jewellery of inestimable value, from a French private owner. A silver tureen, from the collection of the former director of a famous French museum. These are only a few of the 23,000 artworks that the American soldiers found here. The National Socialists took from the people they overran not just their peace, their freedom and their bread - they took from them also that which they loved and were most proud of: the works of their country's great men.

A PRISONER OF WAR COMES HOME

In the barracks square at Plauen, German prisoners of war are summoned for the last time to the administration building. One of them is Private Fritz Riedel. After thorough checking of his reliability, he is to be released from the Wehrmacht to work on the land. He is examined by British and German doctors. Everything is in order; the release paper is presented for signature. The German military insignia, now meaningless, are removed from his uniform. He is a free man - free from the duties of soldiering, and free to return to his family. From soldier Riedel to Fritz Riedel, whose important job it now is to help avert the danger of famine this year in Germany - a danger which Germany's irresponsible continuation of the war has brought so near.

AIRFIELDS FREED FROM FOG DANGER

Safe landings for allied aircraft even in thick fog have now become possible. Through this device, fuel oil is pumped through a special pipe system along the runway. When burning, the oil warms the air and causes the fog to disperse. The oil can be ignited within one second. This development was the invention of British engineers, and enabled allied bombers to continue their day-and-night attacks without interruption during the last winter of the war. It has a double purpose - the fog is dispersed, and the pilot returning from his mission can see the landing strip outlined in flames and so put down safely. In peacetime, this will make possible a safer air service - faster air traffic, not dependent on the weather, for passengers and freight.

MILITARY GOVERNMENT

Water supplies have received the first interim assistance from allied Military Government. From the banks of the Ruhr, water is pumped up to the bomb-damaged city of Essen. The inhabitants come to fetch water and carry it home in buckets. Because the Ruhr chlorine-treatment plants are still not working, as the result of considerable damage, the citizens are warned of the danger of infection. Every pail-full must be boiled before use. Meanwhile, repair of the water system is being carried out by civilian labour; slowly but purposefully, under the direction of the allies, order is made out of chaos. Water flows once more in the town.

In this classroom, Germans - under the direction of the Military Government - are learning to become responsible citizens again. They learn, for example, the tasks of traffic policemen. Conscious of his responsibility, he carries out his duty. This man is proud to become a useful member of the new Germany.

Hamburg: production of a newsheet in five languages, German, Italian, Dutch, French and Polish. Written by men and women of these different nationalities in the premises of the Hamburger Anzeiger, Victory Herald is published by the Military Government for the many thousands of people brought by the Nazis to Hamburg as slave labourers who will soon be returning to their homelands. The papers are packed and distributed in the camps where these people are living under the protection of the allies. After almost six years of darkness, they are learning to see the light of the world again.

INVESTIGATING COMMISSION FOR WAR CRIMES

In London, the conference of the United Nations on proceedings against war criminals opened. Delegates from sixteen countries took part. On the list of war criminals are nearly 3,000 Germans.

In Norway, Quisling fights for his life. Quisling, whose name has become universally known in the vocabulary of the free peoples of the world as an international synonym for 'traitor'. For Quisling, the long-awaited day of reckoning has arrived.

Near Brunswick, two German spies were tried before an allied military court. In February they were smuggled over the Ruhr in civilian clothes to collect information on the state of readiness of American troops. They were captured within 24 hours. The military court sentenced them as war criminals to death by firing squad. Soldiers of the American 9th Army carried out the sentence.

DRAMA OF AN AIRCRAFT CARRIER

In the endless expanse of the Pacific lies the theatre for one of the greatest actions of this war. An American fleet, including the aircraft carrier Franklin is locked in combat with swarms of Japanese aircraft. The Franklin was hit, and caught fire. Powder magazines began to explode. In the tumult of battle the wounded are rescued. A priest comforts the dying on deck. A destroyer comes alongside. It seemed no more could be done to save the Franklin. The sailors were exhausted. One after another they were brought to safety from the flames and twisted steel of the deck. A few of the crew stayed at their posts. But the Franklin did not sink. The flag is still flying. The listing ship is stabilised, and the bulkheads secured, and slowly, slowly, the Franklin and her remaining crew members began the difficult journey homewards. The dead were committed to the sea. In Pearl Harbour, temporary repairs were carried out. Then,

170

at the triumphant entry into the Panama Canal, at a ceremony on the sunny flight deck the medals were presented that had been won for heroism and selfless duty on the burning vessel. The first memory for these men is that of giving of their strength and heroism in the hour of need. The carrier Franklin and her crew return home from halfway round the world. The Franklin will be repaired, and then the ship that was abandoned as lost will be ready for new feats.

2. Welt im Film - die Welt blickt auf Berlin, June 1948
(This is a transcript of the English language version of this film, entitled Berlin - World Focal Point. Stories from this Berlin film unit compilation were carried in Issue No. 165 of the main newsreel).

It was a quiet Sunday in Berlin. The sun shone for the first time in days, and overhead as usual the planes were droning. Then came Monday, and many began their working week without work. Quiet chimneys dramatised the plight of industry in the western sectors as many factories fell victim to the Soviet-sponsored coal shortage. The Borsig plant in the French sector strove to sustain all West Berlin. To fully exploit its limited resources, allocations were set up which sometimes turned the working day into a working night. The latest word in coiffure now came very late for Berliners, and when electric power gave out altogether, there was always manpower. The Russians, concerned as always with the city's welfare, announced the dismissal of two high German railroad officials. Now, they implied, the Helmstedt-Berlin track would be repaired in no time. Then, a new tactic: only Soviet-written interzonal passes were valid. But Berlin could not be cut off from the rest of the world. All week, big planes brought big names into the city. From Australia came Prime Minister J.B. Chifley; after inspecting the air bridge operation at Gatow, he told Berliners 'Australia stands firmly behind the western allies'. After him, Mr Lewis Douglas, US Ambassador to Great Britain, here greeted by General Clay. Another visitor - Mr Arthur Henderson, British Secretary of State for Air. One thing was certain - these men did not come to Berlin to discuss the weather. Next day, Anthony Eden, Deputy-Leader of the Opposition in Parliament, attended a special reception at the British Information Centre. Seen arriving at the meeting are Berlin's acting Mayor, Louis Schroeder; Franz Neumann of the SPD; Kaiser and Landsberg of the CDU; and Brigadier Benson, British Deputy-Commandant for Berlin.

> [Eden speaks] 'How essential it is, if we are to build peace on firm foundations, that there should be respect for international engagements.' [Interpreter] 'Therefore we of the Opposition in Parliament in Britain strongly endorse the action which the British Government, together with its western allies, is taking in Berlin.' [Interpreter] 'In this you are showing that you are not prepared to be

intimidated by methods wholly alien to our conception of democracy.' [Interpreter]

Later, LDP leader Schwennicke said 'Berlin will remain not only the German capital, but the symbol of the new democratic order in a Germany that hungers after peace'. That night, western allied planes set a new record: more than 2000 tons of food and supplies over the air bridge in 24 hours. Each US crew on landing reports to the operations room, nerve centre of all Tempelhof air traffic. Around the clock, these pilots and their British partners bring flour, sugar, potatoes, medicine, coal and oil in one of the most unique air operations of all time. To these men, the impossible has become the routine. Not Soviet sanctions, but the weather is their chief headache. These are the faces of some of the American pilots now helping to feed Berlin... [ranks, names and home towns not transcribed]...American names, American towns, American effort. And finally it came – the Soviet answer to the western allies' note: eight days and fourteen hundred words, just to say 'Nyet'. Meanwhile, Britain, France and the USA continue to build a bigger and better air bridge. A new strip is constructed at Gatow, new bases being prepared in the west, new planes coming from England and America. At Tempelhof too a new strip will soon be ready. Rain or shine, the work went on. American, British, French, German, working together so the Soviet blockade of Berlin serves only to intensify the determination of democratic peoples everywhere.

Chapter Eight

AMERICAN FILM POLICY IN THE RE-EDUCATION OF GERMANY
AFTER 1945

DAVID CULBERT

> The idea that the nation should look back, questioning and
> repenting, was the concept of a conqueror...the people
> only worried about how to fill their stomachs and their
> stoves.

Hans Habe

Apologists blame changing policy directives and administrative
wrangles; everyone else denounced the operation from start to
finish. Nobody, in retrospect, finds much to praise in American
efforts to re-educate Germany after 1945. Because of such a
consensus, amply documented at the time, there has seemed little
reason for elaborate reappraisals. As a result, the ever-increasing
flood of books about Nazi Germany turns into a tiny trickle for the
years between 1945 and 1952; to understand why American
occupation policy failed, one need go no further than the
carefully-documented studies by James Tent, John Gimbel and
Edward Peterson. Tent notes the 'naivete implicit in the assumption
that one people can "re-educate" another toward democracy'.
Peterson argues that 'the occupation, soon after it had begun,
became largely irrelevant to its goals. It could prevent some things
from happening, but it could by itself make very little happen... The
occupation succeeded when it stopped trying. It advanced
retreating.' [1]
    Many of the problems surrounding American occupation
stemmed from a muddled sense of what should be accomplished. The
very idea of re-education seemed a 'conqueror's catchword', not a
method of instruction but a 'panacea for all of the perceived
weaknesses in society'. It may be true, as Hans Habe argues, that
the idea was bungled in its implementation: 'I regard the fashionable
identification of re-educator and pederast as one of the most
disgraceful falsifications of history.' But the remark of one
American occupation officer to Robert Birley finds many supporters:
'You British have been occupying countries all your life. We have
only done it once before, and then it was our own country after the
Civil War—and look what a mess we made of it.' [2]

Re-education, as wartime American planning evolved, had much to do with punishment. Official occupation policy was outlined in JCS/1067, an elaboration of the notorious Morgenthau Plan calling for the pastoralization of Germany, an arrangement which Roosevelt and Churchill agreed to at the 1944 Quebec conference. Five specific goals were set out in JSC/1067; ironically, not a single one was carried out. The goals were:

1. Demilitarisation. No army was to be allowed the German people. Military uniforms and parades - even newsreel coverage of such things - were to be banished. Unfortunately for the planners, the Americans found themselves frantically selling the virtues of militarism to the German people by early 1949, when the Cold War made an army in West Germany seem advisable. Germans had all too vivid a memory of the destruction of their country in 1944-45 to hail this latest bit of good news.

2. Denazification. The hearts and minds of the German people were to be purged of Nazism through an elaborate plan to remove from power and punish the millions of Germans who had supported Hitler. Governmental institutions would be placed in the hands of Germans who had either fled Germany during the Hitler years, or who could demonstrate a political purity. Germany would learn the virtues of democracy, American-style, with heavy doses of instruction in how good government worked in the United States.

Locating leaders of stature who had no Nazi past proved much harder than the planners had envisioned. As Forrest Pogue recalls, aside from Konrad Adenauer, it was hard to come up with many names. Germans felt Willy Brandt had fled the battle, only sneaking back when it was safe. Those who had opposed the Nazis more often than not emerged from concentration camps with no will, or no health. Hans Habe notes with pleasure the fallacy of assuming that all inside camps had belonged to Hitler's opposition. He describes a denazification tribunal judge sent to a Nazi camp for criminal behaviour - selling pornographic literature to the 'sex-starved' Wehrmacht.

Americans gave up denazification when the reality of investigating the past of millions of persons became apparent. George Patton put the matter candidly in a notorious public statement made to a reporter in October 1945: 'The Nazi thing is just like a Democrat-Republican election fight.' In March 1946 the matter was turned over to German nationals, who rapidly abandoned a hopeless assignment. Teaching the virtues of democracy continued at a more modest level, in particular by sending Germans to the United States to live and study. Pogue recalls his second assignment in postwar Germany, 1952-54, where his pragmatic Amerika Haus lectures told Germans 'We're not New Dealers now, we're practical men.' [3]

3. Deindustrialisation. The plan to strip Germany of its industrial plant never got off the ground. Already in 1946 many realised a strong German economy would serve as a buffer to the Soviet Union. The decision, in 1948, to return giant Ruhr industries to the very Nazis who had owned them under Hitler enraged those

who continued to hate Germans, but the Marshall Plan called for rebuilding a strong West German economy, no questions about the past asked. [4]

4. Collective Guilt. The reality of the Death Camps, which became public knowledge to the entire world in 1945, encouraged a significant change in policy towards the nature of the enemy. All during the war an effort - not always successful - had been made to condemn only the Nazi leadership, not all of the German people. the reality of the Death Camps changed things; now all Germans were equally to blame for such atrocities. Thus VE Day in 1945 was accompanied by an orgy of official German-baiting, eagerly seized upon by those making official films.

When American occupation forces entered Germany, the futility of such feelings became apparent. The physical destruction of so much of the country in 1944-45 meant that practical matters relating to food and housing obviously took precedence. Officially, the policy of collective guilt was abandoned in January 1946. Pogue remembers that in Frankfurt it took two full years for the stench of dead bodies to go away following each thaw. [5]

5. Nonfraternisation. A totally unenforceable regulation, such a failure that nobody can be found, in retrospect, who officially advocated such a thing. Occupation forces were not to speak a word to a single German, a command easy to issue if hard to enforce. This policy was officially abandoned in August 1945; Americans would become 'ambassadors of democracy'. Lucius Clay adopts some ludicrous genteelisms to explain what went wrong. 'The soldier who could not be kept away from the opposite sex', he writes 'was forced to meet German girls in dark halls and alleys and under cover of darkness. Obviously only the lowest type of girl, the tramp, would meet with soldiers under such conditions.' [6]

The problems which developed in the American film programme cannot be blamed on lack of planning, though any programme would have been hard-pressed to re-educate German civilians, instruct American occupation forces about correct behaviour, while at the same time beefing up popular support back home, either for leniency or harshness towards things German.

Film communicates through emotional stereotypes, which meant that trying to depict only some Germans as evil was never as popular in Hollywood as the typecasting of an entire nation. Immediately after Pearl Harbour, Hollywood director Ernst Lubitsch, who had been forced to leave Germany, agreed to make an official film for Frank Capra's unit, Know Your Enemy Germany. Lubitsch believed that all Germans were naturally militaristic; he prepared and shot a dull sermon on the lessons of the German past which was never released. By 1944 such a film also needed to instruct the occupation forces; after numerous changes Lubitsch's film was released as Here is Germany in 1945. The timing of course ensured that virtually nobody saw the finished product. Instead, a short official film, Your Job in Germany, got the military viewing audience. First completed by the Capra unit in the fall of 1944, it had to be redone to accommodate a new timetable Hitler imposed through the successes of the Battle of the Bulge. Also, before Your Job in Germany was released in April 1945, it had to reflect the reality of one major success in film used to re-educate Germans, arguably the most significant use of film and still photographs as factual evidence yet seen. [7]

In October 1944 the German Committee of the Office of War Information learned from an employee of the Army Motion Picture Center on Long Island of footage taken at the liberation of the first concentration camps the Allies reached. The next month, Signal Corps photographic teams were directed to collect visual documentation of concentration and prisoner-of-war camps for use in prosecuting Nazi war criminals. This documentation, literally more shocking than eyewitness reports could hope to be, turned out to be the most significant use of film in the occupation of Germany. Most significant because it proved the most compelling evidence in the War Crimes Trials held in Nuremberg, 20 November 1945, to 1 October 1946, and most compelling because parts of the most grisly footage were shown to every German civilian as part of the denazification process.

In World War I, faked atrocity photographs had given photography a poor name in making a moral indictment. This time footage from movie cameras and photography would not be ignored. In April 1945 special motion picture groups were specifically assigned to provide 'complete photographing in both still and motion pictures of each enemy POW and concentration camp...above the priority of combat photography'. Instructions included coverage of 'at least one grave,' plus 'piles of garments, shoes, jewelry, false teeth, etc.', and cameramen were told to photograph 'any escape attempts which had been made'. More important for use in a criminal proceeding, 'the Judge Advocate General will take affidavits from cameramen'. SHAEF's Pyschological Warfare Division assigned professional journalists on its staff to accompany the special photographic units to assure complete documentation. [8]

To increase credibility - itself evidence of how much the cry of faked atrocity photographs was feared - special efforts were made to link visually American generals, particularly Dwight Eisenhower, George Patton, and Omar Bradley, with such evidence. The presumption was that symbols of credibility seen walking through the death camps, or pointing to piles of bodies, would allay fears that the visual evidence had been doctored.

The result was Nazi Concentration Camps, a one-hour film produced by the American Counsel for the Prosecution of Axis Criminality, including footage which an Office of War Information official termed not 'within the realm of common decency'. He particularly did not like 'demonstrations and re-enactments of Nazi tortures', and urged the 'deletion of exposed genital organs on exposed bodies in sequences in Leipzig, Pengi, Nordhausen and Buchenwald prisons' before releasing the footage to American civilian audiences. [9]

Stuart Schulberg, a member of the Documentary Evidence Section of the American prosecution at Nuremberg, provided an extraordinary eyewitness account of the impact of this footage when screened for Nazi leaders in the courtroom at Nuremberg. He arranged to have indirect lighting installed so it would be possible for him to observe the immediate reaction of the most notorious Nazis. Hjalmar Schacht turned around and stared at the projection booth for the entire six reels. Julius Streicher 'watched the entire picture with fiendish fascination. If the world were peopled with Streichers, that evidence film would have become a box-office smasheroo.' Schulberg insists that Wilhelm Keitel was the most visibly affected, openly weeping during much of the screening, by the end 'bent over and broken, mopping his lined face with a soggy ball of handkerchief.

The next step involved using such footage to convince German civilians that Nazism represented a moral horror of unprecedented proportions, a programme which mostly relied on radio and pamphlets during May and June 1945, though Welt im Film, the Anglo-American newsreel for occupied Germany, devoted its entire fifth issue, released 15 June 1945, to the most horrifying footage from the death camps. [10]

At the same time, a more elaborate attempt was underway to convey the meaning of the death camps through film, a story carefully described in Brewster Chamberlain's fine article about Todesmühlen (Death Mills). A film depicting the horror of the death camps was an idea whose time had come. Sidney Bernstein and the British Ministry of Information worked on one; Americans assembled footage at the Army Motion Picture Service on Long Island; and Burger was told to make the film on orders from SHAEF's Psychological Warfare Division in Luxembourg.

Hanus Burger (as he now calls himself) directed Todesmühlen. He was born in Prague of German-Jewish parents. Attracted to left-wing causes, he left Germany for New York in 1938. Moving to Hollywood, he directed Seeds of Freedom (1943), then entered the Army, where he wound up at Camp Ritchie, Maryland, the special Psychological Warfare training centre which recruited political exiles. In 1944 Burger worked with Hans Habe for Radio Luxembourg, though he was investigated by the American Counter-Intelligence Corps because of his Communist sympathies.

In May 1945 Burger was sent to London to look at death camp footage assembled at the PWD film centre. 'When today, over thirty years later, I have a nightmare,' he writes, 'I see the bulldozer from Bergen-Belsen...I see mountains of teeth...cleaned with German thoroughness.' He screened such footage three to five hours every day, working with cutter Sam Winston, the man who edited The Blue Angel (1930) in Hollywood. According to Burger, whose account must be subjected to the same scrutiny one reserves for all Hollywood memoirs, he originally planned a longer film, with scenes showing Germans returning to their war-devastated cities. In the final film all the additional footage he shot on location in Germany was cut. [11]

The villain, according to Burger, was Hollywood director Billy Wilder. Chamberlain simply says that Wilder's role in the film cannot be clearly determined. Burger presents such a damning indictment of Wilder (nobody else receives such treatment) that obviously there was considerable friction. Both were Hollywood directors, both middle-European emigrés, both in their thirties. But in 1945 Wilder was riding high. His Five Graves to Cairo (with Peter Van Eyck and Erich von Stroheim as Rommel) had been a big commercial success in 1943, as was Double Indemnity, released the same year. Burger had no such credentials - one unimportant feature film and the lowly rank of lieutenant. When OWI officials in London asked Wilder to give his advice, he found much to criticise. He screened the opening of the rough-cut, which depicted refugees in their camp uniforms returning home, then gave some frank advice: 'Looks like pyjamas. Four seconds. No more. The rest in the bucket.' Burger's PWD mentor, a Colonel Powell, was far-off in Germany. Wilder's hand contained all the high cards. The film was cut to twenty minutes of documentary footage though Burger did succeed in having his own man assigned to write the commentary. Oskar Seidlin had also written for Radio 1212, the 'black' radio station which caused so much confusion inside Germany in 1945. [12]

Burger did the final editing of Todesmühlen in Munich at Geiselgasteig; Sam Winston continued as cutter. The final version, twenty-two minutes long, was completed at the end of October 1945. Technically it was released by OMGUS. 114 prints went to German theatres, beginning 25 January 1946, the intended 'psychological capper' of the denazification programme. Theatres ran it as part of a sixty-minute programme including the current issue of Welt im Film, and an unidentified American documentary.

Todesmühlen was overtaken by events. A film insisting on collective guilt went into distribution just as OMGUS abandoned the policy. As a result, civilian attendance was not mandatory. [13] Burger does not discuss the reception of his film save for the response of some thirty Germans working at Geiselgasteig who attended an official preview. According to Burger, all present insisted they had known nothing of the death camps. A German girl accused the others of lying: 'On your desk is a photograph from Traunsee because you and your family often travel to Ischl. The concentration camp at Ebensee is close by. You must have known of it.' Burger shortly after married the accuser.

Chamberlain cites not remembered verbatim conversation, but surviving OMGUS surveys of German audience response, first pointing out the fragmentary nature of the evidence and inadequate sampling techniques involved. Who would express himself openly on every controversial issue to a pollster wearing the uniform of an occupying power? Actor Peter Van Eyck served as OMGUS Films Officer in Berlin. His 28 March 1946 report tried a touch of irony in reporting audience response: 'Although the Mills of Death grind slow, they do not get any customers at all. As predicted by this section fifty-two times Todesmühlen within the US Sector of Berlin are too many to take.' Van Eyck reported that in the American Zone, of a population of 944,000, only 157,120, or 16%, saw the film, while a regular feature film attracted 26% of the population. He also noted the inconclusive results from handing out a questionnaire one afternoon to 2000 Germans attending a screening of Todesmühlen in ten different theatres. Of the 1040 who responded, 91% said what they were supposed to, urging the film be shown to all German civilians. But the heart of the film's message, the collective guilt of every German for what happened in the death camps, received a more honest response: 70% said the German people did not share responsibility; 82% said they had no knowledge of the death camps. [14]

Another OMGUS survey, even worse in terms of statistical reliability, concerns citizens of the city of Eichstätt, roughly halfway between Nuremberg and Munich. 'The local popoulation,' an OMGUS official noted, 'as seems to have been general all over Bavaria, stayed away in droves'. It was arranged to require all city employees to attend some extra screenings. 3462 saw it; 1500 received an elaborate questionnaire; 214 filled it out. 'Have no fear,' respondents were told. 'If you have no typewriter and fear your handwriting might be recognised, write in block letters!'

Comments were uniformly unflattering. 'For the next propaganda performance,' a sixteen-year-old girl noted, 'Take Dr Goebbels as adviser'. One person asked why in a democracy one should be required to see the film. Many spoke of Allied air attacks as worse than what appeared in the film. Others claimed the Sovet Union was doing worse things to POWs in Silesia. 87.5 % of the respondents felt no sense of collective guilt. One fourteen-year-old boy had friends in Auschwitz and Belsen who told him 'it wasn't as bad as in the film'. A twenty-two-year-old man termed the film nothing but 'swindle and humbug'. [15] I believe these 214 responses reflect the outrage of all those who turned in nothing at all. The evidence is overwhelming that nobody in Germany bought the idea of collective guilt. As a re-education device, Todesmühlen was a failure.

The film offers a hammer-and-tongs assault. The musical score, an insistent ostinato, matches the ham-handed narration. 'In the hell of Auschwitz, Allied physicians study marks of the Nazi beast... In Dachau, in Auschwitz, in Nordhausen, in Maidenek - the German murder trust standardized the procedure of slaughter - the death gas was always the same - Zyklon.' The narrator tells us that ashes were 'ground up and sold to German farmers as fertilizer'. Hatred of German civilians reached fever pitch at the conclusion: 'The farmers received tons of human bones as fertilizer...but apparently never suspected it came from human beings...manufacturers received tons of human hair...but apparently never dreamed it came from the heads of murdered women...no nightmares ever haunted those who lived near concentration camps...the cries and moans of the tortured were no doubt believed the wailing of the wind.' [16] The film cuts to crowd scenes from Leni Riefenstahl's Triumph of the Will, as we are told that Germans who 'plead for your sympathy' still 'bear heavy crosses now...the crosses of the millions crucified in Nazi death mills!' [17]

Some of the footage from Todesmühlen appears in every documentary film about the horrors of the concentration camps, particularly the charred remains of the human being whose head and arm pressed under a warehouse door at Gardelegen before being burned to death. Motion picture footage allows us to see humanity walking with death-skeletal figures obviously unable to stand erect as they are half-carried by allied soldiers. Nobody forgets such images, seen by the vast majority of German civilians, albeit not only in Todesmühlen.

With an English soundtrack, the film was released in March 1946 as Death Mills, to be seen by troops sent to occupy Germany. The English version makes a studied omission of all references to Jews. Fears of anti-Semitism in America explains why we are told that the victims were 'of all religious faiths, of all political beliefs'. [18] Excerpts of the atrocity footage appears in every American, British, Russian, and French newsreel; the depiction of the death camps in the Anglo-American official film, The True Glory (1945), is immensely effective; footage was cut into Your Job in Germany. And atrocity footage did get shown, in 16mm film, to American audiences. Congressman Marion T. Bennett of Missouri went to Germany in April 1945, at Eisenhower's invitation, to view the concentration camps. He reports that in July 1945 he showed 'some 25,000 people' in his home district both Nazi Concentration Camps and Your Job in Germany. [19] Death Mills was released to American civilian audiences in June 1946. A film in which the collective guilt of the German people is so forcefully argued was released as an official film long after the government that ordered it made had taken up a very different policy in Germany.

Your Job in Germany also argues a policy - this time nonfraternisation - abandoned well before the film completed its original run. This Capra-unit film was already in production in May 1944, when Walt Disney provided inserts for a policy of nonfraternisation: 'Don't make friends; be suspicious.' The argument about collective guilt through a national addiction to militarism was explained by reference to chapters of German history - 1870, 1914, 1939, and 'chapter IV?' [20]

George Marshall felt the completed film would needlessly alarm the American soldier about the perils of occupying enemy territory. Paul Horgan, on 7 December 1944, suggested deleting one sentence from the narration: 'In occupied Germany, your life may be in greater danger than it is in battle.' This done, the final version was personally seen and approved by Assistant Secretary of War John McCloy on December 26. As Lyman Munson, Frank Capra's chief, wired him, 'present version...considered by all present to be even better than the original'. [21] The film was mandatory viewing for all American soldiers in the ETO, though no doubt some field units missed it.

Your Job in Germany offers effective documentation of the policy of collective guilt and nonfraternisation. 'Take no changes...You are up against German history. It isn't good!... It was written by the German people. It can happen again!' The film specifically warns soliders to ignore children, all steeped in Nazi propaganda, suggests that nazi SS-types are watching from the anonymity of the civilian mass, then makes policy specific: 'Every German is a potential source of trouble; there must be no fraternization with any of the German people.' The narration reflects the realities of the vocabulary of the average American soldier by adding: 'Fraternization means making friends.'

In one of the most effective visual parts of the film, collective guilt as a reason for nonfraternisation is depicted through a hand suited to Frankenstein's monster superimposed over a sea of German faces: 'That is the hand that dropped the bombs on helpless Rotterdam...that held the whip over the Norwegian slaves...that murdered Greeks, Czechs, Jews...that killed and crippled American soldiers...Don't clasp that hand.' This sinister combination of narration with special effects is quite extraordinary, and stays with anyone who sees the film. In the conclusion we learn that Americans will stay in Europe for a long time until, through denazification, demilitarisation, and deindustrialisation, Germans 'have been cured beyond the shadow of a doubt'. [22]

Once the film had been shown in Europe, a number of generals, shocked by revelations of the death camps, urged that Your Job in Germany be shown to civilian audiences back home. This recycling of official films originally intended for some specific military purpose, raises fascinating questions about what happens when an official release is seen by audiences for whom it was not originally intended. [23] The idea was to justify a policy of continued military occupation in Germany by showing American civilians atrocity footage plus Your Job in Germany. General Walter Weible explained his opposition: 'My main fear is...that we are teaching the American soldier to hate other people. This is the part that might provide ammunition to the opponents of Universal Military Training.' The Army's Bureau of Public Relations felt the film should have distribution to civilians through local theatres. Other generals said no. The solution was typical of an era in which the military had taken the plunge about scientific methods for gauging response - a survey of public opinion.

Assistant Secretary of War John McCloy had the J.Walter Thompson Agency of New York conduct market research by showing the film to civilians in the New York area; nine out of ten urged the film be shown to civilians. But the reponse of the one-in-ten suggested caution: 'Those who do not approve of this film reveals that many people consider it the same sort of "hate propaganda" fostered by the Nazis. Their opinions which are intelligently and forcefully expressed offer a hint to violent reaction of a considerable section of the press if this film were forced on the public as a government document.' The survey, the Army also learned, lacked statistical validity since the sample used only 198 persons. [24] The film seemed destined for nontheatrical distribution to groups which requested it, preceded by 'the atrocity film', seen largely by those who already hated Germans.

At this point Warner Brothers entered the picture in a story compounded of one part Army bureaucratic ineptitude and nine parts Hollywood chutzpah. What happened is of interest in and of itself, but also because it shows how an official documentary film advocating collective guilt and nonfraternisation could hit the commercial circuit in America and Britain long after both policies had been abandoned officially.

In early 1945, Jack L. Warner decided to have his shorts department prepare a film warning viewers that fascism could still lead to some future war. Warner jotted down a few ideas for what he suggested calling The Ghosts of Berchtesgaden. Hitler and Hirohito, along with their top aides, sit in a projection room looking happily at footage of the destruction of Poland. 'Have screen go dark and big head close-ups,' Warner suggested. 'Have Protestant, Jew and Catholic represented...At very finish show soldiers of Allied Nations saying we have fought to stop this and you at home owe it to us to see that it will not happen again.'

When a mogul has an idea, his staff snaps to attention. Writer Saul Elkins produced just such a story, proposing to recycle the lobby set from Hotel Berlin (1945) and a cast of so-called look-alikes including Bobby Watson as Hitler and Martin Koslick as Goering. Don Siegel was assigned as director, a logical choice for a film intended to incorporate stock newsreel footage. Siegel did much of the montage work for Warner Brothers, including Mission to Moscow (1943). Shooting began on May 8 and was completed four days later.

The big problem for Elkins was creating a 'docudrama' when fact needed to be communicated. At first he called for a Nazi doctor to take blood from a Russian child. He argued the collective guilt of the German people without a profound knowledge of German history: 'the inbred German lust for power has ever been thus...since Frederick the Great in 1888'. His narration concludes by claiming that 'already Axis military cliques are secretly preparing again to dominate the world'.

Trying to decide what to say about the Jews proved especially ticklish. His original draft included two references. A 'Jewish man' says he is 'the wanderer in exile' who 'died in the gutter of the ghetto in Warsaw'. Then a 'Mother' testifies as to 'the abominations of Buchenwald's notorious concentration camp. Who saw the Nazis when they jeered and killed my son.' Script B, 18 April 1945, cuts the mother, and frees the Jewish man from any connection with Warsaw ('the distress of the defenceless ones'). Script C, dated April 28, restores the exact contents on this sensitive issue from Script A. Script D substitutes Ohrdruf for Buchenwald; script E makes no changes about the Jews but calls for one shot of a dead sailor to be a Negro. The revised final script F, of June 4, adds two full mimeographed pages using footage from the concentration camps, and an extended narration discussing human fertiliser, shots of 'warehouses' of shoes, and terms the Nazi camps 'in every phase of their depraved fury a rotten record of ruthlessness'. [25]

In other words, the stale script for The Ghosts of Berchtesgaden was overwhelmed by factual newsreel footage of the

182

death camps, released to American newsreels on April 26. As a surviving memorandum of that week indicates, 'Colonel Warner told me to tell you that Colonel Lord has some wonderful Russian atrocity film'. Such 'wonderful' footage just could not be introduced into a production which looked so totally improbable (and surviving stills make clear that what Siegel shot on the set belonged on the cutting room floor).

Jack Warner was horrified by pictures of the death camps which ran in the Los Angeles Examiner on April 24. When he saw the photographic essay which appeared in Life on May 7, including the human being who died in the warehouse near Gardelegen, he called his shorts supervisor, Gordon Hollingshead, to urge that The Ghosts of Berchtesgaden take this documented reality into account. Joseph Breen of the Hays Office was not pleased. He warned that just because atrocity footage appeared in newsreels - not subject to his censorship - would not mean he could allow such gruesome things to appear in a Hollywood short. Warner decided to wait until he had completed his film before going back to Breen. [26]

Four writers were assigned to try to bail out the Elkins script, and what had been shot by Siegel: Emmet Lavery, Howard Koch, Delmar Daves, and Alvah Bessie. On June 8 they recommended that 'all staged scenes' be eliminated. They suggested relating Hitler's fascism to domestic fascism inside America: 'anti-Semitism, anti-Negro prejudice, anti-labour agitation, anti-foreignborn and anti-Catholic sentiment.'

Meanwhile Jack Warner accepted an invitation from Eisenhower to tour Europe with a small group of leading film executives. Before leaving Washington on 17 June 1945, Warner saw Your Job in Germany at the screening room in the Pentagon. Warner told an aide to locate a print as soon as possible, ordering that it be seen by 'all the people working on the Berchtesgaden picture, and also by Delmar Daves and his Committee'.

During July, scriptwriters Koch, Daves, Bessie, Lavery, and producer Jerry Wald spent odd moments reworking the Elkins script, now in fact adding a strong ending about domestic fascism. They especially hoped to attack Gerald L.K.Smith, once Huey Long's lieutenant. Koch reported that he attended two Smith rallies at the Shrine Auditorium in Los Angeles, and 'had a private half-hour talk with him'. Also during July the decision was made to seek Army permission to incorporate scenes from Your Job in Germany. The Signal Corps' Curtiss Mitchell was the man who could make the decision; Robert Lord in Hollywood, who had worked with the Capra Unit, had a fine grain negative right at hand.

First the Army agreed. 'Select any army-owned footage,' Mitchell wired Gordon Hollingshead at Warner Brothers on August 11. Plans to include an attack on Gerald Smith had to be dropped on August 20, when Richard de Rochemont, head of March of Time, told Warners 'sorry but we were sued by Smith and part of settlement was our agreement not to use material'.

The more Gordon Hollingshead looked at Your Job in Germany, the more he liked it - and the more he persuaded himself that he ought to get the entire film for his commercial short. He ordered his New York representative to 'bring to Colonel Mitchell's attention the fact that there is nothing in this picture shot by any studio...A good percentage is...from our own film library that we gave gratis to the Signal Corps for this picture...As far as using the Army's narration on this, I know the Army men that wrote it were very highly complimented that we wanted to use that same dialogue...A needed job for the Army, and it will make the public understand why we need occupational forces.'

After lots of internal discussion by Army officials, punctuated by telephone calls to Warner Brothers, an official decision was reached on September 27: 'War Department cannot grant your request for production shots, edited material, or narration material...Warmest Regards.' [27] At first Hollingshead decided to go along with the Army's decision, promising to have his writer 'rewrite the complete narration'. But someone at Warners decided instead on a simpler plan – pinch the entire film and to hell with the Army. The memoranda for such a decision do not survive, but obviously Jack Warner made the decision, based on the fact that originally the Army had agreed, and no doubt first persuading himself that Warners would be helping the Army by getting a fine film out to commercial audiences.

True, Hitler Lives? as The Ghosts of Berchtesgaden was finally named, adds four minutes of new material at the end, directly relating the dangers of fascism to the domestic scene: 'The ghosts of Berchtesgaden still walk; right here, in America, the evil spirits of these ghosts still haunt us...They hope for reconversion to be handled badly. They hope for unemployment.' But fully four-fifths of the film is matched frame-for-frame, using the exact narration of the Army film, all without even a hint in the credits as to what happened. Jack Warner had the nerve to rush his short into competition for an Academy Award, and received Best Documentary for 1945. Such a manoeuvre required finesse. At the Academy Awards ceremony, he selected for screening only the conclusion which he had made himself; none of the 'Army film which he wanted to stay away from'. [28]

Lyman Munson was livid when he found out what happened. Having recently moved from being head of Army film production to a similar position at Twentieth-Century Fox, he wrote on his new letterhead to his successor at the Signal Corps. 'I was startled, to say the least,' he began, 'when I saw a picture last night called Hitler Lives. It was produced and released by Warner Bros., and screen credit was given to Hollingshead as producer. There was no credit whatsoever given to the Army, to the Signal Corps, or to the Army Pictorial Service; yet at least seventy-five percent of the picture was lifted bodily, word by word, frame by frame, from a picture that APS made last year...Last summer, when a group of film executives went to Europe on Eisenhower's request, I ran the picture for the group before they left the U.S.A... Early last fall Colonel Swarthout of the Bureau of Public Relations brought up to me informally a proposed script of a picture to be produced by Warner

Bros.; this script, like others which deal with the Army...was submitted for war department clearance. When I saw the script I laughed for the bulk of it was a verbatim copy of the Army picture. At that time I said that obviously no script which had been lifted bodily from an Army picture should be approved. I also said that our policy had been, and would continue to be, that no edited footage would be made available for commercial purposes.' [29] Warner judged the bureaucrats correctly - no official action was taken.

Jack Warner aggressively promoted his short, and the reviews were generally favourable. In January and February 1946, few in America realised that nonfraternisation and collective guilt were no longer official policy. Most reviews and some surviving newspaper editorials thought the film was just the reminder Americans needed for a get-tough policy towards Germany. The Akron Beacon Journal, without explaining what the competition consisted of, termed Hitler Lives? 'one of the most enlightening motion pictures to come to Akron in many months'. The Jewish Advocate, in an editorial, termed this 'the answer to those who cry for the quick return of our occupation forces in enemy lands'. The Tulsa Tribune suggested that 'we can be sorry for the Germans but in good time. Their victims have a stronger claim on us.' In what strikes one as an exercise in tongue-in-cheek, Warner Brothers even showed Hitler Lives? free to 'Ministers-Rabbis-Catholic Priests' as part of American Brotherhood Week. [30]

Nor was foreign distribution ignored. Max Milder, in London, assured Warner that the film would 'play, not only the Warner Theatre, but the A.B.C. Theatres and like-wise get a good showing in every first-class House throughout the country. We will go after this as if it were a feature.' And as an example of the way films find all sorts of audiences - in Paris, 28 June 1946, some 3,000 representatives of the French press and publicists saw Hitler Lives? with superimposed titles in French. As a Warner representative noted, 'this picture was greatly applauded'. Not, however, by those who had turned denazification over to the Germans in March 1946, and were having hell's own time getting French co-operation for a tolerant attitude towards Germans. [31]

A third example, Policing Germany, a This is America release for 27 July 1945, suggests another way in which occupation policy was made vivid for American audiences. There is no reason to believe that German civilians saw this film, but it certainly made the rounds of the entire RKO chain in the United States, aggressively promoted as well in This Week, a Sunday supplement to many American newspapers. What is particularly fascinating about this quasi-newsreel is where it was shot. Cologne of course was in the British Zone, but Americans were in temporary control when the story was filmed. Marya Mannes wrote a tough, hate-filled script to accompany the footage, which included re-enactments using the city of Cologne. Policing Germany thus is a form of 'docudrama', but interests us because the sets are real. We see rubble everywhere; the narrator, Dwight Weist (who played Hitler for the March of Time) tells us 'these were not tattered, exhausted crowds, sprayed by machine guns; these were well-dressed Germans, sturdy with nourishment stolen from other peoples. Many of the women wore silk stockings'. [32]

We see the use of ropes attached to fire trucks to pull down the walls of buildings ready to collapse; we see Americans creating a civilian German police force; we see civilians being dusted with DDT 'every ten days'. And then we see what only a fictional film can do - we see that denazification works like magic. All it takes, in Policing Germany, is a 'detailed questionnaire' to 'ferret' the Nazis out. We see kids helping burn piles of Nazi emblems. To eradicate Nazism, a new system of education is introduced - using, the narrator informs us with unintended irony, 'new American kindergartens'. Best of all, Nazis look like criminals, and, conveniently enough, carry concealed weapons. A scruffy specimen is rounded up, but not for enough pay to put his heart into playing the heavy. In a handy instance of recycling buildings, the 'irreconcilable' Nazi is taken to the old Gestapo prison to serve a stiff sentence.

Policing Germany should be gauged as helpful in two ways: as a good example of why Americans were to hate all Germans (and why occupation policy would accomplish its ambitious goals with ease) and as an instance of surprisingly rare footage showing just what took place in major German cities in the first two months following surrender.

The next time This is America took a look at Germany was its issue of 13 December 1946. Germany Today, according to a release sheet at the Library of Congress, revealed a dramatically changed situation: 'Long months after the war's end...the gigantic clean-up program has made but a dent in the terrific destruction caused by the war.' There are shots of Americans teaching American sports such as baseball to children; hunger, we learn, is 'the greatest destructive force in Germany today'. Better still, 'Germans are fast learning a touch of freedom'. Best of all for exhibitors, the release is 'thoroughly entertaining throughout'. For This is America editors, how times change in eighteen months. Gone is collective guilt; now the problem is hunger. For denazification, try 'a touch of freedom'; for nonfraternisation, teach a kid to play baseball; instead of demilitarisation, rebuild a strong Germany (though no reference is given to the Soviet Union as the reason why). [33]

So much for examples of re-educating Americans back home. What about specific efforts to use film to re-educate the German civilian population? A plan was ready in May 1945, a plan with three components: Hollywood feature films, documentary films to be produced in occupied Germany, and a joint Anglo-American newsreel to take over the audience for Goebbels' elaborate production.

The first part of the plan involved thirty-two feature films, some out-of-date, designed to instil in German civilians a love of things American. [34] Hollywood declined to provide the latest releases, fearing the government might prevent its regaining its prewar exhibition circuits in Germany. The list included One Hundred Men and a Girl (1937), Rene Clair's I Married a Witch (1942), and Going My Way (1944) with Bing Crosby as the Roman Catholic priest. Films depicting American military power such as <u>Air Force</u> (1943) and <u>The Sullivans</u> (1944) were withdrawn when Japan surrendered more quickly than expected. <u>Gone with the Wind</u> (1939) and <u>The Grapes of Wrath</u> (1940) were omitted as containing unflattering portraits of American life.

Robert Joseph, Film Officer in Berlin, adopted a rather defensive posture in describing this list of films for an article assessing the success of the American film programme as of late 1946. 'Today the selected films look foolish and inept,' he concluded. 'When they were selected and first shown, they were excellent for the needs of that moment.' [35]

<u>New York Times</u> correspondent Gladwin Hill accepted with glee the assignment to write an article describing the failure of the American film programme in Germany. The thirty-two films received short shrift: 'As a group of films originally selected for being non-committal, what changes were they expected to work with the considerably less than receptive Germans?' He cites a <u>New York Times</u> report from Frankfurt, in July 1946, which quotes a group of Information Control Division officers as saying the feature films 'had no observable effect in the political and psychological re-education of the Germans'. He then cites a 17 November 1946, OMGUS report which concludes that the films 'had served little in the re-education of the Germans, and had held Americans up to public ridicule, and had hurt the reputation of the American film industry in Germany'.

Sometimes the posture of hard-bitten newspaper man masks misinformation. The thirty-two films indeed did have an impact not discernible to American observers. Nicholas Pronay reports that <u>Going My Way</u> was <u>the</u> big hit in Budapest in 1946. The meaning of Hollywood escapist fare was not lost on German audiences, who had seen no American films for the best part of a decade. Germans wanted to escape the bitter reality of the harsh winter of 1945-46; to them the American films represented a form of cultural propaganda for America which worked all the better for being unobtrusive. Nor should one ignore the entertainment aspect.. Peter Van Eyck, in Berlin, reported the only play to open during a typical week in March 1946, a production of <u>Fair and Warmer</u>, 'the ancient (1916) comedy by Avery Hopwood...No one liked it but the audience; they howled with amusement.' [36]

Gladwin Hill is malicious about the other two parts of the American film programme. Most documentaries produced in occupied Germany 'had not stirred a ripple among the German people' by the time he left in February 1946. <u>Welt im Film</u>, the Anglo-American newsreel intended to be a major part of the film programme for the re-education of Germans, receives withering sarcasm. 'The ones I saw,' Hill writes, 'made the standard American bathing-beauty-and dog show nonsense look like Academy winners by comparison.' He claims to have watched a 'German audience sit in forbearing, bewildered silence' as they saw a 'British Army track meet in Holland; Washington welcoming Admiral Nimitz (replete with men marching, tanks rolling) ...Military Government lieutenants applauding a Military Government captain's speech at the reopening of the Frankfurt stock exchange; a London dog track; a Norwegian square-rigger sailing from Florida.' [37]

A full appraisal of Welt im Film is not possible here, but Roger Smither has provided a brief introduction in his Chapter 7. He notes that some 369 issues were released between 18 May 1945, and 27 June 1952. The production was, he states, compulsory viewing for all theatres in the British and American Zones until September 1949. As to its impact, he concludes by quoting the words Helmut Regel remembers as a kid singing to the theme of the newsreel:

> Chuck 'em out, the Tommies
> Chuck 'em out, the Americans
> Chuck 'em out, the Russians
> Chuck 'em out, the Allied rabble

Surviving OMGUS records suggest the special problems the newsreel encountered. For example, as late as December 1945, all raw stock was controlled in Germany by the Russians, who demanded the Americans and British turn over needed chemicals as a quid pro quo. At a Joint Newsreel conference held in London in November 1945 the Americans and British agreed that Welt im Film should have priority over all other aspects of film in occupied Germany, including feature films, and that nothing should be said about tensions among the occupying powers. The latter requirement helped assure a certain fatuousness in many of the releases.

In September 1948, a tri-zonal film distribution scheme, even with the Berlin airlift in effect and Cold War tensions at their greatest, failed to get the full support of the French, who insisted that they would distribute their own IFA newsreel in their zone. And the president of the German Producers' Association admitted that his colleagues had yet to show much enthusiasm for screening informative officially-produced documentaries, though originally the intent had been to show feature films only to entice civilians in to learn about the virtues of re-education. [38]

An official report for the Motion Picture Branch of OMGUS dated 21 March 1949, suggests, sometimes indirectly, some facts about the operation of the American film programme shortly before the formal creation of an independent West Germany led to the rapid dismantling of outside production. Welt im Film still enjoyed mandatory viewing status, but by issuing only 296 copies per release even at that late date, some theatres did not play the newsreel until three full months later. The 1949 report speaks of allowing foreign newsreels into Germany from 1 January 1950, though still subject to OMGUS approval.

The American documentary film unit, finally fully established in July 1947, had managed to produce eight short subjects, plus a feature-length documentary about the Nuremburg war crimes trials. The anonymous author of the report claimed the film on the trials enjoyed 'amazing box office success' in the major cities but not in smaller towns. This unit also produced twenty-five special newsreels on the Berlin situation, all of which found substantial circulation.

Every film shown in German theatres had to have a Film Exhibition Certificate issued by OMGUS. Exhibitors were allowed to use approved German feature films from the Nazi era. In 1949 some 250 such films still lacked licences. To take care of this matter, OMGUS resorted to a field expedient: 'an experienced and reliable German man' looked at three a day and made the judgement in the name of OMGUS.

Much of this report involved administrative wrangles among representatives of the European Recovery Administration, OMGUS, and the Motion Picture Export Association, which represented Hollywood. OMGUS said that through gentlemen's agreements it had been able to 'hold down' English feature imports to thirty-five, French to thirty-five, while the MPEA was allowed fifty-two. That did not suit Hollywood, where producers demanded a 'convertibility guarantee' of one million dollars per year from the ECA to insure profits from the German market. OMGUS thought such governmental support for private enterprise fully justified. [39]

What may be concluded from the American experience in using film to re-educate Germans after 1945? First, there is the absence of consistent policies. Quality films take time to complete; as a consequence, wartime planning saw the completion of films designed to show why a get-tough policy, and long-term occupation were in order. The rapid collapse of denazification, collective guilt, nonfraternisation, deindustrialisation, and demilitarisation as official policy meant that those making films had no idea of just what policies they were supposed to promote. If you cannot figure out what your product is supposed to accomplish, then product persuasiveness and distribution will amount to very little.

Second, there is the matter of personnel. As Forrest Pogue recalls, the only Americans eager to accept assignments in occupied Germany were 'old fuddy-duddies' the miliary assigned to 'guard Nebraska' while the war was on. American GIs rioted in Germany in 1946; inductees had no interest in re-educating Germans, just a tremendous urge to get back home. James Tent suggests that grim economic conditions in postwar Britain encouraged able English civilians to accept employment in the British zone.[40] Given the American career officer's scepticism towards public information assignments, it is not surprising that the least able of the least able occupied positions involving film utilization. Certainly, Hollywood distribution experts who had helped out during the war went right back to civilian assignments at large salaries following VE Day.

Third, there is what might be termed the impossible dream. What, one must ask, did the Americans intend films to do in re-education? Once the emphasis shifted to non-ideological, pragmatic matters such as getting people enough to eat, a place to sleep, and the rebuilding of roads and cities, was there truly any need for a film programme designed to instil a spirit of democracy in the German people? I think not. Even stranger is the almost complete lack of coordination between film officers in ICD and OMGUS as a whole. [41] One looks in vain, to give but an obvious example, for any reference, even in passing, to Todesmühlen or Welt im Film in Lucius Clay's Decision in Germany, or the thorough surveys of American occupation policy by Peterson, Gimbel, and Tent. In the complete absence of evidence to the contrary, one must conclude that film played a minor role in the political re-education of Germans in the American Zone, with one terribly significant exception. Film documented the atrocities of the death camps to every German civilian. If the physical destruction of Germany in 1945 did not convince Germans that Nazis had been a catastrophe, the visual documentation of the death camps made the moral failure of Hitler appallingly clear.

Fourth, there is the ironic effect of time-lag in showing official films to civilian audiences. Todesmühlen told Germans of collective guilt just after the policy had been abandoned. Films such as Your Job in Germany, reconstituted in 1946 as Hitler Lives?, in combination with official atrocity films, told Americans that all Germans were evil, that they were unrepentent, and that punishment was the order of the day, even as policy-makers in Washington pondered the implications of the containment doctrine outlined in George Kennan's Long Telegram from Moscow. [42] While everyone directing occupation policy in the American Zone turned to the practical matter of feeding a starving German populace, groups in America learned emotional reasons to oppose such largesse. It is impossible to state the precise impact of such outdated doctrine in terms of promoting or hindering policy; but only if one takes the attitude that message films, officially sponsored, never affect anyone can one fail to see a lesson for policy-makers in the dangers of showing official films containing outdated doctrine. Some films may indeed need to be withdrawn from circulation for a time. Of course one reason they were not is the understandable outrage Jews in particular felt about the death camps. Those who saw Hitler Lives? during Brotherhood Week in 1946 could be counted on to return home comforted by the fact that somebody was keeping alive the idea of collective guilt and the need for retribution. Such strong medicine could have a helpful cathartic effect.

For historians, the surviving films themselves offer fascinating visual glimpses of how policies that in reality could not work, could be made to work through film's ability to seemingly make real a planned future. Get-tough films from 1945-46 allow us to see what the Morgenthau Plan might have meant had it been put into effect, or what official American policy might have been had the Cold War not intervened.

Not every film succeeded in proving its point. The effort at proving the collective guilt of all Germans for the death camps, as in the case of Todesmühlen, points to a lesson about the dangers of relying on the expertise of those with too much emotional interest in their subject. Stories are legion of howlers committed by those making films to use in a foreign country who do not know nuances of language and custom. The example of Todesmühlen suggests that using the talents of political exiles can create other problems as well. Todesmühlen really represents an exercise in moral stereotyping, and points to the dangers of using assertion in a visual medium where there is insufficient evidence. I am persauded by Sebastian Haffner's argument. Hitler 'did not take his fellow countrymen fully into his confidence because he did not trust them... He did not expect them to be ready for the mass murder of their Jewish fellow citizens.' [43]

The one great success of the American film programme is of course shared by camera teams from all of the Allied powers. By documenting the final moments of the death camps, the camera laid to rest arguments that America fought the wrong enemy. Even with the changes in the balance of power which took place between 1945 and 1950, and even with the reality of Communist purges inside the United States, nobody successfully argued that Hitler had not been a moral evil. Visual documentation of the death camps, shown in every newpaper, discussed on every radio station, shown in every newsreel, the subject of all manner of documentary and feature films, the subject of innumerable books and articles - all collectively created a world guilt about the death camps, and that in turn had a specific result. It is impossible to imagine the creation of the state of Israel in 1948 without taking into account the shame of the entire world about the destruction of so much of European Jewry.What particularized and defined that guilt was the pictorial record, so exhaustively assembled in 1945. The visual is a compelling method for documenting that which cannot otherwise be imagined.

NOTES

1. Hans Habe, Off Limits: A Novel of Occupied Germany (London, 1956), p. 136; John Gimbel, A German Community Under American Occupation: Marburg, 1945-52 (Stanford, CA, 1961); James F. Tent, Mission on the Rhine: Re-education and Denazification in American-Occupied Germany (Chicago, 1982), p. 318; Edward N. Peterson, The American Occupation of Germany: Retreat to Victory (Detroit, 1977), p. 351-2. See also Lucius D. Clay, Decision in Germany (Garden City, NY, 1950); and the helpful daily entries in Major General John J. Maginnis (ed. Robert A. Hart), Military Government Journal: Normandy to Berlin (Amherst, MA, 1971). For an overview of the difficulties in planning effectively for the occupation of Germany, see Michael Balfour, Propaganda in War 1939-1945; Organisation, Policies and Publics in Britain and Germany (London, 1979), pp. 411-15.

2. Tent, Mission on the Rhine, pp. 1,3,51; Habe, All My Sins: An Autobiography (London, 1957), p. 365; Robert Birley, 'British Policy in Retrospect', p. 48, in Arthur Hearnden, ed., The British in Germany: Educational Reconstruction in Germany after 1945 (London, 1978). Birley was Educational Adviser to the Military Governor in the British Zone, 1947-49.

3. Habe, Off Limits, p. 285; Tent, Mission on the Rhine, p. 51. Interview with Forrest Pogue, Arlington, VA, August 31, 1982. Pogue, Marshall's official biographer, was in Germany with American

occupation forces from November 1945 to June 1946, returning again briefly in November 1946. He was assigned to the OMGUS staff in Heidelberg at the Amerika Haus, 1952-54. British exchanges are described in Dexter M. Keezer, A Unique Contribution to International Relations: The Story of Wilton Park (London, 1973).

4. See the Cold War rationale for this decision in Clay, Decision in Germany, p. 331.

5. Interview with Pogue, 31 August, 1982.

6. Clay, Decision in Germany, p. 62; Maginnis, Military Government Journal, p. 250, notes on 28 May 1945, that such a rule was going to be unenforceable; Peterson, American Occupation, p. 155.

7. Examples of the scripts for Know Your Enemy Germany and Here is Germany may be found in David Culbert, 'Note on Government Paper Records, pp. 235-43, in Bonnie G. Rowan, Scholars' Guide to Washington, D.C. Film and Video Collections (Washington D.C., 1980); prints for Here is Germany and Your Job in Germany may now be purchased from the National AudioVisual Centre in Washington, D.C. See William J. Blakefield, Documentary Film Classics Produced by the United States Government (2nd ed., Washington D.C., n.d. [1983]), pp. 29-31.

8. Brewster S. Chamberlain,'Todesmühlen: Ein früher Versuch zur Massen - "Umerziehung" in besetzten Deutschland 1945-1946', Vierteljahrshefte für Zeitgeschichte, XXIX (July, 1981), p. 421. See memoranda, including John Weir to Chief Signal Officer, 16 November 1944, in 'Pictorial Evidence of War Crimes 44-45' folder, 062.2 ocsigo, Box 750, A43-B28, Washington National Records Centre, Suitland, MD [hereafter WNRC Suitland]; K.B.Lawton to Signal Officer, 6th Army Group, 12th Army Group, and Special Motion Picture Coverage Unit, 25 April 1945; telegram SHAEF MAIN to G (P&PW), 21st Army Group, 26 April, 1945; both in 062.09, PR DIV SHAEF, Box 3, RG 331, Modern Military Records, National Archives, Washington D.C. [hereafter MMR-NA].

9 Nazi Concentration Camps may be purchased from the National AudioVisual Centre; Taylor Mills to Gordon Swarthout, 19 May 1945, entry 269, Box 1488, RG 208, WNRC-Suitland.

10. Letter, 'An Eyewitness Report', Hollywood Quarterly II (July 1947), pp. 412-14. Hans Habe, Off Limits, pp. 132-33, effectively expresses the feelings of Germans indignant at the Nuremberg Trials' 'unfortunate proportion of fact and accusation'. Roger Smither, Welt im Film 1945-1950: A Microfiche Catalogue of the Imperial War Museum's Holding of Material from the Anglo-American Newsreel Screen in Occupied Germany, 1945-1950 (London, 1981); Stephan Dolezel, '"Welt im Film" 1945: Ausgewählte Stories zu "Reeducation"', mimeo, Institut für den wissenschaftlichen Film, Göttingen, 1982, p. 2., copy kindly provided by Dolezel; Morris Janowitz, 'German Reactions to Nazi Atrocities', American Journal of Sociology LII (September 1946), pp. 141-46, describes the massive PWD campaign to inform Germans about the death camps in May and June 1945, but makes no mention of the special issue of Welt im Film.

11. Chamberlain, Todesmühlen,, p. 421; Hanus Burger, Der Frühling war es wert: Erinnerungen (Munich 1977), p. 232, 237. Burger devotes a full chapter to Todesmühlen, pp. 232-66, a source Chamberlain did not consult.

12. Chamberlain, Todesmühlen, p. 427; Burger, Der Frühling war es wert, p. 257, 259. Chamberlain 'Todesmühlen, p. 427, mistakenly gives the name as "Sridlin"'. Credits for Todesmühlen are found in Klaus Jaeger and Helmut Regel, Deutschland in Trümmern: Film Dokumente der Jahre 1945-1949, Eine Dokumentation (Oberhausen, 1976), p. 81.

13. Chamberlain, Todesmühlen, p. 431, notes that in a few places, civilians could not get their ration cards stamped until they had seen the film.

14. Burger, Der Frühling war es wert, p. 264; Peter Van Eyck, 'Film-Theatre-Music Sub-Section Report No. 27', 28 March 1946, Film Theatre and Music Branch 8-1/4; Van Eyck, 'Statistics on Todesmühlen with Intelligence Sub-Section Report on Todesmühlen', ICD 16-2/10, both in RG 260, OMGUS, WNRC-Suitland. Richard Wood kindly provided me with copies of OMGUS surveys relating to Todesmühlen.

15. Felix Scherke, 'A Psychological Survey of the Effects of the Film Todesmühlen', n.d. [February 1946], 32 pp., Bavaria Intelligence Division, III-1/10, RG 260, OMGUS, WNRC-Suitland.

16. The omission of the theme of collective guilt - which cannot be documented visually - is but one reason why Alain Resnais' Night and Fog (1958) remains the most brilliant film about the death camps. A comparison of the heavy-handed musical score in Death Mills with the one Hanns Eisler provided for Resnais' film also explains the latter's successful use of understatement.

17. The final English narration for Death Mills, OF-19, 26 March 1946, is found in Box 11, RG 111, Audiovisual Archives, NA. Public distribution in the United States was approved on 6 June 1946; see memorandum of that date, 062.2 ocsigo, Box 20, A52-248, WNRC-Suitland.

18. A letter to Warner Brothers from W.F.Flowers, Encino, CA, 21 May 1943, regarding Mission to Moscow suggests a theme which particularly concerned Jews in Hollywood: 'Allow me to congratulate you on a very open faced piece of communistic propaganda. I believe you have done a good job from the stand point of propaganda work, but a work that is going to backfire not only on Warner Bros, but on the Jewish race as well.' Box 684, Warner Brothers Archive, Department of Special Collections, University of Southern California, Los Angeles, CA [herafter WA-USC] .

19. Bennett to Jack L.Warner, 7 February 1946, production files for The Ghosts of Berchtesgaden, WA-USC [hereafter Ghosts file] .

20. Walt Disney secrecy agreement, 26 May 1944, 160 as, Box 751, A43-B28, WNRC-Suitland. Lubitsch had proposed the chapters of German history for Know Your Enemy Germany.

21. Horgan to Frank McCarthy, 7 December 1944; 062.2 ocs, Box 133, RG 165, MMR-NA; telegram, Munson to SCPC, 26 December

1944, production files, Here is Germany, OF-9, Box 8, RG 111, Audiovisual Archives-NA.

22. Your Job in Germany, OF-8, was released on 4 April, 1945, and released for public exhibition only on 16 July 1946; see memoranda in 062.2 ocsigo, Box 19, A52-248, WNRC-Suitland. A typed copy of the final narration is located in Ghosts file, WA-USC.

23. For an example of this process, see Thomas Cripps and David Culbert, 'The Negro Soldier (1944): Film Propaganda in Black and White', American Quarterly XXXI (Winter, 1979), pp. 616-40.

24. Weible to Frank McCarthy, 23 May; Hodes to McCarthy, 30 May; Luther Hill to McCarthy, 6 June, 1945; all in 062.2.ocs, Box 133, RG 165, MMR-NA.

25. All of these revisions (some, technically speaking, revised inserts) and the memoranda which help date the development of the story are found in the Ghosts file, WA-USC.

26. The photographs, with memoranda documenting Jack Warner's having seen them, production memoranda, and stills from the Berlin Hotel set - even publicity stills for 'fake newsreel' shots of dead American sailors - are found in the Ghosts file, WA-USC.

27. Memo, Gordon Hollingshead to William Guthrie, 12 September, telegrams and letter, Curtis Mitchell to William Guthrie, both 27 September 1945, Ghosts file, WA-USC.

28. A complete release continuity for Hitler Lives? (the name was changed on 9 November 1945) which makes possible an exact word-by-word comparison with Your Job in Germany may be found in Ghosts file, WA-USC. Warner even had the audacity, in accepting an award for Hitler Lives? from the Hollywood Foreign Correspondents Association, to call the film a 'hard-hitting job well carried out by many able and sincere people at our studio'. Transcription of Warner speech, n.d. [1946] Ghosts file, WA-USC.

29. Munson to W.W.Jervey, 7 February 1946, Box 9, Lyman Munson Papers, University of Wyoming, Laramie, WY.

30. Journal, 28 January; Advocate, 7 February; Tribune, 8 February 1946; copy of Warner Brotherhood Week display ad., all in press file, Ghosts file WA-USC.

31. Milder to Warner, 28 January; Joseph Westreich, Paris, to G.R.Keyser, 9 July 1946; both in distribution records, Ghosts file, WA-US.

32. For an introduction to the This is America series see Richard Meran Barsam, 'This is America: Documentaries for Theatres, 1942-1951', in Barsam, ed., Nonfiction Film Theory and Criticism (New York, 1975), pp. 115-35. Additional information about the series and its relation to Pathe News may be found in Raymond Fielding, The American Newsreel, 1911-1967 (Norman, OK, 1972), p. 193; and Fielding, The March of Time, 1935-1951 (New York, 1978), p. 282. The Motion Picture Section of the Library of Congress has most of the This is America Series.

33. Patrick Sheehan of the Motion Picture Section, LC, kindly sent me copies of the relevant This is America release sheets.

34. The list is as follows: (*means withdrawn as too-militaristic or to balance number from each studio): The Maltese

Falcon (WB 1941); Remember the Day (20th CF 1942); *Action in the North Atlantic (WB 1943; withdrawn, re-edited, re-introduced); Seven Sweethearts (MGM 1942); It Happened Tomorrow (UA 1944); Pride and Prejudice (MGM 1940); All That Money Can Buy (RKO 1941); Madam Curie (MGM 1944); One Hundred Men and a Girl (Univ 1937); Thirty Seconds Over Tokyo (MGM 1945); *Air Force (WB 1943); *The More the Merrier (Col 1943); Across the Pacific (WB 1942); The Human Comedy (MGM 1943); Abe Lincoln in Illinois (RKO 1940); Dr Ehrlich's Magic Bullet (1st Nat 1940); Young Tom Edison (MGM 1940); The Gold Rush (UA 1942 reissue with sound): It Started with Eve (Univ 1941); You Were Never Lovelier (Col 1942); Appointment for Love (Univ 1941); *The Navy Comes Through (RKO 1942); Hold Back the Dawn (Para 1941); I Married a Witch (UA 1942); Christmas in July (Para 1940); *Corvette K-255 (Univ 1943); Tales of Manhattan (20th CF 1944); Shadow of a Doubt (Univ 1943); *The Sullivans (20th CF 1944); My Sister Eileen (Col 42); *Tom, Dick, and Harry (RKO 1941); Going My Way (Para 1944).

    35.   Joseph, Our Film Programme in Germany: I. How Far Was It a Success?, Hollywood Quarterly, II (January 1947), p. 125. Maginnis, in a diary entry for 26 October 1945, notes 'went to first civilian movie tonight on Kürfurstendamm - I Married a Witch'. Maginnis, Military Government Journal, p. 310.

    36.   Conversation with Pronay at London Conference, April 1983. Pronay was in Budapest in 1946. Van Eyck, 'Report No.27', 28 March 1946, RG 260, OMGUS, WNRC-Suitland.

    37.   Hill, 'Our Film Programme in Germany: II. How Far Was It A Failure?', Hollywood Quarterly, II (January 1947), pp. 134-5.

    38.   United States Group Control Council, Information Control in Germany as of 25 September 1945, mimeo; typed minutes, 'Meeting to Discuss PID/OWI Joint Newsreel Held at Bush House on Thursday, 39.ll.45'; OMGUS Plans and Directives Branch, ICD, OMGUS, (Report to the Smith-Mundt Committee on Interpreting the United States to the American Zone in Occupied Germany' VI, Film Control, 19 September 1947; Report on OMGUS Film Conference, Stuttgart, 24 September 1948; all in RG 260, OMGUS, WNRC-Suitland.

    39.   'Operation Report as of 21 March 1949' Motion Picture Branch, RG 260, OMGUS, WNRC-Suitland.

    40.   Interview with Pogue, 31 August 1982; Clay, Decision in Germany, p. 62; Tent, Mission on the Rhine, p. 313.

    41.   See chapter 9.

    42.   A reworked version of the 'long telegram' appeared in Foreign Affairs, July 1947, as 'The Sources of Soviet Conduct', by 'X'.

    43.   Sebastian Haffner, The Meaning of Hitler (Cambridge, MA, 1983), p. 141.

Appendix

Two Film Narrations

1. Death Mills

LEST WE FORGET

1. On a day in April 1945, the townspeople of Gardelegen, Germany, carried 1100 crosses to a local barn. Eleven hundred, about the number of people in a small town like Centreville, Mississippi. Only these eleven hundred were no longer living. The crosses were for eleven hundred fresh graves, the victims of Gardelegen.

2. But these eleven hundred were a small fraction of the twenty million men, women and children murdered by the Nazis. Twenty million human beings equal to the population of twenty-two American states. Twenty million corpses: the product of three hundred concentration camps all over Germany and in occupied territories.

3. Death mills that ground out their dead until the very day Allied Armies broke through their gates.

4. Those who survived could answer the roll call of all the nations of Europe, of all the religious faiths, of all political beliefs condemned by Hitler because they were anti-Nazi.

5. And now they were free. the liberators had smashed through the barbed wire at Dachau, at Buchenwald, at Ohrdruf, at Belsen and at Sachsenhaasen. The killers had fled from Auschwitz, Maidenek, Ebensee and Ravenbrueck.

6. Many were freed only to die. Years of imprisonment, starvation, torture and forced labor had broken them. They had been beaten down to live like animals - far worse - for few animals had lived in the terror, hunger and filth of these victims...People who once had been human beings like you and me.

7. When the Allies came, survivors were taken out of dungeons where rats had been their companions and vermin their bedfellows. Despite the desperate efforts of Allied doctors and medical aids help came too late for many.

8. In the hell of Auschwitz, Allied physicians study marks of the Nazi beast - wounds more ghastly than anything they had seen on the battlefield.

9. Children and infants died the slow death of deliberate starvation.

10. Allied leaders came to the camps, soon after the troops overran them.

11. First was General Eisenhower, who visited Ohrdruf.

12. The inmates demonstrate the 'bock', a torture instrument with which they were well acquainted. This was just one of many torture devices of Himmler's henchmen.

13. Military leaders were followed by church dignitaries like the Archbishop of Canterbury.

14. And civilians of the Allied investigation commission came to authenticate to the world horrors that human beings found hard to believe, such as dungeons where this sort of 'atrocity' - 'five with operations in each box' was routine.

15. And everywhere was the repeated, monotonous sight and stench of corpses - shriveled bodies like old bones picked over by dogs - piles and heaps like the litter of a boneyard. These are the foul, wretched, remnants of human beings, human beings - like you and me.

16. Not all died slowly and horribly by starvation. Millions died quickly - and horribly - by burning in the furnaces of Poland - such as Maidenek.

17. Or the crematoria of Buchenwald...

18. This is what is left of their agony - a handful of ash to swirl into oblivion on a puff of wind.

19. Here is the 'folterkammer' torture chamber in Maidenek. It is a lasting monument to German scientific genius. Gas chambers were the principal agent of death - and their use was admirably organized. Prisoners were told to prepare themselves for a shower bath. They were given towels to make them believe this story. But when the doors of the bathroom were closed behind them, poison gas Zyklon was released through the shower ducts.

20. In Dachau, in Auschwitz, in Maidenek - the German murder trust standardized the procedure of slaughter - the death gas was always the same - Zyklon.

21. Cremation was the chief means of disposal of the great mass of bodies. Auschwitz alone had four of them going night and day like the blast furnaces of Pittsburg. Having been put to all this expense of murder, the Nazis were determined to make a profit. The charred remains were ground up and sold to German farmers as fertilizer.

22. The death mills were made to pay in many ways. Thousands of garments were stripped from prisoners - women's clothes, infants' shoes, even toys and dolls.

23. Human hair - women's hair - cut before death dulled its luster. Methodically packed, it was ready for sale to manufacturers.

24. Every murder mill had its storage room, like this one at Buchenwald. Each contained jewelry - watches-wedding rings-heaps of eyeglasses and gold teeth...torn from the mouth of the dead. These were the instruments used to pull the teeth. In their slaughterhouses, the Nazi butchers wasted as little of the body as possible.

25. When Allied armies approached, the Nazis often tried to rush their prisoners elsewhere.

26. Thousands were suffocated in overcrowded freight cars. Many of the dead - and the dying - were flung into the water.

27. If the Allies moved too rapidly, the Nazis attempted to kill their prisoners so that no witnesses of their crimes were left behind.

28. In Maidenek...in Ohrdruf...in many other camps, thousands were murdered just before liberation.

29. This man was killed with a bayonet-

30. This man with a spade-

31. Here is a typical German barn at Gardelegen. Eleven hundred human beings were herded into it and burned alive. Those who in their anguish broke out - were shot as they emerged.

32. What sub-humans did these things? Here is one captured at Matthausen.

33. At Belsen, we caught the camp commander, Joseph Kramer, the 'Beast of Belsen'.

34. Men or women - they were the Nazi elite - Himmler's own. Amazons, turned Nazi killers, were merciless in the use of the whip, practiced in torture and murder...deadlier than the males.

35. Here are more concentration camp guards, commandents and the so-called physicians, killers instead of healers.

36. In the interrogation room at Hadamar, a witness testifies. The camp commander and chief physician are brought into the room. They can explain everything of course. Of course, the prisoners were used as guinea pigs. Of course, poison was injected into their blood stream and they died. Herr Doktor seems surprised that anyone should find anything wrong with this.

37. The camp cemetery discloses hundreds of victims of this Nazi research in murder.

38. This was a woman.

39. Allied members of the war crimes commission opened thousands of bodies. The record of their autopsies showed the same murder system at work everywhere - slow suffocation, starvation, poison injections, burning, shooting - Hitler's henchmen tried them all.

40. Matthausen tells the same story. Those dead were starved or shot. Often prisoners still alive - or rather not quite dead - were thrown among the corpses.

41. Mass killing methods were standardized for efficiency.

42. In Ohrdruf, shooting -

43. In Naumbach - shooting -

44. In Landsberg - starvation -

45. In Dachau - Burning, poison gas, starvation -

46. In Auschwitz - shooting, poison gas, starvation, even for new-born babes.

47. In Ebensee - starvation -

48. In Belsen - shooting, starvation -

49. In Nordhausen - shooting, poison gas, starvation -

50. In Leipzig - burned to death on high voltage wires -

51. A few thousand of those twenty million victims survived the years of horror. The faces of these women at Nordhausen tell the story of their sufferings.

52. In Remsdorf six women were found alive among thousands of corpses. Six women - with wounds like this...

53. These are children who survived at Auschwitz. Their parents and relatives had been murdered by poison gas. Most of them

have forgotten their names and have nothing left to identify them except the numbers the Nazis tattooed on their arms.

54. Holzen had a handful left. One of these men had his eyes gouged out by the Naizs.

55. Ebensee's survivors were walking skeletons. Most of them couldn't even walk - or crawl.

56. In Offenburg -

57. In Fehrballin -

58. In Belsen -

59. Thirteen thousand people died in the weeks following liberation. For them Allied medical science and nursing came too late.

60. Nazi Party leaders and office holders were commanded by Allied military authorities to visit concentration camps in the neighbourhood of their cities. They were forced to see with their own eyes crimes whose existence they had indignantly denied.

61. At Weimar, all citizens were ordered to visit the concentration camp. They were called from their homes, assembled in the streets and marched off.

62. They started the trip as though they were going on a picnic. After all, it was only a short walk from any German city to the nearest concentration camp.

63. But there was no picnic behind the barbed wore. Death was the only one who had feasted here.

64. None of these victims had died naturally. Each and every one had been murdered - on orders of the Nazi High Command.

65. But these Germans - the ones who said they didn't know - were responsible, too. They had put themselves - gladly - into the hands of criminals and lunatics.

66. They tell you now they meant no evil - that they knew nothing of what was going on - or could do nothing even if they knew.. The farmers received tons of human bones as fertilizer...but apparently never suspected it came from human beings...the manufacturers received tons of human hair...but apparently never dreamed it came from the heads of murdered women...no nightmares ever haunted those who lived near concentration camps...the cries and moans of the tortured were no doubt believed the wailing of the wind.

67. Yesterday, while millions were dying in concentration camps, Germans jammed Nuremberg to cheer the Nazi Party and sing hymns of hate.

68. Today, these Germans who cheered the destruction of humanity in their own land...who cheered the attack on unarmed neighbors...who cheered the enslavement of Europe...plead for your sympathy. They are the same Germans who once 'Heiled Hitler'.

REMEMBER...if they bear heavy crosses now, they are the crosses of the millions crucified in Nazi death mills!

2. <u>Your Job in Germany</u>

Reel 1.

The problem now is future peace.[That is your job in Germany. By your conduct and attitude while on guard inside Germany, you can lay the groundwork for a peace that could last forever, or just the opposite, you could lay the groundwork for a new war to come. And, just as American soldiers had to do this job twenty-six years ago, so other American soldiers, your sons, might have to do it again another twenty odd years from now. [1] <u>Germany</u> today appears to be beaten. Hitler out. Swasticas gone. Nazi propaganda off the air. Concentration camps empty. <u>You'll see</u> ruins. <u>You'll see flowers.</u> <u>You'll see</u> some mighty pretty scenery. Don't let it fool <u>you</u>. You are in enemy country. Be alert! - Suspicious of everyone. Take no chances. You are up against something more than tourist scenery. Your are up against German history. It isn't good! This book was written chapter by chapter; not by one man or one fuhrer. It was written by the German people.

Chapter One: The fuhrer: Bismark, the title- Blood and iron, the armies: German. Under the Prussian Bismark the German empire was built, the German states combined serving notice to all that their religion was iron and that their God was blood. Bismark's German empire built itself by war. At the expense of Denmark, Austria, and France, it became in 1871, the mightiest power in all Europe. - Enough conquest for a while. Time out to digest it. Europe relaxes. The danger's over. Nice country, Germany. Tender people the Germans. Very sweet music indeed.

Chapter Two: A new fuhrer: Kaiser Wilhelm, new title: "Deutschland Uber Alles" - Germany over all. And, the same tender German people slapped us with their World War One Against Servia, Russia, France, Belgium, Italy, Britain and the United States of America. It took all of us to do it, but we finally knocked that fuhrer out, defeated the German Armies. Second chapter ended.

We marched straight into Germany and said, (new voice) "These people are O.K. It was just the Kaiser we had to get rid of. You know, this is really <u>some</u> country. When it comes to culture, they lead the whole world."

We poured in our sympathy. We pulled out our armies, and they flung Chapter Three in our faces. Fuhrer number three, slogan number three: Today Germany is ours, tomorrow the whole <u>world</u>. And the tender, sorry German people carried the torch of their culture to Austria, Czechoslavakia, Poland, France, England, Norway, Holland, Denmark, Belgium, Luxembourg, Russia, Yugoslavia, Greece, and the <u>United States of America</u> [Over the shattered homes, over the broken bodies of millions of people who had let down their guard.] We almost lost <u>this</u> one. It took everything we had. Measure the cost in money. There <u>isn't</u> that much money! Measure the cost in lifes. You can only guess at that figure. It took burning and scalding, drenching, freezing. It took legs, fingers, arms, and it took them by the millions. It cost hours, days and years that

will never return. It ruined our health and wealth, our past and our future. it took every last ounce of our courage and guts. Now, what happens?
(New voice) "Oh, this is where we came in!"
(Narrator) "Yeh! this is where we came in! And, Chapter Four. will be: It can happen again!"

Reel 2

The next war. That is why you occupy Germany, to make that war impossible. No easy job! Keep your wits about you. [Don't relax that caution now. The Nazi party may be gone; Nazi thinking, Nazi training, Nazi trickery remains.] The German lust for conquest is not dead. It has merely gone undercover. Somewhere in this Germany are the SS Guards, the Schutztruppe, the Gestapo gangsters out of uniform. You won't know them, but they'll know you. Somewhere in this Germany are stormtroopers by the thousands. Out of sight, out of the mob, [still watching you]. Somewhere in this Germany there are two million ex-Nazi officials, out of power, but still in there thinking and thinking about next time. Remember that only yesterday every business, every profession was part of Hitler's system. The doctors, technicians, clock-makers, postmen, farmers, housekeepers, toy-makers, barbers, cooks, dock workers. Practically every German was part of the Nazi network. Guard particularly against this group: These are the most dangerous: German youth, children when the Nazi party came into power. They know no other system but the one that poisoned their minds. They're soaked in it. Trained to win by cheating. Trained to pick on the weak. They've heard no free speeches, read no free press. They were brought up on straight propaganda. Production of the worst educational crime in the entire history of the world. Practically everything you believe in, they've been trained to hate and destroy. They believe they were born to be masters, and that we are inferiors designed to be their slaves. They may deny it now, but they believe it and will try to prove it again. [Don't argue with them. Don't try to change their point of view. Other allied representatives will concern themselves with that. You are not being sent into Germany as educators. you are soldiers on guard. You will observe their local laws, respect their customs and religion, and you will respect their property rights. You will not ridicule them. You will not argue with them. You will not be friendly. You will be aloof, watchful and supicious. Every German is a potential sources of trouble; therefore, there must be no fraternization with any of the German people. Fraternization means making friends. The German people are not our friends. You will not associate yourself with German men, women or children. You will not associate with them on familiar terms either in public or in private. You will not visit in their homes, nor will you ever take them into your confidence.] However free, however sorry, however sick of the Nazi party they may seem, they cannot come back into the civilized world just by sticking our their hand and saying 'We're sorry'. Not sorry they caused the war, but only sorry that they lost it. That is the hand that heiled Adolph Hitler. [That is the hand that dropped the bombs on helpless Rotterdam, Brussels, Belgrade. That is the hand that destroyed the cities, villages, the homes in Russia.] That is the hand that held the whip over the Polish, Yugoslav, French and Norwegian slaves. That is the hand that took the food. That is the hand that starved them. That is the hand that murdered, massacred, Greeks, Czecks, [Jews. [2] That is the hand that killed and crippled American soldiers, sailors, marines. Don't clasp that hand. It is not the kind of hand you care to clasp in friendship.]

(New Voice) "But there are millions of Germans. Some of those guys must be O.K."

(Narrator) Perhaps, but which ones? [Just one mistake may cost you your life. Trust none of them.] Some day the German people might be cured of their disease, the super-race disease, the world conquest disease, but they must prove that they have been cured beyond the shadow of a doubt before they ever again are allowed to take their place among the respectable nations. Until that day, we stand guard. We are determined that their plan for world conquest shall stop here and now. We are determined that they shall never again use peaceful industries for warlike purposes. We are determined that our children shall never face this German terror. We are determined that the vicious German cycle of war - phoney peace, war - phoney peace, war - phoney peace shall once and for all-time come to an end. [That is your job in Germany.]

NB. 1. All the expressions in brackets were marked 'out'. 2. The word 'Jews' was marked 'N.B. out'.

Chapter Nine

THE RE-EDUCATION OF IMPERIAL JAPAN

GORDON DANIELS

In 1868 Japan already possessed the most effective system of
education in Asia. Each domain provided official schools for warriors
to study Confucianism and the literary arts, and temple schools
taught 'reading, writing and the abacus' to increasing numbers of
peasants, traders and artisans. Literacy rates were higher than in
large areas of Europe and Western observers praised the high
educational standards of the common people. [1]
    Against this background it was natural for the founders of the
modern Japanese state to give education a central place in their
programme of Westernisation. [2] A nationwide system of schools
would replace provincialism with national unity, and bring knowledge
of the modern world to the humblest citizen. In 1871 the Ministry of
Education was established and in the following year a system of
compulsory primary schooling was inaugurated. Like European states
the Japanese government used schools to instruct children in
patriotism and loyalty and the Imperial Rescript on Education (1890)
urged students to 'offer themselves courageously to the State' to
'maintain the prosperity of ... [the]... Imperial throne co-eval with
Heaven and Earth'. [3] However, economic and political
modernisation also required more sophisticated institutions of higher
learning. To produce significant numbers of officials, technicians and
businessmen the regime created a series of educational ladders
including middle and higher schools, educational and technical
colleges and imperial universities. Entrance to higher education was
on the basis of merit and the hard path from farming household to
college and university brought a significant stream of talent into
Japanese public life. [4]
    In the twelfth century economic growth and imperial expansion
created new educational needs. Compulsory education was extended,
further universities were created, and some private colleges received
university status. Japanese education was highly centralised but
within it were vivid differences of atmosphere and regulation.
Primary schools emphasised obedience, rote learning and conformity;
but in elite high schools and universities there was relatively free
discussion, and student residences were often self-governing. [5]
Undergraduate societies discussed such varied ideas as Christianity,

203

socialism and democracy and the 1920s witnessed the growth of student internationalism and criticism of authority. Such novel ideas attracted official disfavour, and contributed to the introduction, in 1925, of military training into schools and universities. [6] Six years later the world recession and a sense of national isolation produced widespread chauvinism among all classes of Japanese. These changes had a rapid impact on most aspects of education. In 1937 the Ministry of Education issued the 'Basic Principles of the National Polity' (Kokutai no Hongi) which stated a new patriotic philosophy. Like earlier proclamations this emphasised obedience and loyalty but it went beyond the nationalism of the nineteenth century. The authors of the new document openly attacked the rationalism and individualism of liberal Western societies and in contrast praised filial piety, the divine emperor and the creation of 'a new Japanese culture...sublimating Western culture with our national polity'. [7] The outbreak of war with China in July 1937 and increasing campaigns for 'spiritual mobilisation' extended this ethos into all levels of education. In schools relatively liberal textbooks were replaced by patriotic readers, and such subjects as history, geography and 'ethics' were dominated by concepts of ultra-nationalism and military glory. Military training and 'war sports' even entered elementary school education and the declaration of war on Britain, the United States and the Netherlands in 1941 accentuated the concept of the garrison state. [8]

Although the war years saw the expansion and development of Japanese technical education, important subjects were surprisingly neglected. In particular the study of English, the language of Japan's main enemies, was largely abandoned. Wartime education also suffered from the effects of air raids, the shortening of courses, and the mobilisation of students to work in factories. Hundreds of schools were destroyed by incendiaries and in the spring of 1945 middle and higher schools were closed to permit pupils to carry out important war work. [9]

Noting the militarism, xenophobia and intolerance of Japan's wartime education, it is hardly surprising that American officials saw it as a major factor in Tokyo's aggressive policies. Indeed as early as 1942 the United States Government began to plan the re-education of the Japanese population and the transformation of the enemy into a peaceful democratic state. However, much of this discussion centred on negative rather than positive aspects of policy. There was widespread agreement on the need to remove government controls from the mass media and to end military training in schools; but, initially, Americans were unsure of their ability to intervene successfully in the details of Japanese education. Consequently it was thought best to retain the existing Ministry of Education and use it as an agency for liberal improvements. Some American diplomats were aware of the efficiency and meritocratic virtues of Japanese schools and universities but by the summer of 1945 increasingly critical ideas had come to dominate American thinking. In July, Gordon Bowles, of the Department of State, drafted a radical series of proposals which were to influence much later policy. [10] Bowles urged the purging of ultranationalists from the teaching profession and positive measures to emancipate new generations of Japanese. These included greater educational opportunities for women, the expansion of higher education, improvements in vocational courses, and an 'internationalist' curriculum. At the centre of these ideas was the encouragement of freedom and individualism which were to be aided by measures to decentralise the control of education. But even these novel principles constituted no more than a framework of policy. Public pronouncements continued to spell out little more than generalities. On 26 July 1945 the allies issued the Potsdam declaration which demanded Japan's unconditional surrender and declared 'The Japanese Government shall remove all obstacles to the revival and strengthening of democratic tendencies...freedom of speech, religion and thought...shall be established'. [11] Although Japan did not concede surrender until 15 August this document indicated the likely direction of allied policy, and unconsciously suggested ways in which occupation plans might be anticipated.

When Japan accepted the Potsdam declaration her situation was very different from that anticipated by American pre-surrender planners. Her early surrender had prevented armed invasion and her administrative system remained intact. Furthermore, America was the only allied power to have made detailed plans for occupying the Japanese mainland; she also possessed sufficient local power to exclude Britain, China or the Soviet Union from any share in administration. As a result, Supreme Commander MacArthur enjoyed total control but would rule through the Japanese cabinet and civil service.

However, even before MacArthur landed in Japan, the imperial government sought to head off American intervention with its own tentative steps towards educational reform. On 17 August a new cabinet including pre-war 'liberals' was formed and a week later the Ministry of Education abolished all wartime regulations, and began the removal of military personnel from schools and colleges. [12] The Minister of Education in the new cabinet was Maeda Tamon, a man of some international experience who had worked in the International Labour Office in Geneva and the Japanese Cultural Centre in New York. [13] He soon appointed other liberal figures to advise him in planning reform of the educational system. On 15 September Maeda issued Education Policy for the Construction of a New Japan, the first lengthy statement on the future direction of Japanese schools and universities. This emphasised the maintenance of the Emperor system, but also called for the elimination of military thought and practice and the encouragement of peace and science. [14] A further contribution to new thinking was a personal memorandum submitted by Tanaka Kotaro, a Roman Catholic who was head of the Law Faculty of Tokyo Imperial University. This also emphasised internationalism and peace and the need to encourage individualism. Tanaka also extended the discussion from ideas to organisation and advocated the abolition of chauvinistic education colleges and the subordination of administrators to teachers and academics. [15]

It was against this background that the American occupation forces began their own intervention in Japanese education. General MacArthur established his headquarters in Tokyo on 17 September but it was not until five days later that an agency was established to supervise the shaping and execution of educational reform. This was the Civil Information and Education Section (CIE) of General Headquarters which was to be responsible for policies in such wide-ranging fields as religion, film, broadcasting, language, schools and universities. [16] CIE's first head Brigadier Kenneth Dyke who had worked in the National Broadcasting Company (NBC) was well suited to the task of liberalising Japan's mass media. However, the censors of Counter-Intelligence also played a significant role.

As early as 10 September MacArthur had issued the first 'civil liberties directive' which ordered the Japanese Government to impose standards of 'truthfulness' upon the press and radio. Unfortunately this produced unexpected results. Some Japanese journalists continued to proclaim the Emperor's virtues while others attacked the American use of atomic weapons. This produced far from subtle reactions. On several occasions in September MacArthur briefly suspended newspapers to punish such transgressions, and on 21 September a ten point 'Press Code' was issued by Colonel Hoover of Counter-Intelligence. [17] This forbade any criticism of the allies, emphasised public tranquillity and condemned any 'propaganda line' in news reporting. All these events demonstrated that press freedom was to be conditional and limited. Censorship was to remain an important weapon of American policy and the occupation authorities often 'suggested' appropriate themes for press attention. [18]

Similarly, in the field of broadcasting, initial talk of freedom was replaced by the 'Radio Code' of 22 September. In many respects this resembled the instructions already issued to newspaper companies, and the Japan Broadcasting Corporation (NHK) was also forbidden to broadcast to overseas audiences. Under CIE pressure radio became a major agency in advocating 'democracy' and denouncing the evils of the old regime. [19]

CIE's policy towards the cinema consisted of a similar mixture of liberalisation and control. On 27 September and 10 October all existing controls and agencies of censorship were abolished, but MacArthur soon showed a heavier hand. In mid-November CIE issued a list of 236 films which were to be banned from cinemas and handed in for SCAP scrutiny and destruction. Not only was this list an arbitrary jumble of historical epics and chauvinistic propaganda but intervention soon went further. CIE began to suggest 'appropriate themes' for new films such as women's rights, trade unions and democracy. Newsreels also became acquiescent aids to 'democratic propaganda'. [20]

Despite these manifold forms of re-education the transformation of the Japanese education system remained the most ambitious and important field of CIE activity. CIE's educational policies, like Maeda's proposals, began with broad demilitarisation. The United

States Initial Post-Surrender Policy, which was issued from Washington on 6 September, had stated that 'militarism and ultranationalism in doctrine and practice, including paramilitary training shall be eliminated from the educational system' [21] and on 22 October this theme was converted into a broad directive to the Japanese Government. This memorandum entitled <u>Administration of the Educational System of Japan</u> called for the screening of teachers and administrators and the dismissal of military personnel and proponents of 'militarism and ultranationalism'. Textbooks and courses were to be scrutinised for unsavoury content and unsatisfactory sections eliminated and replaced. But this document also suggested that far more drastic changes were afoot. The Japanese Ministry was directed to establish practices 'in harmony with international peace, representative government, the dignity of the individual and fundamental human rights' while, for the first time, students and teachers were to be permitted 'free and unrestricted discussion of issues involving political civil and religious liberties'. Even more dramatic was an order to the all-powerful Ministry of Education to furnish regular reports on its compliance with American instructions. [22]

Initially CIE was handicapped by acute shortages of staff but as this was gradually remedied American action became more overt. Further instructions from Washington aided this process, and on 15 December the state-supported Emperor cult (Shinto) was condemned and government assistance forbidden. This directive had an immediate impact in Japanese schools for all references to Shinto were removed from textbooks, visits to shrines were forbidden and circulation of 'Basic Principles of the National Polity' was prohibited. [23] By the end of the year an even more sweeping directive temporarily banned the teaching of existing courses in Japanese history, geography and ethics, all of which were heavily coloured by extreme nationalism.

Despite this vigorous attack on the most chauvinistic aspects of Japanese education MacArthur lacked a comprehensive plan for the reconstruction of schools and universities. Furthermore the relatively conservative Ministry of Education still appeared a barrier to extensive reform. These two factors combined to produce the next major steps in American policy. After much discussion within the CIE, on 6 January 1946, MacArthur requested the United States government to select and organise a mission of educational specialists to tour Japan and furnish advice on democratic reform. [24] Three days later the Japanese Government was instructed to create a parallel committee of experts to cooperate with the visiting mission. In response to this request a group of twenty-nine distinguished Japanese educators and laymen was chosen and approved by CIE This committee - the Japanese Education Committee (JEC) - included some of the most liberal figures in Japanese intellectual life. Its head was Professor Nambara Shigeru, a Protestant who had opposed the military during the war and had recently been appointed Principal of Tokyo Imperial University. [25] Among other influential members was Tanaka Kotaro who had already furnished advice on future policy. In the ensuing weeks the JEC produced a detailed programme of suggestions which was to prove remarkably influential. The committee's written 'Opinion' began with the hope that the Emperor's prestige could be used to assist new educational ideas, but most of its proposals marked a complete break with tradition. It proposed the reduction of the Ministry's powers and the transfer of much administrative power to prefectural and metropolitan committees. These would be elected by ordinary citizens and teachers and would contain no more than one or two administrators. This theme of decentralisation was affirmed in a plan to end the ministerial control of textbooks and teaching instructions. Perhaps the committee's most important blueprint concerned the basic structure of the school system. [26] The committee found the system of stratified educational ladders extremely inflexible and in its place proposed a single comprehensive system which would extend compulsory education from eight to nine years. According to this a full course from elementary education to university degree would embrace six years at junior school, six years at middle and high schools and four years at university. The JEC also favoured a less standardised curriculum, less emphasis upon textbooks and more freedom for pupils to express their natural creativity. It also proposed that teachers should have the legal right to form unions and professional associations.

In parallel with these Japanese discussions, the American Government had slowly gathered together members of the United States Education Mission. This process was not only hampered by the busy schedules of numerous academics but by active political pressures to include prestigious Roman Catholic educators in the party. The eventual Mission consisted of twenty-seven scholars, administrators and laymen under the leadership of Dr George Stoddard, Commissioner of Education for the State of New York. Accompanying the party was Gordon Bowles, of the Department of State, who had already exerted an early influence on occupation education policy. The Mission arrived in Japan on 6 March and was to explore the themes of 'Education for Democracy', 'Psychology in Re-education', 'Administrative Re-organisation' and 'Higher Education'. All these concepts were interpreted in extremely broad terms so as to embrace language reform, libraries, museums, and the social sciences as well as the familiar theme of decentralisation. [27]

At the Mission's first meeting with Japanese leaders, the new Minister of Education, Abe Yoshishige, made a courageous attempt to assert Japanese interests. He declared: 'It must be a very difficult thing to be a good victor...we believe that you...are not going to be needlessly proud and arrogant as a victorious nation...I hope I am not too bold in expressing the wish that America will not avail herself of this position to impose on us simply what is characteristic of America...this is a mistake which a victorious people is always apt to make'. In reply Stoddart stated: 'We shall look for what is good in the Japanese education system...our hope is that we may study these tasks together formulating the joint outcomes of our work'. [28] In a sense these Japanese and American comments symbolised the complex relationship which underlay the Mission's activities. Of course, victors and vanquished could never be equals but in the Mission's four week investigation it absorbed ideas and schemes from CIE, the Japan Education Committee, the Ministry of Education and a wide variety of individuals.

The Mission's Final Report ignored the centralised educational systems of various allied countries and claimed that decentralisation was essential to democracy and the elimination of militarism. This was linked to a broad philosophical analysis which emphasised the importance of the locality, the individual and choice, in the development of a free system. Any morality taught in schools should not be imperial ethics but 'equality', 'the give and take of democratic government' and 'pride in individual workmanship'. If this were to be achieved, new textbooks would be needed as well as programmes to re-educate the teaching profession. The healthy growth and development of pupils would require improved courses in hygiene, more relevant vocational courses and increasing attention to modern technology. Many of these ideals appealed to Japanese liberals but in one respect the Mission pursued a notion which was anathema to virtually all Japanese. [29] Under the influence of ill-informed enthusiasts in CIE, Stoddard proposed the total transformation of the Japanese writing system. Arguing that the mixture of Chinese characters and two syllabaries was a barrier to literacy and international communication he advocated the adoption of total romanisation. The Mission may have been motivated by high ideals but a minority in CIE had more sinister objectives. Such officers as Robert K. Hall believed that such a move would isolate all future generations of Japanese from traditional culture and thereby prevent the revival of militaristic sentiments. [30] Perhaps of more value was the suggestion that many nuances of spoken Japanese should be replaced by a simpler 'democratic' style; and this may have contributed to the later streamlining of much everyday language.

Of all the Mission's proposals the most important and influential was its plan for the reshaping of the school system. Despite Japan's enormous financial problems it followed the JEC's proposal for the extension of compulsory schooling to nine years. It also adopted the related Japanese idea of a single comprehensive educational ladder for all children. Under this so-called '6.3.3.system' all would attend co-educational primary schools for six years and middle schools for three years. for those who wished to continue their education, three-year high school courses would be available - as the necessary preliminary to higher education. [31] Parallel with this single ladder school system the Mission proposed the simplification and expansion of higher education. Favouring the opening of educational opportunities and the destruction of privilege, the Report advocated the replacement of varieties of higher schools, colleges and universities with a standardised system of four-year universities.

In supporting a policy of decentralisation the Mission reflected American and liberal Japanese ideas. It proposed the control of education by elected committees and sought to link the general public with educational agencies. This ideal was further expressed in imaginative plans for the promotion of adult education and the development of libraries and community halls. [32]

General MacArthur received this humane and idealistic report favourably but implementation was to be a complex and selective process. Not only was it impossible to impose complicated reforms on an intricate alien society but the survival of any changes would depend upon generating substantial public support. As a result, MacArthur sought to continue the element of cooperation in educational reform which had already produced significant results. In practical terms this meant the eventual replacement of the Japan Education Committee by the Japan Education Reform Council which was created at CIE's behest. [33] Like its predecessor this was a generally liberal body which might aid the occupying army in its dealings with the conservative Ministry of Education. Although the US Education Mission Report was now to form the basis of most educational changes its ideas were only transformed into detailed legislation after discussion by the new body. At first the officials of the Ministry tried to cling to a large measure of autonomy but by 3 September 1946 American pressure had given the JERC an autonomous and powerful position in the refinement of reform. Coordination between the Council, the Ministry and the CIE was provided by a permanent steering committee which enabled MacArthur to sway policy without overtly intruding in the Council's activities. [34] In theory the Council was to be responsible for general policy while the Ministry was confined to matters of administrative detail.

In one important respect the new Council differed from the opinions of its liberal predecessor. Members of the JEC had believed that the basis of the new democratic education should be enshrined in a new Imperial Rescript. This would replace the statement of conservative principles which had been issued in 1890. [35] However, American disapproval, and democratic propaganda philosophy, had destroyed this idea and in place its place had developed the notion of a Fundamental Education Law which would be enacted by Japan's new democratically elected parliament. Finally, in March 1947, the Fundamental Law of Education was enacted. This echoed both Japanese and American ideals of the construction of a peaceful state and society and emphasised equality of opportunity, co-education, 'political education for intelligent citizenship' and the secular character of the public education system. [36]

To any sceptical observer the gulf between Japan's physical poverty and expensive reform proposals must have appeared unbridgeable. But American pressure prevented conservatives utilising economic conditions to justify resistance to reform. [37] The skilful formula which prevented obstruction was an agreement 'that reforms would be accepted in principle'. Thus their implementation was taken out of the realm of immediate difficulties. In this setting the JERC not only adopted the 6.3.3. system but assisted in the drafting of the 1947 School Education Law. This second legal foundation of postwar education covered all levels of teaching from kindergarten to university and provided a much needed strengthening to provisions for blind and handicapped people. [38]

The enactment of legislation to implement the philosophy of decentralisation was to prove a far more difficult problem. Not only did this concept threaten the fundamental basis of ministerial authority but history provided an unfortunate precedent. In 1879 Japan had briefly experimented with local autonomy and confusion had resulted. Furthermore, there were legitimate fears that popularly elected committees might lack the professional expertise which characterised Japanese education administration. [39] In fact even liberals who might agree on the general principle of decentralisation could differ drastically about ways and means. Tanaka Kotaro believed that Japan's small area made American-style devolution inappropriate. He favoured regional rather than local decentralisation, and fearing the chauvinism which the Japanese population had shown in the recent past, believed that membership of elected committees should be confined to professional educators. Morito Tatsuo, Minister of Education in 1948, similarly believed that implementation of the principle should be slow and that Japanese laymen would not give their services to committees without financial reward. All these arguments certainly created delay but ultimately they were of no avail. On this issue the unofficial entente between occupationaires and liberal Japanese was replaced by a far harsher relationship. The Japanese were virtually compelled to enact the 1948 School Board Law with its system of popularly elected local committees. [40]

Perhaps the most fundamental challenge to Japanese ways and customs lay in the carrying out of decentralisation. Few Japanese were happy at the radicalism of the School Board law, and by 1949, the year of the first elections, even some Americans were apprehensive lest Communists or traditional political bosses would come to dominate local committees. [41] Lack of local financial resources and suitable personnel remained a significant obstacle to local control; and it is hardly surprising that this major education reform was reversed following the restoration of Japanese independence.

Although reports and legislation constituted the main landmarks of re-education policy they were never more than a small element in the activities of CIE and Japanese officials and pedagogues. From the outset of the occupation both Japanese and Americans faced physical as well as policy difficulties in rehabilitating Japanese education, and both sought to return education to normality as soon as possible. To this end textbooks were rewritten, published and distributed with remarkable speed.

This activity was not confined to such politically sensitive fields as history and geography but covered virtually every subject in the curriculum. The creation of such an extensive range of materials was obviously beyond the abilities of CIE staff so a complex system of review was adopted whereby each draft was translated into English while American suggestions and corrections were, conversely, translated into Japanese. Clearly occupation officials retained a veto in this process but some textbook authors claim that the volume of American intervention was small, and instructions often concentrated upon clarity of style and presentation. [42] However, CIE also had an important political role in resisting the demands of left-wing teachers for the insertion of a large quantity of Marxist material in new teaching materials. At its peak this textbook programme involved the simultaneous preparation of more than eighty works and though many books merely sought to provide up-to-date information, new works on history were dramatically original. These presented scholarship rather than myth and for the first time devoted a significant space to the history of the common people.

In one major field, language reform, occupation activity was half-hearted and ambiguous. For MacArthur this issue was always too intimately linked with Japanese culture to warrant crude intervention. The Japanese government was encouraged to introduce the teaching of the roman alphabet into all schools but this was always in addition to, rather than instead of, the existing scripts. Yet in raising the language issue the occupation force may have given encouragement to Japanese who sought a simplified script, and who reduced the number of characters in everyday use. [43] Even so, this sector of policy was not without its ideological absurdities. Some members of CIE saw calligraphy as inextricably linked to the evils of the old regime and clumsily sought to reduce its place in the school curriculum. [44]

Another field in which America ultimately left much responsibility to the Japanese was the much vaunted screening of teachers and educational administrators. The scale of the task was too great for American manpower and it was carried out by committees of Japanese. As all teachers had effectively supported the war effort a drastic purge was educationally impossible. What was ultimately a very selective process removed a mere 3151 staff from Japanese schools. [45]

Parallel to the varied attacks on old ideas went equally determined programmes to strengthen new thinking. To this end CIE carried a large-scale programme of teacher education and novel courses for educational administrators. These efforts began in the autumn of 1945 with radio broadcasts on democratic education; and expanded into large-scale film programmes in public halls and schools. In its most typical form the re-education of teachers took the form of conferences and workshops throughout Japan, and as the war was slowly forgotten selected Japanese teachers were allowed to visit the United States for study tours and more detailed training. [46]

One of the most lasting elements in occupation reform was the revised curriculum. This not only removed archaic and chauvinistic materials, but introduced new subjects and a new coherence to school courses. Social studies effectively replaced history and geography, and increasing efforts were made to link the subject matter of various subjects to create what was termed a 'core

The Re-education of Japan

curriculum'. [47] The new scheme gave increasing importance to science, foreign languages, and international studies - all characteristics which have remained unchanged throughout the postwar period.

Although the transformation of Japan's school system was always CIE's major concern, higher education gradually assumed an increasing importance in occupation policy. MacArthur's advisers believed that the expansion of higher education would have three important virtues. It would aid the liberation of talent, be economically valuable and end the notorious 'examination hell' of university entrance which had marred the elite prewar system. [48] Despite the criticisms of Japanese who lamented the alleged loss of academic standards, American plans were successfully carried out. The notion that Japanese prefectures, like American states, should each have a public university was often ridiculed; and the resulting institutions were condemned as 'station lunch-box universities' but educational opportunities were drastically expanded. Hundreds of colleges and higher school were transformed into new style universities to create a system which has come to resemble the open varied American pattern of higher education rather than the more traditional systems of Western Europe. Despite these radical changes of structure attitudes changed much more slowly. Most Japanese continued to regard the erstwhile imperial universities as the most desirable and economical of academic destinations so that competition to enter them increased rather than slackened. Thus their elite character survived, and examination hell remained an essential preliminary to entering Japan's most famous universities.

Inherent in most educational reform were political objectives; not only democratisation but the maintenance of American influence over Japan. This not only implied the exclusion of non-American models from educational change but the limiting of Communist influence in the educational system. [49] Fear of Communism was unimportant in 1945 when militarism seemed the greatest enemy; but by 1949 a divided Korea and the advance of Chinese Communism had created new alarms. Furthermore the left-wing attitudes of the Japan Teachers Union added to American fears. [50] Occupation officials exhorted Japanese teachers to exclude Communists from their ranks and Walter Eels of CIE toured universities to condemn the presence of Communists in a liberal education system. Yet for many Japanese political freedom had become an important virtue and academics were alarmed by talk which recalled the intolerance of pre-war days. Many scholars still saw militarism and central control of education as their worst enemies, while Communists retained some prestige from their wartime resistance to authority. In Japan it was difficult to reproduce the simplicities of American anti-Communist analysis.

Yet despite political and educational frictions American educational reforms were the product of a surprising measure of cooperation between occupiers and occupied. Plagued by language difficulties, lack of expert personnel and immense material problems Americans were often dependent upon Japanese cooperation. In particular, liberal, internationalist Japanese who shared important American ideals played a significant role in transforming broad concepts into legislative realities. Without a residue of Japanese liberalism reform would have had far less prospect of popularity or success.

Following the 1951 peace treaty the Japanese Ministry of Education defeated decentralisation and regained much of its former control over textbooks and the curriculum [51], but Japanese education had been fundamentally changed. Today the Japanese system has little in common with the narrow meritocracy of pre-war days and the occupation's creation of mass higher education has proved irreversible. Large scale universities and colleges combined with American-style vocational studies have contributed much to Japanese prosperity, and made a return to crude authoritarianism impossible. Now, as in 1868, Japan possesses the most efficient education system in Asia. Her society has become one of the most open in the contemporary world.

NOTES

1. For the best account of Japanese education in the era before modernization see R.P. Dore, Education in Tokugawa Japan (Routledge & Kegan Paul, London, 1965). E.g. 'Mr. Macfarlane, quoting from M. Meylan, a more recent authority, states that children of both sexes and of all ranks are invariably sent to rudimentary schools, where they learn to read and write, and are initiated into some knowledge of the history of their own country. To this extent, at least, it is considered that the meanest peasant should be educated...it will appear that a more widely diffused system of national education exists in Japan than in our own country, and that in that respect at all events, if no other, they are decidedly in advance of us.' Laurence Oliphant, Narrative of the Earl of Elgin's Mission to China and Japan (Blackwood, Edinburgh and London, 1859), Vol. 2, p. 117.

2. 'With the opening of Japan to Western thought, the literature of Confucianism was temporarily put aside to enable the people to master a great body of information in a brief time. Education which had been a by-product of moral training became one of the major purposes of life. It was no longer a private road to accomplishment for a few, but an essential preparation for youth to take their part in building a modern state. There was little time for aesthetics. There was strong pressure to acquire knowledge, so that Japan could grow strong and face other powers on equal terms.' R.S. Anderson, Japan: Three Epochs of Modern Education (U.S. Department of Health Education and Welfare, Washington, D.C., 1959), p. 3.

3. For the full text of the Rescript see General Headquarters, Supreme Commander for the Allied Powers, Civil Information and Education Section, Education Division, Education in

Japan (Tokyo, 15 Feb. 1946), p. 111 - reprinted in M. Kodama (ed.) Educational Documents of Occupied Japan, Vol. 1, CIE (15 Feb. 1946) Education in Japan (Meisei University Press, Tokyo, 1983) - afterwards cited as Education in Japan.

4. 'Replacing family background, performance in impartial entrance examinations determined matriculation beyond the universal and compulsory primary school. The promise of social mobility through the national educational system is often cited as an effective measure by which the Meiji leadership liquidated arbitrary class privileges... To simplify drastically: rational standards of performance regulated admissions to each ascending level of the school system, provided that the applicant was male and came from a family that could cover the nominal costs of tuition and board.' Donald Roden, Schooldays in Imperial Japan. A Study in the Culture of a Student Elite. (University of California Press, Berkeley, 1980), pp.4-5.

5. For a vivid picture of elite student life in the early twentieth century, see Henry D. Smith, Japan's First Student Radicals. (Harvard University Press, Cambridge, Mass., 1972).

6. General Headquarters, Supreme Commander for the Allied Powers, Civil Information and Education Section, Education Division. Education in the New Japan, Vol. 1 (Tokyo, 1948), p. 31.

7. R. Tsunoda, W.T. de Bary, and D. Keene (eds.), Sources of Japanese Tradition (Columbia University Press, New York, 1958), p. 795.

8. E.g. Thomas R.H. Havens, Valley of Darkness, The Japanese People and World War Two (W.W. Norton, New York, 1978), pp. 25-31, 138-142.

9. Mombusho (Ministry of Education) Gakusei Hyakunen-shi (Hundred Year History of the Education System) (Tokyo, 1972), vol. 2, p. 138.

10. See Marlene Mayo, 'Psychological Disarmament: American Wartime Planning for the Education and Re-education of Defeated Japan, 1943-1945' in Thomas W. Burkman (ed.), The Occupation of Japan: Educational and Social Reform (MacArthur Memorial, Norfolk, Virginia, 1982), pp. 61-67.

11. For the text of the Potsdam declaration see Supreme Commander for the Allied Powers, Government Section, Political Reorientation of Japan, September 1945 to September 1948, Vol. 2 (U.S. Government Printing Office, Washington, D.C., 1948), p. 413.

12. 'The Ministry of Education... Issued Order No. 20 on 25 Aug. 1945 abrogating all those orders designed to promote militarism and ultra-nationalism in the schools which came under the Ministry of Education.' Education in Japan, p. 63. See also Joseph P. Trainor, Educational Reform in Occupied Japan, Trainor's Memoir (Mesei University Press, Tokyo, 1983), p. 20. (afterwards cited as Trainor)

13. Oe Shinobu, Sengo Kaikaku (Postwar Reform), Nihon no Rekishi (History of Japan), Vol. 31 (Shogakkan, Tokyo, 1976), p. 174. Maeda (1884-1962) served as Minister from 18 Aug. 1945 to 13 Jan. 1946. Mombusho (Ministry of Education) (ed.) Gakusei Hyakunen-shi

(Hundred Year History of the Education System) (Tokyo, 1972), Vol. 2, p. 365.

14. Oe Shinobu, Sengo Kaikaku, p. 174. For the full text of this document see Gakusei Hyakunen-shi, Vol. 2, pp. 52-53.

15. Sengo Kaikaku, p. 174-175. 'Tanaka was a distinguished professor of Tokyo Imperial University's Law School, a Catholic, and an advocate of universal values in Japan's educational system' - Harry J. Wray, 'Decentralization of Education in the Allied Occupation of Japan, 1945-1952' in T.W. Burkman (ed.), The Occupation of Japan Educational and Social Reform, p. 150. (afterwards cited as Wray)

16. The best brief account of CIE's organisation and activities is Takemae Eiji, GHQ (Iwanami Shinso, Tokyo, 1983), pp. 115-128 and pp. 183-197.

17. Toshio Nishi, Unconditional Democracy, Education and Politics in Occupied Japan, 1945-1952 (Hoover Institution, Stamford, 1982), pp. 86-91, afterwards cited as Nishi.

18. Ibid. pp. 88-89.

19. Ibid. pp. 89-90. For the most detailed study of radio reform see D.G. Smitham 'The Reform of Japanese Broadcasting 1945-1952' in Historical Journal of Film, Radio and Television (forthcoming).

20. For the history of cinema policy see Supreme Commander for the Allied Powers, History of the Non-Military Activities of the Occupation of Japan, Theatre and Motion Pictures (Tokyo, 1950) (available on microfilm from the National Archives, Washington, D.C.).

21. See Political Re-orientation of Japan, Vol. 2, p. 424.

22. For the test of this document see Education in the New Japan, Vol. 2, pp. 26-28.

23. William P. Woodward, The Allied Occupation of Japan and Japanese Religions (E.J. Brill, Leiden, 1972), pp. 295-299.

24. Education in the New Japan Vol. 2, pp. 36-39.

25. For the background to the Education Mission see Edward Beauchamp, 'Education and Social Reform in Japan: The First United States Education Mission to Japan, 1946' in T.W. Burkman (ed.) The Occupation of Japan: Educational and Social Reform pp. 175-192 (afterwards cited as Beauchamp). The instruction to the Japanese Government is reproduced in Education in the New Japan Vol. 2, pp. 40-42. See also Sengo Kakaku, pp. 177-80.

26. Ibid. pp. 179-180

27. See Beauchamp and Nishi pp. 188-190. For a valuable review of Nishi's work see Harry Wray's review in Monumenta Nipponica Vol. XXXVIII, No. 1 (1983) pp. 102-104. For the full text of the Mission's report Report of the United States Education Mission to Japan see M. Kodama (ed.) Educational Documents of Occupied Japan (Vol. 1) Education in Japan (Meisei University Press, Tokyo, 1983).

28. Trainor pp. 77-79.

29. See 27.

30. The Report's treatment of language reform occupies pp. 20-23 of the document. See also Nishi pp. 199-206.

31. For the Mission's ideas and its links with Japanese suggestions see Sengo Kaikaku pp. 179-181.

32. Report of the United States Education Mission to Japan pp. 44-47.

33. For a useful discussion of the JERC see Trainor pp. 101-119 and Sengo Kaikaku pp. 181-182.

34. Trainor p. 107.

35. Ibid. pp. 108-109.

36. For the text of the law see Education in the New Japan Vol. 2, pp. 109-111.

37. Trainor p. 111.

38. For the text of the School Education Law see Education in the New Japan Vol. 2, pp. 112-130.

39. For a sympathetic view of Japanese resistance to this policy see Wray pp. 144-192.

40. Nishi pp. 210-211.

41. Ibid. p. 212.

42. Takemae Eiji, GHQ pp. 184-185. For discussions of textbook revision see Trainor pp. 120-138, and Nishi pp. 176-180.

43. GHQ pp. 185-186.

44. Nishi pp. 206-208.

45. Nishi p. 175. Though over 110,000 teachers who were likely to be purged retired voluntarily.

46. Trainor pp. 203-220. Education in the New Japan Vol. 1, pp. 281-299.

47. Takemae Eiji and Kinbara Samon, Showashi (Showa History) (Yuhikaku, Tokyo, 1982) pp. 258-259.

48. For higher education see Trainor pp. 221-241 and Education in the New Japan Vol. 1, pp. 253-281. For the problem of entrance examinations - Peter Frost 'Examination Hell, the Reform of Entrance Examinations in Occupied Japan' in T.W. Burkman (ed.) The Occupation of Japan: Educational and Social Reform, pp. 211-218.

49. Trainor pp. 327-361.

50. Benjamin Duke, Japan's Militant Teachers (University of Hawaii Press, Hawaii, 1972).

51. The content of history textbooks continues to be a significant political issue. In 1982 the governments of both Korean régimes and the People's Republic of China made public complaints regarding the toning down of accounts of wartime atrocities in Japanese textbooks.

Chapter Ten

FROM 'RE-EDUCATION' TO THE SELLING OF THE MARSHALL
PLAN IN ITALY

DAVID ELLWOOD

No-one in the capitals of those Allied countries, Britain and
America, which had done most to liberate Italy from Nazi-Fascism
ever thought seriously about 're-educating' the Italians. For one
thing it was so hard to decide whether Italians really were Fascists
or not, a point which history itself has not found easy to deal with.
Allied propaganda had long insisted that the armies were in the
country to fight the Fascist system not the Italian people, but Allied
soldiers and journalists often felt like Lieutenant Nately in Catch
22, who in a Roman bordello found the vile old man whose proud
boast it was that he had been fanatically pro-German when the
Germans were protecting him against the Americans, and was now
fanatically pro-American as long as the Americans were there to
protect him against the Germans: 'But', Nately cried out in disbelief,
'you're a turncoat! A timeserver! A shameful, unscrupulous
opportunist!' 'I am a hundred and seven years old', the old man
reminded him suavely. [1]

The country had of course changed sides when the Fascist war
effort collapsed and had been awarded the deliberately ambivalent
status of 'co-belligerency', along with a punitive armistice designed
by the British to settle the accounts of 1940 and before. [2] But the
end of Fascism and the breakdown of the traditional State at the
moment of the surrender left an ideological vacuum which demanded
new ways forward, visions for the future, plans for reconstruction
and progress. When, after spring 1944, it appeared that the most
likely force to fill this vacuum was the Communist Party, armed
with the kind of mass support and paramilitary apparatus which
might bring political power within its reach, then the British and
Americans thought again about the democratic evolution of the
Italians. For a while, in 1947-48, there was genuine fear of an
imminent Communist take-over, by fair means or foul, and every
propaganda and political device which the Americans and their allies
in the Italian political class could lay hands on to prevent this was
mobilised in one of the first great set-piece dramas of the Cold War,
the national elections of April 1948. Afterwards, in a different
climate, fundamental long-term choices were finally made by the
Christian Democrats and their American supporters, in favour of

structural reform and modernisation aimed at attacking the mass discontent where its social and economic roots lay. This was the meaning of the Marshall Plan: a vision of consensus and prosperity conveyed by a programme of action which brought material aid and propaganda together as never before.

The results were not quite what was expected - the Communist Party for instance continued to grow - but by the time the Korean War started, when the whole emphasis of the effort changed, the first signs of solid economic recovery were beginning to show. The country was in fact on the verge of changing dramatically, in a way no-one would have predicted in 1948, let alone 1945 or 1943. That was why it came to be called a 'miracle'.

The purpose of this paper then is to trace and explain the three crucial phases of British and especially American 'ideological' relations with Italy after the collapse of Fascism: first we have the end of the war and a hiatus in 'democratisation' which lasted from mid-1945 until the spring of 1947; then come the months of panic and of American mobilisation down to April 1948; finally the season of the Marshall Plan arrives lasting to mid-1950. The first two of these phases were years of confusion and fear; the final phase from our point of view is the most interesting and will receive most attention here, since we see a coherent long-term propaganda strategy being applied by the US in a European country on a scale and with an intensity never seen before or since, and with a story to tell which was essentially economic.

*

No-one was satisfied with the results of the propaganda offensive carried out in Italy during the war. When the balance sheet was drawn up by men such as the Supreme Allied Commander, Harold Alexander in July 1945, he said: 'On what we do now will depend whether Italy goes left or right, and on how our ideology - which at the moment is both incoherent and very badly propagated - is (organised) to permeate this country'. [3] The head of the Allied Commission, a body set up under the armistice to supervise the Allied military government and the transitory Italian governments of the time, wrote in a wide-ranging report on 'Future Policy Toward Italy' that, 'the education of the minds of the Italians towards a democratic way of life' was 'a duty of the Allies' and that 'not enough (had) been done in this direction'. The author of these words, the American Admiral Stone, was convinced that Italian behaviour at the side of the Allies since the armistice and especially in the Resistance showed that 'they are willing to abandon totalitarianism and work for the same freedoms as the Allies who liberated them'. But he also insisted that 'the people, the Government and the local authorities, after twenty years of Fascism, (needed) advice on the interpretation of democracy': the Allies 'still have much to teach and the Italians much to learn'. Unless this educational process took

220

place, concluded the Admiral, 'they will inevitably turn to the USSR and join the group of "police" states, united by Communism, which is extending westwards from Russia'. [4]

The British Executive Commissioner of the Allied Commission, Brigadier Lush, was even more explicit: 'We have granted freedom of speech and writing, we have ensured freedom from hunger: we have not ensured freedom from fear', he wrote in May 1945:

> ...the two democratic countries have stood by in this country and watched the spread of Communism and still more the spread of fear of Communism. We have failed adequately to present to Italians the other alternative - a democratic way of life. Much has been done in the field by (military government) officers. But direction has been lacking. By distribution of literature, through the medium of films and radio, by visits of democratic leaders, more could and should have been done. [5]

Yet remarkably little was done about these warnings and very little effort put into a post-liberation drive for democratisation, in spite of the dangers of social breakdown, civil war and even insurrection - on the Greek model - which Allied and Italian observers all agreed were the risks facing the country in 1945-46. Why was this?

Although no study exists of the wartime propaganda campaign in Italy by the Allies, the difficulties and contradictions of British and American efforts in this direction are quite clear. Sworn to defeat and eradicate Fascism, the Allies had immediately compounded with Fascism's protector and its retainer King Victor Emmanuel III and Field Marshal Badoglio to expedite the surrender. They had then insisted on keeping these two veterans in their places to legitimise their own actions vis-à-vis the traditional Italian State machine and had done much to rehabilitate them politically. Partly as a result of this, partly out of political diffidence - in the British case - they had fended off until the last minute contact with the reborn anti-Fascist political forces and while Fascists were very often kept on in the South in the name of administrative convenience, aid to the northern Resistance was scarce and largely channelled - at least at first - to its minority conservative elements. Meanwhile the military effort, the Allied Commission and the post-war political planning - to the extent there was any - were largely controlled by the British, and they made it quite clear that they had very little interest in the difference between a Fascist and an anti-Fascist Italy. Their purposes hinged on having a peace treaty to match the armistice, and it was embarrassing to them that the military campaign took so long, that the Americans pulled the greater part of their forces out of it half way through, and that the Italians gained time to put a substantial Resistance movement into the field and an anti-Fascist government in the saddle in Rome.

It was also irritating to the British that they should be united in wedlock in Italy with American partners who had quite different interests and attitudes. The Americans had no accounts to settle but had 4.5 million Italo-American voters; they were looking for markets and talked as though a total reform of international security and trade was just around the corner - as long as everyone followed their plans. They saw Italy's troubles as a question of development and economic progress, and although they were still vague in 1945 about how to do anything concretely in these areas, they were the ones sending the aid, the food and the cash which alone prevented total social breakdown. Above all they acted as though they believed in self-determination, which to them at that time meant less not more propaganda, less not more aid to Italian political friends, in spite of the pleas of these same friends for sustenance and protection which began to mount from the end of 1945, when the first elections approached and the crucial constitutional test between monarchy and republic. [6]

So when the Allies finally turned over the remaining portions of Italian territory to the jurisdiction of the Rome government in December 1945 (excepting the Trieste region), they left very mixed memories. In June the former Assistant Secretary of State Sumner Welles had charged that: 'In no part of Europe has our recent policy been more inept 'than in Italy, where a radical programme of political and economic rehabilitation was necessary immediately, he felt, to undo the effects of British control and to prevent a swing either to the extreme right or to Communism. There had been elements in the Allied control machinery who understood the essential dilemmas, and the spring 1944 judgement of the Allied Commission's Political Section, talking of the impact of the Resistance, Russian military successes and the rise of the Communist Party, would be a refrain of Anglo-American political analysis until the 1950s: 'These cumulatively powerful influences are superimposed on a country already ripe for that swing towards extremes which is the inevitable corollary of a shattered economy and the threat of inflation.' [7] In the aftermath of the First World War this situation had produced Fascism, everyone agreed, and Greek events showed just how great were the dangers in similar circumstances 25 years later.

Yet when the American political scientist and former military government officer Maurice Neufeld came to write on the Italian situation in spring 1946, some of the worst predictions seemed to be coming true. The first broad-based post-liberation government headed by a northern Resistance leader (Ferruccio Parri) had collapsed to be replaced by a man of the Catholic establishment at the head of a new bloc of conservative forces. The Resistance movement, to its astonishment, found itself powerless and empty-handed when this took place. But much worse starvation, banditry and political violence seemed to be becoming endemic in parts of the country, and there was a new political movement of the far right, the Uomo Qualunque, or Common Man Party, nationalist, populist, wholly cynical, ready to exploit the situation at the national level. Neufeld saw these developments as the direct outcome of Allied failures, blaming chaotic military government, national governments without policies, a defascistisation process which had made too many compromises with the Fascists it found and military men who had neither knowledge or interest in what Neufeld called 'the moral issues of the war and our role in Italy', which were essentially how to make possible 'stable, democratic and anti-Fascist government'. [9]

Yet dangerous and threatening as the Italian atmosphere felt in the crucial two years after the liberation, this was the hiatus period in Anglo-American propaganda activity in the country. The wartime joint effort died down even if it did not disappear completely (the Allied Commission itself remained until January 1947). Each of the erstwhile Allies meanwhile sought space for independent lines of propaganda and political influence. But only the British actively occupied this space, stepping up information activities and the work of the British Council. Italy and Greece were 'to be allocated first priority in the postwar development of our news and cultural services', the Daily Telegraph had reported in September 1945, and an explicit link was made with forthcoming political tests: 'It is felt that wider knowledge of Anglo-Saxon ideas of democracy and methods of government will help the nation in shaping the future for which it is groping after two decades of Fascism', the paper reported. [10]

But there is almost no indication of what if any impact this British effort had in 1946. In those days the currency of power and influence was material aid: emergency food and money to stave off a total social breakdown, and this only the Americans could provide in quantity, which they did largely by way of UNRRA. [11] Moreover at the political level the British continued to think in terms of 1943, refusing to facilitate the re-entry of Italy into the international community, and negotiating a peace treaty which aimed to remove from Italy the last trace of any impulse to act as an autonomous Great Power. When its details came out in 1946-47 the blow to Italian pride and British prestige in particular was very great, since the tone and contents of the document effectively ignored all the efforts Italians had made to atone for their past and pull themselves up by their bootstraps since 1943. This development, together with the complete lack of interest or knowledge shown by the Labour government put Britain largely out of the Italian propaganda picture by 1947.

*

1947 was the year when the hiatus ended and when the Americans stepped decisively into the situation. The process began in Italy, however, not in Washington. The immediate circumstances were the significant rise in the Communist vote in the municipal elections of November 1946, an increase repeated in regional elections in Sicily in April 1947. Along with these developments went a dramatic escalation in political violence, culminating in the

Portello della Ginestra massacre when a May Day parade was fired on leaving 6 dead and 20 wounded. [12]

But it was a public reference by the Communist leader Togliatti to the possible need for 'direct action' which attracted most attention in the Government and the American Embassy, where an energetic new ambassador, James C. Dunn, former head of the European Affairs Office of the State Department, had recently taken up residence. These were the months of the Truman Doctrine and of a dramatic flight by De Gasperi to Washington in search of more emergency supplies and new loans for reconstruction. Yet there was still little sign of a coherent, incisive approach to Italian difficulties in an American capital torn by the advent of a Republican Congress, the setbacks to the grandiose plans of wartime for world re-construction, and the growing tension with the Soviets. In the first instance the policy gap was filled by the new ambassador, who throughout the spring of 1947 bombarded Washington with a series of messages indicating the strategy needed in the menacing circumstances. From our point of view the most significant aspects of Dunn's formulations are:

1) Emergency aid on a hand to mouth basis was not enough; long-term structural intervention was needed.

2) This structural intervention, as with all other crucial aspects of the situation, revolved round economics, in other words reconstruction, stabilisation, employment, living standards.

3) Nothing could be done with any hope of lasting effect unless accompanied by a large-scale, specially designed propaganda effort. [13] On this last point Dunn said in May:

> Our practice of holding back from expressing ourselves on ideological views has given all the advantage to the other side and they have not hesitated to use it and abuse it. With all the efforts which have been made here since the war very little presentation of United States policies and positions has appeared in the Italian press...We have assumed a passive role as regards the growth of Italian Communism. [14]

To fill the gap in the short term Dunn began to tour the country himself, speaking to friendship groups, Chambers of Commerce, exhibitions and making great publicity in particular out of the arrival of the aid ships. Inaugurating a practice which lasts to this day, the American Ambassador himself became a prominent public figure in the country, speaking on Italian-American relations, on Italy's place in the world and Italy's future.

In a typical speech of mid-1947, to the Rotary Club of Palermo, the Ambassador began by reminding his audience of the traditional ties linking Sicily to the US, and the respect of Americans for what he called Sicilian 'forthright individualism'. He then illustrated American aid since the war, noting that aid would go only to peoples who had demonstrated their democratic sincerity, not a casual remark coming but a month after the final exclusion of the left wing parties from the Rome government and the announcement of the Marshall Plan. General Marshall himself was quoted as saying 'Everyone who comes back from Italy remarks upon the vitality of the people, their will to work and their very real attachment for democracy'. And the Ambassador concluded with a confirmation of America's support for Italian entry into the United Nations, and a eulogy for Sicily's 'noble love of freedom acquired through centuries of heroic combat against oppression.' [15]

But in spite of the Ambassador's voice, in spite of the galvanising effect of the Marshall Plan announcement and a new aid programme which brought 200 ships more to Italy between August and December 1947, as autumn turned to winter the political and economic situation became more and more precarious. Against a background of riots and widespread strikes, a total financial crisis broke out in September precipitated by the British suspension of sterling convertibility. In October the left attempted to force a vote of no-confidence through Parliament and were widely believed to be ready to 'seize' northern Italy if the manoeuvre should fail. While the parliamentary crisis was fended off and no take-over of the north occurred, these months saw the foundation and consolidation of an openly neo-Fascist party, the Movimento sociale italiano. On the left the establishment of the Cominform was accompanied by a state of almost continuous Communist mobilisation culminating in the seizure of the Prefecture of Milan, which gave the government and the Embassy the impression that a general revolt could occur at any time up to or even after the national elections fixed for March 1948. When the new National Security Council started work in Washington its very first paper concerned Italy, the 'pre-revolutionary' conditions said to exist there, the possibility that the Communists could come to power by legal or extra-legal means, and the impression that Italy had first priority in Cominform strategy. [16]

The NSC was convinced that 'the majority of the Italian people...are ideologically inclined towards the Western democracies, friendly to the United States and conscious of the fact that US aid is vital to Italian recovery'. The Council was also clear that 'the prevailing economic distress' was what gave the Communists their mass support. [17] As the national elections came nearer the emphasis in NSC deliberations in fact changed: the greater threat was now seen to be not an insurrection but an electoral victory by the Left Bloc. So the propaganda front immediately became crucial and an unprecedented wave of American activity suddenly built up: Congressmen were mobilized, the Peace Treaty partially abrogated, the arms of the British and French prised open to embrace Italy in new talks on West European unity. But this was just the beginning.

It turned out to be 'the most hectically fought political campaign that ever took place in Europe', according to the knowledgeable CBS journalist Howard K. Smith writing a year later. and it was Smith's view too that the most important factor giving the Christian Democrats their overwhelming victory was the 'frank, open entrance of America into the campaign'. Once the American effort got under way, 'not a day passed without the anti-Communist majority of the Press having a new, effective American gesture to put in its headlines'. Merchant ships were given as a gift, Nazi gold returned, Communist voters banned from emigration to the United States and there were shows of naval and air strength. [18] The private Italo-American campaign was even more remarkable, not least for its originality. Ten million letters and cables were sent from individual Italian-Americans 'to relatives and acquaintances in Italy begging them to vote against the Communists'. Famous stars such as Sinatra and Gary Cooper recorded radio programmes; the Church and the American propaganda agencies USIS and the Voices of America ran campaigns in parallel. 'Freedom flights' carrying airmail from America were organised with the cooperation of the US Post Office and TWA, and the red, white and blue 'Friendship Train' distributed piles of gifts gathered on its tour of America. Above all the United States held out the long-term promise of the European Recovery Program and made quite clear that Italy would not be a beneficiary if its government was made up of Communists and Socialists. [19]

When the uproar died down and the true impact of this confrontation could be measured, it became clear that one side had won a battle but not a war. The Christian Democrat victory was based on getting out the abstainers and faint-hearted not on reducing the left, which basically held its vote. Moreover liberals such as Howard K. Smith saw a very high price being paid for the result by the US: compromising its long-held faith in self-determination, plunging into an open-ended commitment to the Christian Democrats and allying itself, in Smith's words, 'with social elements in Italy whose aims have nothing to do with democracy'. Smith concluded: 'Democracy is on very infirm feet when such methods are required to keep the people from voting for a dictatorship'. [20]

Like most American observers Smith was convinced that democratisation as such was not a problem: 'I know of no people in Europe (he wrote) who so painfully want to be democratic. They have had their dictatorship, and it is my firm impression that from right to left the whole people is deathly sick of it...But the naked circumstances of earning a livelihood are against them.' In eloquent detail Smith went on to list the age-old problems of over-population, under-development, poverty and alienation between North and South, and showed how badly the impact of world war and civil war had disturbed the fragile web of improvisation which alone had conserved stability up to that time. 'The social consequences of this dire struggle of man against man for jobs and survival inside Italy are obvious', Smith went on, echoing long-standing American official analyses; 'It induces the privileged to hold on blindly to every advantage they possess in the struggle; to the point, if necessary, of supporting right-wing dictatorship to guard it for them. In desperation it drives the poor to the other extreme - towards Communism and confiscation. The slack necessary for social compromise, which is the first requisite for democracy, does not exist.' [21] And so we come to the Marshall Plan, Italian version.

*

Two points need to be emphasised before we go any further. The first is that although we know a good deal about the origins of the European Recovery Program and its strategic and economic intentions, we know relatively little about what happened during the Marshall Plan, its impact in the various countries and the results sector by sector. One reason for this is the lack of accessible, coherent documentation. Most of the records are still classified, and what is available leaves a lot to be desired. Fragments of the Italian story are available but no more, and among these fragments are not to be found the records of the ERP Italian Mission's Information Division. Parts of the Mission files have now been located - though not declassified - but they do not include the publicity sections. So what follows is largely based on the correspondence between the Rome Information Division and the European coordinating office in Paris, or the headquarters in Washington. The result is that the overall plans and the intentions emerge much more clearly than the substance of the ERP team's relationship with Italian reality.

But before we look into this certain general remarks on the nature of the European Recovery Program are also in order. In the short term the ERP, or Marshall Plan, was as its chief European coordinator Ambassador Averill Harriman said in 1950, a fire-fighting operation, designed to halt once and for all the advance of Communist parties, the process of political and economic disintegration in Europe and galvanise the Europeans into organising together their own recuperation.[22] Its specific meanings in relation to Germany, to the danger of an American internal recession and to the dollar gap between European necessities and American production are well-known.[23]

But from our point of view its most important dimensions are undoubtedly the long-term ones. The ERP, I believe, brought forward and developed ideas of economic progress for the advanced world first thought of during the war, and turned them for the first time into an operative plan. These ideas all revolved round the notion of raising living standards everywhere, of economic well-being as the key to social and political stability, of Fascism and Communism as roughly the mirror image of each other, produced by backwardness, under-development and misery. The Marshall Plan, I would like to suggest, launched the idea of economic growth in the sense we know it on its distinguished European career, and it did so by means of a devastatingly simple yet unprecented message: 'You too can be like us.' [24]

America was at the height of its power in the 20th century, economically, politically, strategically. Europe was in ruins and showed few signs of healthy recovery in 1947-48. Everywhere there was evidence of the ideological exhaustion and demoralisation of the European ruling classes and their governments: 'Who hasn't heard remarks', asked an ERP Information Officer in Paris in 1950, 'such as "Why rebuild when the Russians will tear it all down again?" or "Why should I stick my neck out by taking sides? When the Commies take over, it won't be healthy to have it on my record."'[25] It was into this psychological void that the Marshall Plan's message stepped so effectively, providing a 'return of hope', a 'psychological blood transfusion' as the programme's Director Paul Hoffmann said in the course of the 20th anniversary celebrations in 1967.[26]To achieve this result propaganda was seen as a fundamental part of the entire operation from the beginning, since the problem was not just to raise production but to raise productivity, not just to bail out bankrupt governments but to modernise the State, not simply to save ailing industries but to change the war between reactionary capitalists and revolutionary workers into a dynamic relationship between enlightened producers and contented consumers. America triumphant showed how all this could be done and projecting this example into Europe was the purpose of the ERP 'Information Program'. If the Europeans weren't interested, then Giuseppe Stalin would be happy to embrace them: that was the choice.

*

In Italy the propaganda operation got under way in the summer of 1948, its authorisation coming from a section of the European Cooperation Masterplan between the US and Italy signed in June. As in similar plans for the other European countries this section, headed 'Publicity', was based on the recognition 'that wide dissemination of information on the progress of the program is desirable in order to develop the sense of common effort and mutual aid which are essential to the accomplishment of the objectives of the program'. Both the United States Government and the Italian Government were empowered to 'disseminate information' under this ruling.[27]

The head of the Information Division in Italy arrived in August. He was Andrew Berding, an energetic former head of the Rome bureau of Associated Press, co-author of Cordell Hull's memoirs and a future Assistant Secretary of State for Public Affairs. At the beginning Berding had one American employee and eight Italians; within a few months he was running not only the largest campaign in all the Marshall Plan countries, but also the one considered 'tops' in Paris, where his boss was the well-known journalist and broadcaster Alfred Friendly.

Berding and his small staff were extraordinarily active and inventive. In the first month alone they established a daily survey of the Italian press, made contacts with radio, film, press and news agency offices, prepared a three-room exhibition with accompanying booklets, postcards and photos, set up documentary film production arrangements, and agreed with the Italian national radio network on

228

an 8-language weekly shortwave broadcast and a 15 minute weekly programme in Italian. [28] They came to think in terms of tens of documentary films, hundreds of radio programmes, thousands of mobile film shows, millions of copies of their pamphlets, tens of millions of spectators for their exhibitions and films. Between June, 1948 and the end of 1950, to quote a typical report, 'the Mission installed and operated 45 exhibits frequented by 6,744,000 visitors. In these exhibits 16,049,555 pieces of (ERP) literature were distributed. Cost of the operation was...$537,239.30. The expenditure was in Counterpart...' (in other words in that part of the funds obtained from the sale of Marshall Plan goods which the administration kept for its own uses, the source of money for almost all the huge effort).[29]

There is no mystery about the operating principles which Berding and his men applied in their campaign. They were arrived at fairly quickly and changed little up to the outbreak of the Korean War. They were similar to the methods used in the other ERP countries but were probably applied more intensively in Italy. A January 1950 report by Berding explained:

> Carry the message of the Marshall Plan to the people.
> Carry it to them directly - it won't permeate down. And give it to them so that they can understand it. [30]

The basic thrust then was for a truly mass programme using 'every method possible...to reach Giuseppe in the factory and Giovanni in the fields', or as the Paris office put it, 'slugging it out way down among the masses'. [31] In Rome the Mission quickly understood that Press and radio, although not negligible, could not bear the brunt of the offensive: only one newspaper was sold for every twelve Italians and the distribution of radios was only half that. The Italian Government in its suggestions had wanted to concentrate on these two media, Foreign Minister Sforza allegedly proposing the purchase of half the country's dailies as an opening move. This notion was dismissed out of hand by the ERP men, who insisted that visual messages were the key to the situation - especially in a country where the illiteracy rate was around 15% - and should be put over in whatever way necessary to penetrate the closed mental world of people such as the Communist worker or the peasant isolated in his remote mountain village. [32]

In his January 1950 summary, prepared for a Congressional presentation, Berding also listed the other key operating principles:

1. to convince the Italians 'that the Plan is his as well as Mr Marshall's, in other words to increase the sense of national identification with the Plan and encourage a personal stake in its outcome.
2. to demonstrate the depth and seriousness of Italian-American cooperation: 'Thus the signs which the Mission has induced the Italian Government to put up by the many hundreds over the ERP

Counterpart fund projects carry the color of both countries, side by side, on the same shield'.
3. to make use of local identities, particularly regional ones, by demonstrating the work done in each area.
4. to direct special attention to key 'target groups', particularly organised labour, Communist and non-Communist; agricultural workers; housewives as runners of 'the economics of the household'; management in business and industry' in whose hands lie the guidelines of productivity', and finally children, following the example of the Church, which 'has always maintained that the best way to win and retain followers is to convince them while they are young'.
5. to avoid direct confrontation with the massive waves of Communist propaganda directed against the Plan. Thus 'when the Communists said the Marshall Plan was a plan of war, the Mission never said it was not a plan of war but over and over again, in thousands of inhabited centers, with every medium at its disposal, the Mission put across the slogan - "ERP means peace and work".' As we shall see, Korea could not have been a more unfortunate event from this point of view. [33]
6. to avoid accusation of interference in Italian internal affairs. Not surprisingly this was the principle which gave the publicity men most difficulty, especially since they were under pressure in Congress to step up their labelling of goods and services originating in the US with American flags. [34]

When applied on the ground these principles proved extremely flexible and no idea seemed too large or too daring for the Information Program in its heyday. Besides the traditional media there were ERP concerts and ERP essay contests, ERP art competitions and ERP variety shows on radio, ERP trains and ERP ceremonials. There were calendars, cartoon strips, postage stamps and atlases. There were troubadours singing the story of ERP sponsored miracles in Sicilian villages and even mobile puppet shows 'to bring the Marshall Plan message ostensibly to children but actually through the children ..to semi-literate or illiterate adults...'. This was 'Operation Bambi', run in agreement with the Ministry of Education, which according to its supporters did not 'bring the children statistics or dry commentaries on international economics. It brings them entertainment they have never seen before and educates them with modern techniques.'[35]

In the traditional media film dominated. By the end of 1950 40 documentaries had been produced most of which were seen in town cinemas attached to the feature films of the moment, but which were also taken into the remotest parts of the country by a fleet of 26 mobile projection units. Most of the shorts concerned the ERP impact in different areas of Italian industry, agriculture and social life, but interestingly there was also a film on the work of the Information Division itself for showing in America. Unfortunately we do not know if this or the majority of the other documentaries survived: very few have so far been located in Italy or in

Washington. An interesting aspect of the film programme was its use of Technicolour: five colour films were produced in 1950, and the Mission justified the expense by saying that colour shorts were a rarity in the country and thus had much greater impact.[36]

Radio was used with some diffidence, since distribution of sets was not high and there was a Parliamentary control committee supervising the network which included Communist deputies. Nevertheless 34 different types of show were produced, mostly of a documentary kind, 'utilizing on the spot recordings, original music and commentary'. The Mission thought that radio was 'ideal for wide, immediate distribution of general information and for stimulating a predisposition to acceptance of a message'. But they thought it weak for explaining the details of difficult problems.[37]

For these purposes the Mission preferred exhibits, which were styled to cater for what the ERP men believed was a particularly Italian love of colour, movement and humour. They did not hesitate to include a 'Mickey Mouse' cartoon if possible, becoming expert at shifting from the amusing to the serious quickly but subtly. This was a particularly pressing necesssity since the substance of the exhibitions, as of the ERP itself, was inevitably heavily technical, economic and abstract. Ideas such as Counterpart, the dollar gap, European integration and productivity were not only quite new to Italian ears and eyes but also difficult to communicate in the best of circumstances. Berding explained the Mission's solution to this problem with an example: 'Instead of using statistics to tell about the Counterpart fund, the exhibits show a huge safe, from which on an endless belt, pours a cascade of thousand lire notes, which dissolve into models of the Counterpart projects financed with the fund.' Little wonder that the ERP information directors in Washington felt that 'we have become in surprising measure...the principal fount for education about the big economic problems and developments disturbing the world today', a challenge which no information service had ever faced.[38]

Opening up an ERP pamphlet or visiting an ERP exhibition in the months down to June, 1950, what were the themes one would always find? What was 'the message'? A booklet distributed at the Venice exhibition on ERP in July–September, 1949 opens with a dramatic quantifaction of the dimensions of American aid: 3 ships a day, $1000 a minute, 2 weeks' salary from every American worker. The goal? A 'higher standard of living'. The text explains:

> By utilising American free supplies of foodstuffs and raw materials, Italy and the other nations included in the ERP plan hope to attain by the year 1952:
> - A higher standard of living for the entire nation.
> - Maximum employment for workers and farmers.
> - Greater production.
> through exploiting all their energies and by a close economic collaboration with all the other ERP countries.

The essential mechanisms of the plan are then outlined: how supplies of wheat and raw materials from the US turn into lira deposited in a special fund at the Bank of Italy, which are then used for public works and other 'productive improvements aiming to diminish unemployment'. The details follow, underlining how work has been restored to lifeless industries, how new machinery has modernised factories and how greater output needed to be integrated Europe-wide to facilitate emigration and stabilise economic life on a life on a continental scale. As for the 'Lira Fund', it is credited with giving employment to some 250-300,000 workers, and there are figures on its effect in the areas of housing, land reclamation, railway reconstruction, industrial reconversion, shipbuilding and the tourist trade. The concluding message states that:

> ERP is a unique chance offered to European nations toward reconstructing their economy, raising the standard of living among the masses, and attaining by the year 1952 an economic stability which is the foundation of political independence...Every worker, every citizen is bound up in this rebirth. The future and the peace of Italy and of Europe, the general well-being of all, depend on the will and the work of each single one of us. [39]

The references to the masses and to workers illustrates the crucial importance the ERP as whole attached to changing the balance of power, the structures and the attitudes in the world of organised labour. Here information activities were only part of a vast operation directly aided by the American trade unions which actively sought to organise non-Communist trade unions where hardly any existed before. Without entering into the merits of this still controversial undertaking, which was largely part of the ERP as fire-fighting operation, it is worth noting that the entire thrust of the effort was to create trade unions with different ideological objectives than those dominated by the Left parties which had emerged after the fall of Fascism. The creation of a single 'non-political organisation devoted to the economic improvement of the job-holder' was to be the aim and a furious propaganda and political battle developed on this front from 1949 onwards. [40]

The theme of ERP information on the subject was that non-party, economically oriented trade-unionism made for 'better working conditions, better wages, peaceful labor-management relations, higher productivity and a more vital democratic life', as a 1950 report explained. [41] But if convincing the workers of this unheard of story in a time of massive unemployment and general dislocation was hard, persuading the industrialists of their role in promoting higher living standards was hardly less difficult.

The key words here were mass production, scientific management and above all productivity. A typical portable exhibition on the subject would explain what productivity was, 'how it has given the United States a high standard of living, how increased per man output can result in betterment of living conditions, social progress, strength and ability to defend democratic institutions'. There were specialised reviews on the subject, joint committees, trips to inspect American factories, conferences and eventually even 'productivity villages' where model factories and workers' communities could be seen in action. [42] And there were constant exhortations and even reprimands for the industrialists, pushing them in the direction of modernising their attitudes and their practices. In October 1950 the ERP Mission Chief in Rome Dayton went as far as accusing business and industrial leaders of giving lip-service only to the need for 'raising the standard of living and to the basic principles of low cost and high production'. And he asked why it was that shoes arrived in the shops with up to 500% profit margins attached, and why an automobile cost the equivalent of 1000 days work in Italy - for an industrial worker - compared with 100 days in the United States. 'Something to justify their support of democracy', Dayton demanded, referring to 'the little men and women who are the backbone of the country', and he recommended to his audience at the Chamber of Commerce in Genoa a new publication called 'Productivity'. [43]

Although financed by Counterpart funds, this review was published by the Italian Government, and it was to the State that the ERP directed a third major effort in modernising attitudes and practices. The efficiency and credibility of the State was seen as fundamental in reconciling individuals to their democracy and to their government, as well as creating the infrastructures and environment in which business operated. 'Soundness and efficiency of government administration, improvement in fiscal systems, correction in taxation policies and administration, social security programs and administration, aids to small business, safeguards against monopoly'; these were just a few of the desirable objectives the Italian Mission saw for an effective reform push in this area. There was no question here of a major publicity operation, but in arranging exchanges, sending expert advisers and dedicating a good part of the 'technical assistance' programme to government reform, particularly in the fiscal sector, the ERP sought consciously to place the relationship between the State and its citizenry on a basis of confidence and mutual respect. [44] But without knowing it, the Mission had stumbled at this point on what would emerge as the crucial historical problem of the first Italian Republic; little wonder then that they had to admit their substantial failure in such areas as tax reform by the end of 1950.

*

The extreme difficulty when not outright failure of plans such as tax reform or agrarian reform, in which the ERP men and the US government had also taken a direct interest, taught them that democratisation was not simply a problem of economic security, or of stopping the Communists nor even of guaranteeing freedom of speech and thought. Inevitably their perplexity in front of the methods of the Italian political and business classes drove them back to their familiar reference points in American practice and to insist that theirs was the only reasonable way forward. Replying to attacks on his allegedly negative attitude to land reform, the first overall head of the Rome Mission, Zellerbach pointed out that reform was crucial to ERP:

> Behind this (he went on) is the basic fact that the United States is probably the 'reformingest' country in the world. As a nation Americans are, and have long been devoted to next year's model of anything and are somewhat scornful of last year's model. Perhaps the reason we at home have avoided having a big revolution for a long time is that we have thousands of changes and reforms which amount to little revolutions every day, every month, every year...[45]

But offering the American example in a thousand ways as the entire solution to Italy's democratisation problems inevitably ran into all those contradictions of Italian life produced not by economics or politics or cussedness, but by Italy's history. There was no way Marshall Plan propaganda could tackle for instance the openly disloyal Fascists it found throughout the State tourist corporation, or the hundreds of employees still nominally working for the Ministry of Colonies when Italy no longer had colonies. [46] More seriously there was no tradition in Italian political history of the kind of left-liberal reformism visible in Scandinavia, Britain or, say, Belgium which the ERP technocrats thought essential to reconcile the working classes to post-Fascist, capitalist democracy. In France a State Department opinion poll asked 2000 varied electors which political party they felt was looking out for the interests of the working man. Twenty-one percent named the Communist Party, 13% named the Socialists, the rest had no opinion: not a single respondent mentioned any other party. The problem was very similar in Italy, where the Christian Democrats would certainly not have been America's first choice for preferred ally, that distinction going to the right-wing socialists. Presenting the results of the French opinion poll, an anonymous writer in the Paris office of the ERP admitted at the end of 1950 that throughout Europe there were doubts on America's motivations, 'and these doubts all revolve in one way or another around the question of whether US policy was aimed at progressive improvement in general living standards or was designed more to shore up economic and social systems which are not popular and to restore to power reactionary and conservative vested interests'. [47]

As the Cold War reached its climax the tension between the fire-fighting priorities of the ERP in Italy and its long-term hopes almost crippled it. It was easy for the opposition to proclaim that Italy was becoming a client state of America in a new kind of imperialism, and that nobody gave something for nothing. But the worst advertisement for the Plan was the disastrous economic situation which persisted in much of the country, aggravated by policy conflicts between the ERP Mission and the Government over industrial expansion versus monetary stabilisation. In a region like Emilia Romagna, for example, heartland of Communist militancy, light engineering, textiles, timber-working and agriculture knew their worst years of the century. In Bologna alone 61 engineering firms were wholly or partially closed down between 1947 and 1952, 48 timber firms, 33 clothes factories, etc.; and there was a terminal crisis of many ancient industries such as hemp and fruit preserving linked to the area's traditional agriculture. On a national level GNP per capita was still only 84% of the 1938 level in 1948-49 and unemployment either 15% of the work force of 30% according to whether one chose ERP or left trade union statistics.[48] Only when the Korean war boom worked its way through and a new international economic situation had developed did the famous miracle begin. But the far-away Korean war, whatever its causes, demanded a transformation of the American effort in Italy, from reconstruction to rearmament, and provoked a great deal of soul-searching and re-thinking among the organisers of propaganda. [49] All this tended not to weaken but to consolidate and even strengthen the left vote, which continued to climb slowly in spite of the post-Korea escalation of the propaganda and political offensive. Meanwhile in the South and Sicily the far right became a serious political force, the Monarchists and neo-Fascists taking between them 16% of the vote in 1951. [50]

Yet not only did the Italian electorate remain largely democratic in the conventional sense but within ten years of the Marshall Plan the country was the scene of an unprecedented transformation in industry and society, of a great boom in production and employment, of an almost frenzied Americanisation in terms of life-styles and patterns of consumption. In 1949 a New York Times correspondent lamented that Italy still had not developed its own authentic capitalism or mass market: 'The idea', he wrote, 'of persuading the low income consumer to feel the need for something he has never had, using advertising, and then to give it to him at a price he can afford, could be the Marshall Plan's biggest contribution to Italy - if it gets anywhere'. [51] In 1951 the ERP administrator Hoffman was convinced the process was happening, as Italians learned from the Information Program's many channels not only about techniques but also about America: 'They learned (Hoffman wrote) that this is the land of full shelves and bulging shops, made possible by high productivity and good wages, and that its prosperity may be emulated elsewhere by those who will work towards it.' [52] By the end of the 1950s Italy was the land of the 'miracle' and although it is clearly impossible to link directly the tumultuous changes of that time with the message of the Marshall Plan, it was not by chance that the motor car was at the centre of the transformation, mass produced by a company called FIAT which had been a major beneficiary of ERP's attention and largesse.

'Prosperity makes you free': that was the slogan on the Marshall Plan Freedom Train as it brought aid and comfort in the dark days of the late 1940s. Ten years later there was prosperity and freedom, and neither the extreme left or the extreme right were the same as they had been. Yet Italy was not a model of a healthy democracy: deep shadows surrounded aspects of the State's life and large numbers of Italians persisted in such anti-social behaviour as tax-evasion. Anti-communism and productivity, it turned out, were not enough. But that was not for lack of trying.

NOTES

1. Joseph Heller, Catch 22, Corgi edition, 1982, pp.263-64.
2. Analysed in D.W. Ellwood, The Enemy Ally: Allied Occupation Policy in Italy, 1943-45, forthcoming.
3. Cit. in tel. Alexander Kirk, American Ambassador to Italy, to State Dept. 31 July 1945, in National Archives, Washington D.C. (henceforth NA), Record Group (henceforth RG) 59, 740.00119 EW/7-3145.
4. 'The Future Policy Toward Italy', 23 June 1945, in NA, RG 331, 10000/136/256; partially cit. in H.L. Coles & A.K. Weinberg, Civil Affairs: Soldiers Become Governors (Washington D.C., 1964) pp.622-23.
5. 'Memorandum on the future of Italy', n.d. but May 1945, by M.S. Lush et. al., in NA, RG 331, 10000/136/256.
6. These are some of the central themes of Ellwood op. cit.
7. New York Herald Tribune, 6 June 1945.
8. Maurice F. Neufeld, 'The Failure of Allied Military Government in Italy', in Public Administration Review, Spring 1946, pp.137-47.
9. Memorandum of 16 Apr.1944 in NA, RG 59, 865.00.
10. Daily Telegraph, 4 Sept.1945.
11. UNRRA's story, which included a not insubstantial information effort, is told in 'Venti mesi con l'UNRRA per la ripresa industriale italiana', Rome, 1948, and in the documentary Italy Rebuilds (1947), conserved in the Motion Picture, Broadcasting and Recorded Sound Division, Library of Congress.
12. The episode is reconstructed in F. Rosi's film Salvatore Giuliano (1961).
13. Dunn's point of view is best seen in his despatches to the State Department of 3 May 1947 and 7 May 1947, in Foreign Relations of the United States (henceforth FRUS), 1947, Vol.III, pp.889-92 & 895-902.
14. Ibid., p.891.
15. James Clement Dunn, Discorsi in Italia (Rome, n.d.) pp.126-29.
16. NSC 1/1, 1 Nov.1947, in FRUS, 1948, Vol. III, p.724.
17. NSC 1/2. Feb.1948, in ibid., p.766.
18. Howard K. Smith, The State of Europe (New York, 1949) pp.205-6.

19. See Robert T. Holt and Robert W. van de Velde, Strategic Psychological Operations and American Foreign Policy, (Chicago, 1960) Ch. VI.

20. Ibid., pp.207-8.

21. Ibid., pp.208-11.

22. See FRUS, 1950, Vol. III, p.800.

23. 'Il Piano Marshall e l'Europa', proceedings of a conference held in Rome, May, 1980; published Rome, 1983.

24. See Ellwood, 'Il Piano Marshall e il processo di modernizzazione in Italia', in Il Piano Marshall e l'Europa, op. cit.pp.149-61.

25. Memo F.V. Norall to Roscoe Drummond, Director European Information Division, Paris, 9 Aug.1950 in NA, RG 286, Office of Special Representative (OSR), Central Secretariat, Information Division, Retired Subject File (OSR 473), 'Mission Memoranda' sub-file.

26. New York Times, 3 June 1967, 5 June 1967.

27. Documents on American Foreign Relations 1948, (Princeton, 1950) p.235.

28. Monthly Report, Information Divn., ECA Mission to Italy, 1 Sept.1948, in RG 286, OSR, Info. Divn., Mission files (OSR 471), 'Italy 1948-49' sub-file.

29. 'A review of the activities and performance of the Information Division of the Special Mission to Italy from June, 1948 to December 31, 1950, with particular emphasis on the last six months of 1950', n.d. but 1951, in NA, RG 286, ECA Washington, Office of Information, Office of Director, Informational country file (W303), 'Italy' sub-file. This lengthy summary has been published by the author in E. Krippendorff (ed.) The Role of the United States in the Reconstruction of Italy and West Germany, 1943-1949 (Berlin, 1981) pp.274-302.

30. Notes dictated by Berding for use in Congressional presentation, 16 Jan.1950, in NA, RG 286, OSR Info. Divn., Information Subject File (OSR 470), 'Previous Testimony' sub-file.

31. Ltr. F.R. Shea, Chief, Field Branch, European Information Divn., to Berding, 24 Feb.1949, in NA, RG 286, OSR Administrative Services Divn., Communications and Records Section, Country Files 1948-1949, Italy 'Publicity and Information. Radio-Film' sub-file.

32. Doc. cit. note 29; the Italian Government's attitude is described in a letter. Berding to Zellerbach, Chief, ECA Mission to Italy, 27 Sept.1948, in NA, RG, 286, OSR, Info. Divn. Mission files, 'Italy II' sub-file. The state of literacy and the media in Italy at this time is also described in Robert T. Holt and Robert W. van de Velde, op. cit., ch.VI.

33. The January 1950 summary should also be compared with an earlier much longer description of 18 June 1949, unsigned, in NA, RG 286, ECA Washington, Office of Information, Office of Director, Informational country file, 'Italy' sub-file, as well as with the doc. cit. in note 29.

34. Both sides of the question discussed in Joseph B. Phillips, 'Italy: Making the ECA Visible', Newsweek, 10 Oct.1949; labelling

debate in Congressional Record-Senate, April, 1949, pp.4209-4213; Info. Divn. views summed up in 'Notes for Ambassador Katz regarding Information', unsigned, n.d. but end 1950, in NA, RG 286, OSR, Central Secretariat, Subject Files 1948-52, 'Public Relations' sub-file.

35. See notes 29, 30, 33.
36. See note 29.
37. Ibid.
38. Ibid: Washington comment in Robert Mullen, (Director, Office of Information). 'Budget Estimate. Fiscal 1950', in NA, RG 286, ECA Washington, Info. Divn., Information Subject File, 'Previous Testimony' sub-file.
39. Copy of pamphlet 'ERP in Italy' in NA, RG 286, ECA Washington, Office of Information, Office of Director, Informational country file', 'Italy' sub-file.
40. Memo on 'Labor Information' 19 Dec. 1949 in NA,RG 286, OSR, Info. Divn., Mission Files, 'Italy: Publicity and Information' sub-file.
41. See note 29.
42. Ibid.; see note 24.
43. Text of Dayton's speech in NA, RG 286, OSR, Central Secretariat, Permanent Country Subject File, 'Italy 1951' sub-file; the speech aroused considerable controversy in Italy and a protest from the head of Confindustria, the employers' association; details in Ellwood, 'Il Piano Marshall nel processo...'
44. Memo from Stone to Zellerbach and Barrows, 19 Apr. 1949, in NA, RG 286,OSR Central Secretariat, Country Subject File, 'Italy: Administration' sub-file; tel. Zellerbach to OSR Paris, 3 May 1949, in NA, RG 286, ECA Washington, European Programme Divn., Mediterranean Branch, Subject files pertaining to France and Italy, 'S-37 Technical Assistance' sub-file (quote from this tel.); W.J.Hoff, Director, Technical Assistance Divn., ECA Washington, to S. McK. Rosen, Bureau of the Budget, 10 Oct. 1950, in NA, RG 286, ECA Washington, Office of Director, Technical Assistance Divn., 'Italy: General' file; further details in Ellwood, see note 24.
45. Extent of U.S.Govt's interest in reforms indicated in memo Luzzato to Bissell, ECA Washington, 15 Dec. 1949, in NA, RG 286, ECA Washington, Office of the Assistant Administrator for Program, Subject File, 'Countries - Italy thru' Dec. 1949' sub-file; draft version of Zellerbach statement, 4 Feb. 1949, in NA, RG 286, OSR, Central Secretariat Permanent Country Subject File, 'Italy 1951' sub-file.
46. Discoveries mentioned in memo from Behoteguy to Quinn, 18 Oct. 1949, in NA, RG 286, ECA Washington, Office of Director, Technical Assistance Divn., 'Italy: General' sub-file.
47. Opinion poll and discussion in 'Notes for Ambassador Katz..', see note 34.
48. Data in Ellwood, 'Il Piano Marshall in Emilia Romagna', in P.P.D 'Attorre (ed.) La ricostruzione in Emilia Romagna (Parma, 1980) pp.238-41; see 'Tre anni di ERP in Italia', ECA Italy Mission, Rome, 1951.

49. The long report 'A review of the activities and performance...' see note 29, was written to assess the impact of the Korean outbreak on information objectives; many other papers tell the same story, in particular the memo from Norall to Drummond, August 1950, see note 25.

50. A. DelBoca - M. Giovana, 'Lo Sviluppo del neofascismo negli anni cinquanta', in M. Legnani (ed.), Profile politico dell'Italia repubblicana (Naples, 1974) pp 117-22; cfr. M.Grindrod, The Rebuilding of Italy (London, Royal Institute of International Affairs 1955) Ch. VIII.

51. New York Times 7 June 1949.

52. Paul G. Hoffmann, Peace Can Be Won (Garden City, NY 1951) p.53; for his summary of the ERP effort in Italy, ibid., pp. 50-52; cfr. G.Hutton, We Too Can Prosper (London, British Productivity Council) 1953.

SELECT BIBLIOGRAPHY

Bach, J. America's Germany (New York, 1946).

Balfour, M.G.L. Four-Power Control in Germany 1945-6 (Oxford, 1956)

—— 'Reforming the German Press 1945-49' Journal of European Studies, 3, 1973.

Barsam, R.M. 'This is America: Documentaries for Theatres, 1942-51' in Barsam R.M. (ed.) Nonfiction Film Theory and Criticism (New York, 1976.

Berghahn, V.R. Militarism: the history of an International Debate 1861-1979 (Cambridge, 1984).

Birley, R. 'Education in the British Zone of Germany' International Affairs, xxvi no.1, 1950.

Bower, T. Blind Eye to Murder. Britain, America and the Purging of Nazi Germany - a pledge betrayed (London, 1981).

Braunthal, G. 'The Anglo-Saxon Model of Democracy in the West German Political Consciousness after World War Two' Archiv für Sozialgeschichte, 18, 1978.

Buckley, R. Occupation Diplomacy: Britain the United States and Japan 1945-52 (Cambridge, 1982.

Bullock, A. Ernest Bevin, Foreign Secretary 1945-51 (London, 1984).

Burger, H. Der Frühling War es Wert- Erinnerungen (Munich, 1977).

Burmeister, W. 'Were the British too neutral' Adult Education, July 1978.

Burridge, T.D. British Labour and Hitler's War (London, 1976).

Calleo, D. The German Problem Reconsidered (Cambridge, 1978).

Carr, E.H. Conditions of Peace (London, 1942).

Chamberlain, B.S. '"Todesmühlen": Ein Früher Versuch zur Massen - Umerziehung in Besetzten Deutschland 1945-46' Vierteljahrshefte Für Zeitgeschichte, xxix, 1981.

Chatham House The Problem of Germany - an interim report by a Chatham House Study Group (London, 1943).

Clay, L.D. Decision in Germany (New York, 1950).

Cockerill, Sir G. What Fools We Were (London, 1944).

Coles, H.L. and Weinberg, A.K. Civil Affairs: Soldiers become Governors (Washington D.C., 1964).

Cowling, M. The Impact of Hitler: British Politics and British Policy 1933-40' (Cambridge, 1975).

Culbert, D. 'Note on Government Paper Records' in Rowan, B.G. Scholars' Guide to Washington D.C. Film and Video Collections (Washington, 1980).

Davies, E. 'Der Britische Beitrag zum Wiederaufbau des deutschen Schulwesens von 1945 bis 1950' in Heinemann M. (ed.) Umerziehung und Weideraufbau (Stuttgart, 1981).

Select Bibliography

Davis, K.S. 'Das Schulbuchwesen als Spiegel der Bildungspolitik von 1945 bis 1950' in Heinemann M. (ed.) Umerziehung und Weideraufbau (Stuttgart, 1981).
Deak, I. 'How Guilty Were the Germans' New York Review of Books, xxxi no 9, 31 May 1984.
Deutsch, H.C. Hitler and his Generals: the hidden crisis, January to June 1938 (Minnesota, 1974)
—— The Conspiracy against Hitler in the twilight war (Oxford, 1968).
Donnison, F.S.V. Civil Affairs and Military Government, North-West Europe 1944-46 (London, 1961)
—— Central Organisation and Planning (London, 1966).
Dore, R.P. Education in Tokugawa Japan (London, 1965).
Duke, B. Japan's Militant Teachers (Hawaii, 1972).

Ebsworth, R. Restoring Democracy in Germany. The British Contribution (London, 1960).
Eiji, T. and Samon, K. Showashi (Tokyo, 1982).
Ellwood, D.W. 'Il Piano Marshall in Emilia Romagna' in d'Attore P.P. (ed.) La Riconstruzione in Emilia Romagna (Parma, 1980).
Eyck, F. 'Psychological Warfare and Newspaper Control in British-Occupied Germany: a personal account' in Travers, T. and Archer, C. (eds) Men at War (Chicago, 1982).

Faulk, H. Group Captives: the Re-education of German Prisoners of War in Britain 1945-48 (London, 1977)
—— Die Deutschen Kriegsgefangenen in Grossbritannien Re-education (Bielefeld, 1970).
Fielding, R. The American Newsreel 1911-1967 (Norman, Ok., 1972)
—— The March of Time, 1935-1951 (New York, 1978).
Fischer, H-D. Re-educations und Pressepolitik unter britischen Besatzungsstatus Die Zonenzeitung 'Die Welt' 1946-50 (Dusseldorf, 1978).
Foschepoth, J. 'Britische Deutschlandpolitik zwischen Yalta und Potsdam' Vierteljahrschefte für Zeitgeschichte, 30, 1980.
Fromm, H. Deutschland in der Offentlichen Kriegszieldiskussion Grossbritanniens 1939-45 (Frankfurt, 1982).

Gelfand, L. The Inquiry: American Preparations for Peace 1917-19 , 1956)
—— All my Sins (London, 1957)
—— Im Jahre Null (Munich, 1979).

Halbritter, M. Schulreformpolitik in der Britischen Zone 1945-49 (Weinheim, 1979).
Harenberg, K-H. Die Welt 1946-53. Eine deutsche oder eine britische Zeitung. Ph.D. F.U.Berlin 1976.
Havens, T.R.H. Valley of Darkness, the Japanese People and World War Two (New York, 1978).
Headlam-Morley, J.W. A Memoir of the Paris Peace Conference 1919 , 1956)

Select Bibliography

Havens, T.R.H. Valley of Darkness, the Japanese People and World War Two (New York, 1978).
Headlam-Morley, J.W. A Memoir of the Paris Peace Conference 1919 (London, 1972).
Hearnden, A. Education in the Two Germanies (London, 1974)
---- Education, Culture and Politics in W. Germany (London,1976)
---- (ed.) The British in Germany: Educational Reconstruction in Germany after 1945 (London, 1978)
---- Red Robert: A Life of Robert Birley (London, 1984).
Heckmann, H.H. Die führenden englishchen Wochen - Zeitschriften und ihre Stellung zum Deutschlandproblem nach 1945 (Berlin, 1960).
Herzstein, R.E. The War that Hitler Won (London, 1979).
Hoffmann, P. History of the German Resistance (MIT, 1977).
Holborn, L. (ed.) War and Peace Aims of the United Nations vol. 1 (Boston, 1943).
Holt, R.T. and van de Velde, R.W. Strategic Psychological Operations and American Foreign Policy (Chicago, 1960).
Hurwitz, H. Die Stunde Null der Deutschen Presse (Cologne, 1972).

Iriye, A. Power and Culture: the Japanese-American War 1941-45 (Harvard, 1981).

Jaeger, K. and Regel, H. Deutschland in Trümmern: Film Dokumente der Jahre 1945-49, eine Dokumentation (Oberhausen, 1976).
Janowitz, M. 'German Reactions to Nazi Atrocities' American Journal of Sociology, LII, 1946.
Jerchow, F. Deutschland in der Weltwirtschaft 1944-47 (Dusseldorf, 1978).
Jürgensen, K. 'Elemente Britischer Deutschlandpolitik' in Scharf, C. and Schroder, H-J. Die Deutschlandpolitik Grossbritanniens und die Britische Zone 1945-49 (Wiesbaden, 1979)
---- 'Entscheidung Fur das Bundesland Schleswig-Holstein zur Entstehung der Landerordnung in der Britische Zone Deutschlands' in Boockmann, H., Jürgensen, K., Stoltenburg, G. (eds.) Geschichte und Gegenwart (Neuminster, 1980)
---- 'Zum Problem der "Political Re-education"' in Heinemann, M. (ed.) Die Bildungspolitik in Deutschland und Osterreich (Stuttgart, 1981)
---- 'British Occupation Policy after 1945 and the problem of "Re-educating Germany"' History, 68, 1983.

Keezer, D.M. A Unique Contribution to International Relations: the story of Wilton Park (London, 1973).
Kettenacker, L. 'Preussen in der Alliierten Kriegszielplanung 1939-47' in Kettenacker et. al (eds) Studien zur Geschichte Englands und der Deutsch-Britischen Beziehungen (Munich, 1981)
---- 'The Anglo-Soviet Alliance and the Problem of Germany 1941-45' Journal of Contemporary History, 17, 1982

——— 'Der Einfluss der Deutschen Emigration auf die Britische Kriegszielpolitik' in Hirschfeld, G. (ed.) Exil in Grossbritannien (Stuttgart, 1983)

——— Krieg zur Friedenssicherung. Die Deutschlandplanung der britischen Regierung 1939-45 (Stuttgart, 1984).

Klewitz, M. Berliner Einheitsschule 1945-51 (Berlin, 1971)

——— 'Allied Policy in Berlin' in Hearnden, A (ed.) The British in Germany (London, 1978).

Knight, J. 'Russia's Search for Peace: The London Conference of Foreign Ministers, 1945' Journal of Contemporary History, 13, 1978.

Kochan, L. The Struggle for Germany 1914-45 (Chicago, 1963).

Kodama, M.(ed.) Educational Documents of Occupied Japan (Tokyo, 1983).

Koszyk, K. Kontinuitat oder Neubeginn? (Siegen, 1981)

——— The German Press under British Occupation (Siegen, 1983).

Krippendorff, E. (ed.) The Role of the United States in the Reconstruction of Italy and West Germany 1943-49 (Berlin, 1981).

Krüger, W. Entnazifiziert! Zur Praxis der politische Sänberung in Nordrhein-Westfalen (Wuppertal, 1982).

Kubina, C. 'Anmerkungen zur Verwendung des Begreiffs Restauration' in Schmoldt, B. (ed.) Zielkonflikte um das Berliner Schulwesen zwischen 1948 und 1962 (Werkstattbericht) (Berlin, 1983).

Kuklick, B. American Policy and the Division of Germany (Ithaca, 1972).

Lange, I. Entnazifizierung in Nordrhein-Westfalen (Siegburg, 1976).

Legnani, M. (ed.) Profilo Politico dell' Italia Repubblicana (Naples, 1974).

Ludlow, P.W. 'The Unwinding of Appeasement' in Kettenacker, L. (ed.) The 'Other Germany' in the Second World War: emigration and resistance in international perspective (Stuttgart, 1977).

McGeehan, R. The German Rearmament Question (Chicago, 1971).

McLaine, I. Ministry of Morale: Home Front Morale and the Ministry of Information in World War Two (London, 1979).

Maginnis, J.J. Military Government Journal: Normandy to Berlin (Amherst Ma., 1971).

Mantoux, P. Les Deliberations du Conseil des Quatre (Paris, 1955).

Marshall, B. 'German Attitudes to British Military Government 1945-47' Journal of Contemporary History, 15, 1980

——— 'German Reactions to Military Defeat 1945-47: the British view' in Berghahn, V.R. and Kitchen, M. (eds) Germany in the age of Total War (London, 1981).

Martin, B. Friedensinitiativen und Machtpolitik im zweiten weltkrieg 1939-42 (Dusseldorf, 1974).

Mayer, A.J. Political Origins of the New Diplomacy 1917-18 (New York, 1970).

Select Bibliography

Mayo, M. 'Psychological Disarmament: American Wartime Planning for the Education and re-education of defeated Japan 1943-45' in Burkman, T.W. The Occupation of Japan: Educational and Social Reform (Norfolk, Va., 1982).

Meiser, H. Der Nationalsozialismus und seine Bewältigung im spiegel der Lizenzpresse der britischen Besatzungszone von 1946-49. Ph.D. Osnabrück 1980.

Merritt, A.J. and Merritt, R. L. Public Opinion in Occupied Germany: the OMGUS Surveys 1945-49 (Chicago, 1970).

Milward, A.S. The Reconstruction of Western Europe 1945-51 (London, 1984).

Mosse, G.L. The Crisis of German Ideology (New York, 1964).

Neufeld, M.F. 'The Failure of Allied Military Government in Italy' Public Administration Review, 1946.

Nishi, T. Unconditional Democracy, Education and Politics in Occupied Japan 1945-52 (Stanford, 1982).

Norman, A. Our German Policy: Propaganda and Culture (New York, 1951).

Pakschies, G. Umerziehung in der britischen Zone 1945-49 (Weinheim, 1979).

Penrose, E.F. Economic Planning for Peace (Princeton, 1953).

Peterson, E.N. The American Occupation of Germany: Retreat to Victory (Detroit, 1977).

Phillips, D. (ed.) German Universities after the surrender: British Occupation Policy and the control of Higher Education (Oxford, 1983)

—— 'Die Wiedereröffnung der Universitäten in der britische Zone: Das Problem Nationalismus und Zulassung zum Studium' Bildung und Erziehung, 36, 1983.

Phillips, M. 'The Nazi Control of the German Film Industry' Journal of European Studies, 1971.

Pilgert, H.P. Press, Radio and Film in West Germany 1945-53 (Historical Division, Office of U.S. High Commissions for Germany, 1953)

—— The History of the Development of Information Services through Information Centres and Documentary Files (ibid. 1951).

Pingel, F. 'Die Russen am Rhein?' Vierteljahrshefte für Zeitgeschichte, 30, 1982.

Reusch, U. 'Die Londoner Institutionen der Britischen Deutschlandpolitik 1943-48 Historisches Jahrbuch, 100, 1980.

Robinson, S.B. and Kuhlmann, J.C. 'Two Decades of non-reform in West German Education' Comparative Education Review, xi no. 3, 1967.

Roden, D. Schooldays in Imperial Japan. A Study in the Culture of a Student Elite' (Berkeley, 1980).

Rothwell, V. Britain and the Cold War 1941-47 (London, 1982).

Rudzio, W. 'Export englischer Demokratie? Zur Konzeption britischer Besatzungspolitik in Deutschland' Vierteljahrshefte für Zeitgeschichte, 17, 1969.

Scharf, C. and Schröder, H.J. (eds) Die Deutschlandpolitik Grossbritanniens und die britische Zone 1945-49 (Weisbaden, 1979).
Schoenbaum, D. Hitler's Social Revolution (New York, 1967)
---- 'American Idealism and the Re-shaping of Germany after 1945' in Bullen, R.J. (ed.) Ideas and Politics (London, 1984).
Schneider, U. Der Kampf um Demokratisierung in Wirtschaft und Gesellschaft (Hamburg, 1980)
---- 'Grundzüge britischer Deutschland und Besatzungspolitik' Zeitgeschichte, 9, 1981-2
---- Niedersachsen unter britischer Besatzung 1945' Niedersachsisches Jahrbuch für Landesgeschichte, 54, 1982
---- Vier-Mächte-Kontrolle Deutschlands von Kriegsende bis Herbst 1945. Documentation' Militärgeschichtliche Mitteilungen, 31, 1982.
Scott, J.B. Official Statements of War Aims and Peace Proposals, December 1916 to November 1918 (Washington, 1921).
Shinobu, O. Sengo Kaikaku, vol 31 in Nihon no Rekishi (Tokyo, 1976).
Sienknecht, H. Der Einheitsschulgedanke (Weinheim, 1968).
Smith, H.D. Japan's First Student Radicals (Harvard, 1972).
Snyder, L.L. Roots of German Nationalism (Indiana, 1978).
Steinert, M. Hitler's War and the Germans (Athens, Ohio, 1977).
Steininger, R. 'British Labour, Deutschland und die SPD 1945-6' Internationale wissenschaftliche Korrespondenz zur Geschichte der deutsche Arbeiterbewegung, 15, 1979.
Stuart, Sir C. Secrets of Crewe House (London, 1920).
Sullivan, M.B. Thresholds of Peace (London, 1979).
Sulzback, H. 'Inside Featherstone Park' in Breitenstein, R (ed.) Total War to Total Trust' (London, 1976).

Tent, J.F. Mission on the Rhine: re-education and de-nazification in American-Occupied Germany (Chicago, 1982).
Trainor, J.P. Education Reform in Occupied Japan (Tokyo, 1983).
Trees, W., Whiting, C., Omansen, T. Drei Jahre nach Null. Geschichte der britischen Besatzungszone 1945-48 (Dusseldorf, 1980).
Tsunda, R., de Bary, W.T., Keene, D. (eds) Sources of Japanese Traditions (New York, 1958).

Vansittart, R. Black Record: Germans Past and Present (London, 1941).

Watt, D.C. Britain Looks to Germany: British Opinion and Policy towards Germany since 1945 (London, 1965)
---- 'Every War Must End: War-time planning for post-war security in Britain and America in the wars of 1914-18 and 1939-45. The

Roles of Historical example and of Professional Historians'
Transactions of the Royal Historical Society 1978.
Wilson, K.M. 'Isolating the Isolator: Grey, Cartwright and the
seduction of Austria-Hungary 1908-12' Mitteilungen des
Osterreichisches Staatsarchiv, 35, 1982.
Wolffe, H. Die Deutschen Kriegsgefangenen in britischer hand. Ein
Uberblick (Munich, 1974).
Woodward, W.P. The Allied Occupation of Japan and Japanese
Religions (Leiden, 1972).
Wray, H.J. 'Decentralization of Education in the Allied Occupation
of Japan 1945-52' in Burkman, T.W. (ed.) The Occupation of
Japan: Education and Social Reform (Norfolk Va., 1982).

Ziemke, E.F. The U.S. Army in the Occupation of Germany 1944-46
(Washington, 1975).

INDEX

In this index WW1 = first world war
WW2 = second world war

de-industrialisation 1-2, 174-5;
see also industry
de-militarisation of Germany 1-3,
7, 13, 26, 63, 71, 174,
206-7; post-WW1 42, 45,
48-9, 52, 141; of schools
99-100
de-militarisation of Japan 204-7
de-nazification 2-3, 63-74, 85-6,
90, 100, 174; see also
National Socialists
Death Mills (film) see
Todesmühlen
de-centralisation see regions
Delmer, Sefton 128, 146
democracy, incompatible with
involvement in education
67, 76
democratisation of Germany 2-3,
11, 13, 18; and newsreels
157; post-WW1 41-51;
post-WW2 65,
69, 87, 91; of schools 100
democratisation of Italy 226,
233-5
Department of Special
Intelligence, War Office 39
Die Welt 121-3
Dillon, John 45
directives, newsreel 155-6
disarmament see demilitarisation
discussion groups 85
dismissal of teachers 68-9, 85,
90
Disney, Walt 180
Dodds, Professor E.R. 68
Douglas, Lewis 171
Draft Directive on Re-education
of Germany 68-70, 110
Dunn, James C. 224-5
Dyke, Brigadier Kenneth 206

EAC see European Advisory
Commission
Eckert, Georg 100, 102-3
economic improvement 98, 234-5;
non-interference 72; see
also Marshall Plan
Eden, Anthony 22, 107, 142, 171
Education Branch 85-94, 145-6;
and schools 97-106

Education Mission 208-9
Educational Advisers 85, 90; see
also Birley
Eels, Walter 213
Eisenhower, General Dwight D.
68, 70, 111, 143, 180,
183-4; and concentration
camps 176, 196;
and Montgomery 113; and
non-fraternisation 116; see
also Supreme Headquarters
etc.
élite in education 1, 9-10, 22, 75
Elkins, Saul 182-3
Elton, Sir Arthur 147
emigrés, German 99; not included
in re-education 69, 107,
113
Enemy Propaganda Department
17, 37, 48, 53-4
ERP see Marshall Plan
European Advisory Commission
109-11
European Recovery Program see
Marshall Plan
European unity 72, 88-9
Evening News and Evening
Standard 45
exhibitions 228, 231-2

faked photographs 176
Faulk, Lieutenant-Colonel Henry
74-5, 140, 149
Federal Republic of Germany,
creation of 83-4, 87, 90-3
films about concentration camps
74, 140, 149, 175-82, 190-1,
196-9; in Germany 173-202;
interwar 19-21; in Italy
228, 230; in Japan 206;
unimportance of 147;
United States policy 173-202;
see also newsreels
finances Marshall Plan 229,
233; newspapers 115, 126-7;
newsreels 153
Foch, General Ferdinand 49
FORD see Foreign Office
Research Department

INDEX

For Product Safety Concerns and Information please contact our EU
representative GPSR@taylorandfrancis.com
Taylor & Francis Verlag GmbH, Kaufingerstraße 24, 80331 München, Germany

www.ingramcontent.com/pod-product-compliance
Ingram Content Group UK Ltd.
Pitfield, Milton Keynes, MK11 3LW, UK
UKHW021008180425
457613UK00019B/848